T0297399

MOBILE SECURITY AND PRIVACY

MOBILE SECURITY AND PRIVACY

Advances, Challenges and Future Research Directions

Edited by

MAN HO AU

KIM-KWANG RAYMOND CHOO

GARY KESSLER, Technical Editor

AMSTERDAM • BOSTON • HEIDELBERG • LONDON
NEW YORK • OXFORD • PARIS • SAN DIEGO
SAN FRANCISCO • SINGAPORE • SYDNEY • TOKYO

Syngress is an Imprint of Elsevier

SYNGRESS

Syngress is an imprint of Elsevier
50 Hampshire Street, 5th Floor, Cambridge, MA 02139, United States

Notices
Knowledge and best practice in this field are constantly changing. As new research and experience broaden our understanding, changes in research methods, professional practices, or medical treatment may become necessary.

Practitioners and researchers must always rely on their own experience and knowledge in evaluating and using any information, methods, compounds, or experiments described herein. In using such information or methods they should be mindful of their own safety and the safety of others, including parties for whom they have a professional responsibility.

To the fullest extent of the law, neither the Publisher nor the authors, contributors, or editors, assume any liability for any injury and/or damage to persons or property as a matter of products liability, negligence or otherwise, or from any use or operation of any methods, products, instructions, or ideas contained in the material herein.

Library of Congress Cataloging-in-Publication Data
A catalog record for this book is available from the Library of Congress

British Library Cataloguing-in-Publication Data
A catalogue record for this book is available from the British Library

ISBN: 978-0-12-804629-6

For information on all Syngress publications
visit our website at https://www.elsevier.com/

Working together
to grow libraries in
developing countries

www.elsevier.com • www.bookaid.org

Publisher: Todd Green
Acquisition Editor: Chris Katsaropoulos
Editorial Project Manager: Anna Valutkevich
Production Project Manager: Punithavathy Govindaradjane
Cover Designer: Mark Rogers

Typeset by SPi Global, India

Contents

7. On Discovering Vulnerabilities in Android Applications

X. LI, L. YU, X.P. LUO

8. A Study of the Effectiveness Abs Reliability of Android Free Anti-Mobile Malware Apps

J. WALLS, K.-K.R. CHOO

9. Timeline Analysis for Digital Evidence on MTK-Based Shanzhai Mobile Phone

J. FANG, Z.L. JIANG, S. LI, S.-M. YIU, L.C.K. HUI, K.-P. CHOW

10. RESTful IoT Authentication Protocols

H.V. NGUYEN, L. LO IACONO

11. An Introduction to Various Privacy Models

X. LU, M.H. AU

12. Performance of Digital Signature Schemes on Mobile Devices

D.Y.W. LIU, G.Z. XUE, Y. XIE, X.P. LUO, M.H. AU

Contributors

M.H. Au The Hong Kong Polytechnic University, Kowloon, Hong Kong

C. Chia University of Melbourne, Melbourne, VIC, Australia

K.-K.R. Choo University of Texas at San Antonio, San Antonio, TX, United States; University of South Australia, Adelaide, SA, Australia

K.-P. Chow The University of Hong Kong, HKSAR, China

J. Fang Jinan University, Guangzhou, China

D. Fehrenbacher Monash University, Melbourne, VIC, Australia

F. Hayata University of Ngaoundéré, Ngaoundéré, Cameroon

L.C.K. Hui The University of Hong Kong, HKSAR, China

Z.L. Jiang Harbin Institute of Technology Shenzhen Graduate School, Shenzhen, China

L. Lau Asia Pacific Association of Technology and Society (APATAS), Hong Kong Special Administrative Region

X. Li Chinese Academy of Sciences, Beijing, China

S. Li Jinan University, Guangzhou, China

D.Y.W. Liu The Hong Kong Polytechnic University, Kowloon, Hong Kong

L. Lo Iacono Cologne University of Applied Sciences, Cologne, Germany

X. Lu The Hong Kong Polytechnic University, Kowloon, Hong Kong

X.P. Luo The Hong Kong Polytechnic University, Kowloon, Hong Kong

Y. Mohanraj Chennai, TN, India

H.V. Nguyen Cologne University of Applied Sciences, Cologne, Germany

F. Schiliro University of South Australia, Adelaide, SA, Australia

F. Tchakounté University of Ngaoundéré, Ngaoundéré, Cameroon

S. Tully Sydney, NSW, Australia

J. Walls University of South Australia, Adelaide, SA, Australia

Y. Xie Xiamen University, Fujian, China

G.Z. Xue Xiamen University, Fujian, China

S.-M. Yiu The University of Hong Kong, HKSAR, China

L. Yu The Hong Kong Polytechnic University, Kowloon, Hong Kong

About the Editors

Man Ho Allen Au received bachelor's and master's degrees from the Department of Information Engineering, Chinese University of Hong Kong, in 2003 and 2005 respectively, and a PhD from the University of Wollongong, Australia, in 2009. Currently, he is an assistant professor at the Dept. of Computing, Hong Kong Polytechnic University. Before moving to Hong Kong in Jul. 2014, he was been a lecturer at the School of Computer Science and Software Engineering, University of Wollongong, Australia.

Dr. Au's research interests include information security and privacy, applied cryptography, accountable anonymity, and cloud computing. He has published over 90 papers in those areas in journals such as *IEEE Transactions on Information Forensics and Security, IEEE Transactions on Knowledge and Data Engineering, ACM Transaction on Information and System Security* and international conferences including the Network and Distributed System Security Symposium (NDSS) and the ACM Conference on Computer and Communications Security (CCS). His work has received various awards, including the ACISP 2016 Best Paper Award and runner-up for a PET award in 2009 for Outstanding Research in Privacy Enhancing Technologies.

He has served as a program committee member for over 30 international conferences and workshops. He is also a program committee co-chair of the 8th International Conference on Network and System Security and the 9th International Conference on Provable Security. He is an associate editor of the *Journal of Information Security and Applications, Elsevier.* He has served as a guest editor for various journals including *Future Generation Computer Systems, Elsevier,* and *Concurrency and Computation: Practice and Experience, Wiley.*

Kim-Kwang Raymond Choo currently holds the Cloud Technology Endowed Professorship at the University of Texas at San Antonio, and is an associate professor at the University of South Australia, and a guest professor at the China University of Geosciences. He has been an invited speaker for a number of events, such as the 2011 UNODC-ITU Asia-Pacific Regional Workshop on Fighting Cybercrime, the Korean (Government) Institute of Criminology (2013), the UNAFEI and UAE Government conference in 2014, and the World Internet Conference (Wuzhen Summit) in 2014, jointly organized by the Cyberspace Administration of China and the People's Government of Zhejiang Province. He has also been a Keynote/ Plenary Speaker at conferences, such as the SERENE-RISC Spring 2016 Workshop, the IEEE International Conference on Data Science and Data Intensive Systems (DSDIS 2015), and those organized by Infocomm Development Authority of Singapore, A*Star, Nanyang Technological University, Singapore Management University (2015), the Cloud Security Alliance New Zealand (2015), CSO Australia and Trend Micro (2015), the Anti-Phishing Working Group (2014), the National Taiwan University of Science and Technology (2014), the Asia Pacific University of Technology &

Innovation (Malaysia; 2014), the Nanyang Technological University (Singapore; 2011), and National Chiayi University (Taiwan; 2010), and he has been an Invited Expert at UNAFEI Criminal Justice Training in 2015, at the INTERPOL Cyber Research Agenda Workshop 2015, and at the Taiwan Ministry of Justice Investigation Bureau's 2015 International Symposium on Regional Security and Transnational Crimes. He was named one of the 10 Emerging Leaders in the Innovation category of The Weekend Australian Magazine/Microsoft's Next 100 series in 2009, and is the recipient of various awards, including the ESORICS 2015 Best Research Paper Award, the Highly Commended Award from Australia New Zealand Policing Advisory Agency in 2014, a Fulbright Scholarship in 2009, a British Computer Society's Wilkes Award in 2008, and the 2008 Australia Day Achievement Medallion, and was on the winning team in Germany's University of Erlangen-Nuremberg (FAU) Digital Forensics Research Challenge in 2015. He is also a Fellow of the Australian Computer Society, and a senior member of the IEEE.

1

Mobile Security and Privacy

M.H. Au*, K.-K.R. Choo[†,‡]

*The Hong Kong Polytechnic University, Kowloon, Hong Kong [†]University of Texas at San Antonio, San Antonio, TX, United States [‡]University of South Australia, Adelaide, SA, Australia

1 INTRODUCTION

Security and privacy are highly dynamic and fast-paced research areas due to rapid technological advancements. Mobile security and privacy are no exception. For example, 10 or 15 years ago, research in mobile security was mainly concerned about securing the Global System for Mobile Communications (GSM) network and communications (Jøsang and Sanderud, 2003). Since mobile phones become user programmable (i.e., the device supports third-party software), the scope for security and privacy research extends to studying the security of such third-party software and associated privacy risks (La Polla et al., 2013) (e.g., whether third-party software will result in the leakage of user data).

It is also in the user's interest to ensure both confidentiality and integrity of the data that is stored on and made accessible via these devices. This is the focus of this book.

Specifically, in this book, we will be presenting the state-of-the-art advances in mobile device security and privacy. Such devices (e.g., Android, iOS, BlackBerry, and Windows devices) are, in fact, "minicomputers," with processing, communication, and storage capabilities. In addition, these devices often include additional sensing capabilities from the built-in camera, GPS, barometer, accelerometer, and gyro sensors. It should be noted that the modern-day mobile devices are generally more powerful than the IBM Deep Blue supercomputer of 1997 (Nick, 2014).

According to research detailed in the report entitled "State of Mobile Commerce," 34% of electronic commerce transactions are conducted over mobile devices globally (Wolf, 2015). In some parts of the world, such as technologically advanced countries like Japan and South Korea, more than half of e-commerce transactions are conducted over mobile devices (Wolf, 2015).

A prominent example of the shift in conventional business processes to mobile is mobile payments. This is evidenced by the significant worldwide trend of using platforms such as Apple Pay, Google Wallet, Samsung Pay, and WeChat Pay. According to Statista (2016), the annual transaction volume for mobile payments is reportedly $450 billion in 2015 and is fore-casted to double in 3 years.

Another emerging mobile application is mobile health, which is the practice of integrat-ing mobile technologies in supporting medical and health care services (Istepanian et al., 2006; Kay et al., 2011). With the anticipated benefits of increased access to point-of-care tools amongst others, mobile devices are becoming commonplace in medical and health care set-tings. It has also been suggested that mobile health supports better clinical decision making and improved patient outcomes (Divall et al., 2013).

Finally, we would also like to highlight the risks associated with the use of mobile devices in the workplace, a practice known as bring your own device or BYOD.

2 THREATS TO MOBILE SECURITY

Mobile threats can be broadly categorized into application-, web-, network-, and physical-level threats, as discussed in the following section.

2.1 Application-Level Threats

Application-level threats appear to be the most widely discussed threats in the literature (Faruki et al., 2015). As mobile devices can execute downloadable applications (apps), it is clear that apps can be a target vector to breach the security of the device and the system it connects to (e.g., a corporate network). The threats can be due to malicious applications (malware), particularly those downloaded from a third-party app store, as well as vulnera-ble apps.

Malware can, for instance, inject code into the mobile device in order to send unsolicited messages; allow an adversary the ability to remotely control the device; or exfiltrate user data, such as contact lists, email, and photos, without the user's knowledge or permission. For example, in a recent work, mobile security researchers demonstrated that it is possible to exfiltrate data from Android devices using inaudible sound waves (Do et al., 2015). As D'Orazio and Choo (2015, 2016) aptly explained, in the rush to reduce the time-to-market, applications are usually designed with functionality rather than security in mind. Hence it is not surprising that there are a large number of applications that contain security loop-holes that can be exploited by an attacker. In another recent work, Chen et al. (2016) dis-cussed how a botnet master issues commands, via multiple message push services, to remotely control mobile devices infected by malware. While vulnerable apps may not be developed with a malicious intent, they can result in significant security and privacy risks to the users. For example, D'Orazio and Choo (2015) revealed previous vulnerabilities in a widely used Australian government health care app that consequently exposed the users' sensitive personal data stored on the device. Other examples include the work of Zhao et al. (2016) and Farnden et al. (2015). Zhao et al. (2016) demonstrated how the geographic coordinates of a location-based social network app user can be obtained via probing at-tack, which resulted in location privacy leakage. Farnden et al. (2015) demonstrated that using forensic techniques, a wide range of data can be recovered from the devices of nine popular proximity-based dating app users, including the details of users who had been discovered nearby.

2.2 Web-Level Threats

While these threats are not specific to mobile devices (see Prokhorenko et al., 2013, 2016a,b for a review of web applications vulnerability and protection techniques), the security and privacy risks to mobile devices due to web-level threats are real. One key web-level threat is phishing, which uses email or other social media apps to send an unwitting user links to a phishing website designed to trick users into providing sensitive information such as user credentials. When combined with social engineering, phishing is one of the top seven security threats identified by Kaspersky Lab for the 2015–16.

2.3 Network Level Threats

One of the distinct features of mobile devices is the ability to connect. Typical connection supported by currently mobile devices include cellular/mobile networks, local wireless networks, and near field-communication (NFC). Security of the connection at the network level is another active research area at the time of this writing.

2.4 Physical-Level Threats

Finally, physical security of mobile devices is equally important, if not more so. Since mobile devices are typically small and portable, these devices can be easily stolen or misplaced. A lost or stolen device could be used to gain access to user data stored on the device or as an entry point into the user's corporate network (Imgraben et al., 2014; Choo et al., 2015).

3 ORGANIZATION OF THE BOOK

The rest of this book is organized as follows.

The use cases of mobile devices within an organization's context and their security implications from a practitioner's perspective are presented in Chapters 2 through 5.

Chapters 6 and 7 explain how malware and vulnerabilities can be identified using state-of-the-art techniques.

Chapter 8 examines the effectiveness of existing antimalware Android apps.

Chapter 9 focuses on mobile forensics.

Chapter 10 presents a security framework on Internet of Things (IoT) security protocols.

Chapter 11 introduces the common security models for generic privacy requirements.

Finally, preliminary experimental results on the implementation of cryptographic algorithms on mobile devices are presented in Chapter 12.

References

Chen, W., Luo, X., Yin, C., Xiao, B., Au, M.H., Tang, Y., 2016. MUSE: towards robust and stealthy mobile botnets via multiple message push services. In: Information Security and Privacy. Lecture Notes in Computer Science. 9722, pp. 20–39.

Choo, K.K.R., Heravi, A., Mani, D., Mubarak, S., 2015. Employees' intended information security behaviour in real estate organisations: a protection motivation perspective. In: Proceedings of 21st Americas Conference on Information Systems, AMCIS 2015. Association for Information Systems. http://aisel.aisnet.org/amcis2015/ISSecurity/GeneralPresentations/29/.

Divall, P., Camosso-Stefinovic, J., Baker, R., 2013. The use of personal digital assistants in clinical decision making by health care professionals: a systematic review. Health Informatics J. 19 (1), 16–28.

Do, Q., Martini, B., Choo, K.K.R., 2015. Exfiltrating data from Android devices. J. Comput. Secur. 48, 74–91.

D'Orazio, C., Choo, K.K.R., 2015. A generic process to identify vulnerabilities and design weaknesses in iOS health-care apps. In: System Sciences (HICSS), 2015 48th Hawaii International Conference on. IEEE, pp. 5175–5184.

D'Orazio, C., Choo, K.K.R., 2016. An adversary model to evaluate DRM protection of video contents on iOS devices. J. Comput. Secur. 56, 94–110.

Farnden, J., Martini, B., Choo, K.K.R., 2015. Privacy risks in mobile dating apps. In: Proceedings of 21st Americas Conference on Information Systems, AMCIS. Association for Information Systems. http://aisel.aisnet.org/amcis2015/ISSecurity/GeneralPresentations/13.

Faruki, P., Bharmal, A., Laxmi, V., Ganmoor, V., Gaur, M.S., Conti, M., Rajarajan, M., 2015. Android security: a survey of issues, malware penetration, and defenses. IEEE Commun. Surv. Tutorials 17 (2), 998–1022.

Imgraben, J., Engelbrecht, A., Choo, K.K.R., 2014. Always connected, but are smart mobile users getting more security savvy? A survey of smart mobile device users. Behav. Inform. Technol. 33 (12), 1347–1360.

Istepanian, R., Laxminarayan, S., Pattichis, C.S. (Eds.), 2006. M-Health: Emerging Mobile Health Systems. Springer-Verlag, New York.

Jøsang, A., Sanderud, G., 2003. Security in mobile communications: challenges and opportunities. In: Proceedings of the Australasian Information Security Workshop Conference on ACSW Frontiers 2003. vol. 21. Australian Computer Society, Inc, pp. 43–48.

Kay, M., Santos, J., Takane, M., 2011. mHealth: New Horizons for Health Through Mobile Technologies. World Health Organization. pp. 66–71.

La Polla, M., Martinelli, F., Sgandurra, D., 2013. A survey on security for mobile devices. IEEE Commun. Surv. Tutorials 15 (1), 446–471.

Nick, T., 2014. A modern smartphone or a vintage supercomputer: which is more powerful? Phonearena News, http://www.phonearena.com/news/A-modern-smartphone-or-a-vintage-supercomputer-which-is-more-powerful_id57149&gt (accessed 08.06.16).

Prokhorenko, V., Choo, K.K.R., Ashman, H., 2013. Intent-based extensible real-time PHP supervision framework. IEEE Trans. Inf. Forensics Secur. http://dx.doi.org/10.1109/TIFS.2016.2569063.

Prokhorenko, V., Choo, K.K.R., Ashman, H., 2016a. Web application protection techniques: a taxonomy. J. Netw. Comput. Appl. 60, 95–112.

Prokhorenko, V., Choo, K.K.R., Ashman, H., 2016b. Context-oriented web application protection model. Appl. Math. Comput. 285, 59–78.

Statista, 2016. Total revenue of global mobile payment market from 2015 to 2019 (in billion U.S. dollars). http://www.statista.com/statistics/226530/mobile-payment-transaction-volume-forecast/&gt (accessed 08.06.16).

Wolf, J., 2015. State of Mobile Commerce Report 2015. Criteo.

Zhao, S., Ma, M., Bai, B., Luo, X., Zou, W., Qiu, X., Au, M.H., 2016. I know where you are! Exploiting mobile social apps for large-scale location privacy probing. In: Information Security and Privacy. Springer International, New York.

Mobile Security: A Practitioner's Perspective

S. Tully*, Y. Mohanraj[†]

*Sydney, NSW, Australia [†]Chennai, TN, India

1 MOBILE SECURITY

In this chapter, we look at how users and organizations interact with mobile devices, as well as the security that is needed to keep abreast of the rapid changes in mobile computing.

After discussing various issues, such as privacy, location and jurisdictional issues, threats, risks and mitigations, and individual versus organizational impacts, this chapter outlines steps to take to ensure that your mobile devices—and everything that's on them— stays safe.

The world is transforming dramatically in a way that is having a significant impact on how people and enterprises operate (Soulodre, 2015). The telephone network has come a long way within the last century, from physical offices attended by technicians in telephone installation trucks to mobile devices and information available, anywhere, at any time.

Today, business is increasingly likely to be a mobile enterprise, conducted using devices that might not have even existed 5 years ago. This is affecting the technology, systems, and processes that are designed and built to support them. Work is no longer a place we "go," instead it's something we "do."

Mobile devices and portable media[1] add significant value to people and organizations through increased efficiency and productivity. However, their proliferation in the workplace is a serious and expanding threat to both security and privacy; that is, keeping corporate information secure and keeping certain data private.

---

[1] Mobile devices referred to in this chapter includes smartphones, tablet computers, laptops, PDAs, storage devices (e.g. USB drives, SD cards), scanners, sensors (e.g., Internet of Things), remote-control drones, autonomous cars, and connectivity devices (e.g., Wi-Fi, Bluetooth). However, smartphones and tablets are the devices referred to in most detail; to cover all of these other devices in detail would require an entire book.

Knowledge workers and the new generation of mobile-first and mobile-only masses are now the 21st century's "digital native" workforce. Besides the corporate environment, the cell phone has become the adult's transitional object, replacing the toddler's teddy bear for comfort and a sense of belonging.[2] Toffler (1970) predicted the relationships between people and machines, including emotional relationships, in his book *Future Shock* back in 1970. Prof. H.D. Block at Cornell University pointed out that people often develop emotional attachments to the machines they use. He suggests that we shall have to give attention to the "ethical" questions arising from our treatment of "these mechanical objects of our affection and passion." A serious inquiry into these issues is to be found in an article by Puccetti (1967) in *The British Journal for the Philosophy of Science*, 1967, pp. 39–51.[3] Other research in this area includes work by Choi, who is writing a piece on the *Emotional Attachment to Mobile Devices*[4] and further work by Cheever, Rosen, Carrier, and Chavez called *Out of Sight is Not Out of Mind: The Impact of Restricting Wireless Mobile Device Use on Anxiety Levels Among Low, Moderate and High Users* in Computers in Human Behaviour.[5] The strength of this attachment to mobile devices was reiterated by Holden, who said "I want to be buried with a mobile phone, just in case I'm not dead."[6]

These agents of change with digital attitudes and real-time expectations influence where, when, and how things are done. Their demands come from an "always-on" lifestyle with instant, on-demand expectations. Executives and employees are expecting, even demanding, access to their work resources through a variety of mobile devices. And, perhaps crucially, this expectation and demand is without time restrictions. It's not just a 9–5 solution, which has both positive as well as negative implications. The potential for abuse of employees by employers who provide this access must be taken into account.

Being connected has made us more efficient, but there is now the risk of reacting so quickly that we don't give the same attention to data protection that we might have given just 5 years ago.[7] Most people have not noticed—or simply ignored—the shift in responsibility. When data/information was managed by centralized IT departments, it was clearly someone else's role to protect it. Now that information is literally in the palm of your people's hands, but people have not caught up with this shift in responsibility; they don't understand it and they don't manage it. Connected with this is the socio-psychological aspect of human nature and the inclination to trust. With people having access to data almost instantly, there is the temptation to keep personal emails, calendar items, notes, mobile banking credentials, and other useful data to get through day-to-day activities, often stored insecurely. Over time, this personal data can quickly build up, and if the mobile device were lost or stolen, it could leave an easy-to-compromise digital footprint of the user, particularly if it is left unmanaged and not cleaned up regularly. Additionally, by being so connected, users are increasingly vulnerable to cyber adversaries.[8]

---

[2] Heffernan, M. Available from: http://www.brainyquote.com/quotes/keywords/cell_phone.html#lTyuvbSK4phtzolc.99.

[3] Puccetti, R., 1967. On thinking machines and feeling machines. Br. J. Philos. Sci. 18 (1), 39–51. Available from: http://bjps.oxfordjournals.org/content/18/1/39.

[4] Choi, Y-J. Available from: http://www.oneonta.edu/academics/research/PDFs/LOTM12-Choi2.pdf.

[5] Cheever, N.A., Rosen, L.D., Carrier, M., Chavez, A. Available from: http://www.csudh.edu/psych/Out_of_sight_is_not_out_of_mind-Cheever,Rosen,Carrier,Chavez_2014.pdf

[6] Holden, A. Available from: https://econsultancy.com/blog/65001-28-inspiring-mobile-marketing-quotes/.

[7] For details, see the book by Davidow, W., 2012. Overconnected: The Promise and Threat of the Internet.

[8] See the book by Zetter, K., 2014. Countdown to Zero Day: Stuxnet and the Launch of the World's First Digital Weapon, Crown, New York, pp. 376–377, ISBN: 978-0-7704-3617-9.

1.1 Global Growth in Mobile Use

It is important to note just how long mobile security has been a real issue. This section provides a brief timeline that helps build a sense of how we got to where we are today.

Cabir, the first Trojan horse for smartphones, was detected in Aug. 2004.[9] The Australian Communications and Media Authority demonstrated the growth and ubiquity of Australian mobile devices in their Communications Report 2011–12, which noted "the total number of mobile services in operation increased by three per cent to reach 30.2 million, approximately four mobile services to every three people in Australia."[10]

Furthermore, online and mobile use in China shows 668 million people access the Internet as of Jun. 2015. Of that, 89% (594 million) access the Internet via smartphones. For context, this means the number of people using smart phones in China is equal to 25 times the population of Australia. Similar trends can be seen in Vietnam, where there are 128.3 million mobile phone accounts for a population of 90.7 million. Vietnam is seeing explosive growth in mobile Internet adoption, as the Vietnamese bypass fixed Internet uptake and moved straight to mobile, creating an environment of innovation.

The security and privacy challenges in this dynamic digital landscape is for enterprise agility to implement a mobile security strategy to keep up with the people connecting with the things that surround them. This is especially true for those mobile device users who struggle to get by from day to day securely, sustained by a kind of security passivity. This security passivity can be summed up by a Japanese phrase "Shikata ga-nai" which loosely translated means "It can't be helped."[11]

2 PRINCIPLES

To minimize the risk of mobile device usage and to maximize the value associated with it, some high-level principles should be applied in order to provide a structure for safer mobile device use. While the guiding principles may not be exhaustive, they provide a reasonable basis for managing the security of mobile devices.

These mobile security principles can be broken into two broad categories: principles for mobile device end-users and principles for organizational mobile device management (MDM), including mobile application software developers.

For *mobile device end-users*, principles include:

- Lock your device.
- Accept the updates (unless it is a fake security update on Android, which is a common malware vector, so be warned!). Keep the operating system fully updated to the latest version available from the vendor. If the vendor has ceased supporting operating system updates on your device, which is a particular Android problem, then upgrade the device.
- Ensure software updates, in general, for all applications.
- Keep a clean machine by removing old, unused apps.

---

[9] See https://en.wikipedia.org/wiki/Cabir_(computer_worm).

[10] See Australian Communications and Media Authority (ACMA), 2013. Communications report 2011–12. pp. 14. http://www.acma.gov.au/webwr/_assets/main/lib550049/comms_report_2011-12.pdf.

[11] See Hershey, J., 1946. Hiroshima, Penguin Books, London, pp. 122, ISBN: 978-0-141-18437-1.

- Avoid questionable apps. Be aware of applications that want to access your data (e.g., by accessing your contacts) and consider using applications such as 1Password or other encrypted content managers to ensure that sensitive data is protected.
- Practice personal data management.
- Protect your personal information by storing the least amount of personal information as possible on devices. Android doesn't give you a lot of control currently, but that may change over time, whereas iOS does give you that control.
- Cleaning up or removing personal information from devices so that you don't leave data on the device if it is lost. This will avoid future users of the device finding information about you left on the device.
- Wipe the data on your mobile device before disposing of it. Also enable a remote wipe feature in case the mobile device is lost or stolen. Understand that using a remote wipe may include features that will delete stored data on your mobile device if a password is entered incorrectly after a certain number of times.
- Back up your data. Mobile devices are easy to backup, and users should make the most of this option.
- Stay safely behind bars. Ensure you do NOT jailbreak/root the device and ONLY install applications from the primary distribution points for the operating system (Apple Store, Google Play, and similar app stores).
- Use malware detection software, which predicts and stops mobile attacks, such as Lookout.
- Install privacy apps that explain all of the access to private data that installed apps require.

For *organizational mobile device security*, principles include:

- Embed security for mobile devices in corporate governance, risk management, and compliance (GRC) strategies.
- Establish security governance over mobile devices.
  N.B. This step may not be necessary, but it is part of the risk-based discussion and GRC strategy that an organization should undertake. Organizations may decide NOT to impose governance over devices, and that is their prerogative. Enforcement comes at a price, and not all organizations are willing to pay that price.
- Perform regular mobile device software testing, such as checking runtime interpretation of code for errors.
- Perform regular mobile device security audits focused on applications and software that run on them. Of course, you are then left with the frustrating problem of "what can I do about it?" when the operating system is not something that most organizations can really customize in any way.
- One of the key areas to search for are device defaults; that is, what services are open, authentication defaults, and so on. This is less focused on smartphones and more on things like portable Wi-Fi/mobile hotspots.

For *mobile application software developers*, principles include:

- Building security and privacy into every phase of development.
- Ensuring sensitive data is protected in transit.

- Ensuring security by design and privacy by design by locking down the security and privacy settings of your mobile device app.
- Ensure source code review and application penetration testing.

Further useful information in this area can be found in ISACA's *Securing Mobile Devices Using COBIT® 5 for Information Security* (See ISACA, n.d.).

3 APPLICATION STORES

Application stores, or app stores, refer to online stores for purchasing and downloading software applications and mobile apps for computers and mobile devices.

The term in most cases refers to Apple's App Store, but it is also frequently used for similar online stores that sell mobile apps, including Amazon's Appstore for its Kindle and other Android-powered devices, the Android Market for Android devices, Google Play, Blackberry's App World for Blackberry devices, and Nokia's Ovi Store.

Official app stores tend to have stricter guidelines as to what sort of apps can be uploaded, as well as how they interact with the device and collect information about users and the device itself. Applications that grab your phone number, call history, GPS location, Wi-Fi password, and other data can be a concern. The point here is to start thinking, "Wow—that's scary. I don't want someone to access THAT!"

Applications can sometimes contain viruses or malware that can steal any important information from the phone. Most official app stores have screening processes that detect malicious software and behavior embedded within applications, but these processes are not perfect and there have been instances of suspicious or malicious apps getting through screening and into general availability. Winn Schwartau, Chairman of MobileActiveDefense.com said, "App stores and mobile apps are the greatest hostile code and malware delivery mechanism ever created."[12]

Recently, various reports have shown multiple exploits of app stores via exploiting flaws[13] and zero-day exploits,[14] as well as by installing malicious apps that bypass app store review processes,[15] such as by sideloading, which means installing applications without using the official app store. The motivations for an end-user to sideload an application from a illegitimate source can be varied, such as empowering the user, allowing the use to fine-tune the app experience, allowing the ability to work offline, avoiding registration, or login to use the app, remove phoning-home code, or remove in-app advertising. The risk is that your phone

---

[12] Schwartau, W. Available from: http://www.itsecuritywatch.com/mobile-security/10-great-quotes-about-mobile-security/

[13] Hacker exploits iOS flaw for free in-app purchases http://www.macworld.com/article/1167677/hacker_exploits_ios_flaw_for_free_in_app_purchases.html.

[14] Zero-day exploit lets App Store malware steal OS X and iOS passwords http://www.macworld.com/article/2937239/zero-day-exploit-lets-app-store-malware-steal-os-x-and-ios-passwords.html.

[15] Researchers sneak 'Jekyll app' malware into App Store, exploit their own code, http://www.imore.com/researchers-sneak-malware-app-store-exploiting-their-own-app.

is now more vulnerable to attacks from applications and that you accept all the responsibility that comes with downloading the app. It makes sense: you can't hold the app store responsible for applications you downloaded elsewhere.

4 APPROVED APPLICATIONS

Poor implementation of a legitimate application's usage of device information and authentication credentials can thereby expose sensitive data to third parties. Some examples of this sensitive data include location, owner identification (e.g., name, number, and device ID), authentication credentials, and authorization tokens. Smartphone apps can give automatic access to near-field communications (NFC) payments, SMS, roaming data, premium rate phone calls, etc. Apps with privileged access to such application programming interfaces (APIs) can allow attackers to take advantage of this to abuse the user's financial resources, with subsequent monetary impact. For example, if an API was able to access the PayPal account details of a user and subsequently use these details to make a purchase from a different device, it shows that the security consequences of mobile security aren't limited to just the mobile device.

Data segregation is an approach whereby personal and corporate data are separated, allowing different controls to be applied to each. Although this is less important on corporate-owned devices used only for corporate work, it can be extremely useful in other ownership scenarios, such as personally owned devices which are also used for work.

Increasingly, mobile operating system vendors and third-party software vendors are implementing features to better support personally owned, mixed-use devices. The challenge with smartphones and tablets is different from that of laptops, as the owner of a smartphone or tablet is not likely to be running as an administrative user on their device. A current approach is "containerization," where corporate data is contained within a single app that can enforce protections from other apps and from the user or attackers.

4.1 App Containerization

Containerization of mobile devices such as smartphones and tablets through the separation of personal applications and data from business applications and data is a control mechanism for either the individual or for the business.

App containerization involves segmenting mobile devices into personal and business regions or domains. If this is done with, for example, a bring your own device (BYOD) phone, it lets employees do whatever they want on their side of the border, while corporate IT retains control of the other.

Applications exist that can containerize complete work environments in a secure sandbox or wrap individual apps within a centrally managed container, such as Teopad, Good, and AirWatch. There are different approaches to containers as well, namely on a per-app basis or on entire groups of applications. Application sandboxes create a secure working environment on the mobile device that holds not only locally installed enterprise apps, but also app data and preferences. The runtime environment is protected from the personal home screen and associated apps and the experience is separate: a user is in either an organizational or personal workspace, as illustrated in Fig. 1. However, when app compartmentalization is implemented poorly, it's actually a leading cause of people trying to work around it. People want the natural flow of information in native ways, which the mobile OS provides. Containers and compartmentalization create barriers that many try to work around, and containerized applications are often quite out of date in comparison to their public versions because of a lack in features and functionality. That gets to be really annoying! There is a security implication here as well; containerized apps may not be updated for security flaws/updates as quickly as public versions.

Mobile app containerization

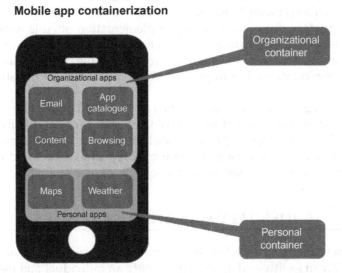

FIG. 1   Mobile app containerization.

A business may want to remotely wipe business data in a business container or a containerized app after someone leaves an organization, for example, but doesn't want to remotely wipe and destroy the unique and personal images that the device owner may have stored.

4.2 Software Watermarking

Software watermarking, which is a form of steganography, involves embedding a unique identifier within a piece of software.[16] Watermarking provides a means to identify the owner of the software and/or the origin of the software and is something that a developer could do for creating enterprise apps. Although originally conceived to discourage software theft, the concept has the potential to be used for validating approved mobile applications. One advantage is that the hidden watermark can be extracted at a later date, by the use of a recognizer to validate the origin of the software. This also has useful applicability for mobile device forensics.

---

[16] See the software watermarking description by Nagra, J., Thomborson, C., Collberg, C., 2002. A functional taxonomy for software watermarking. In. Oudshoorn, M.J. (Eds.), Proc. 25th Australasian Computer Science Conference 2002, ACS, pp. 177–186, January 2002. Available from: http://crpit.com/confpapers/ CRPITV4Nagra.pdf.

4.2.1 *Online-Based Services (Accessible Via Mobile)*

If it is possible for data from a mobile device to be emailed to an external account or uploaded to an online-based service such as Dropbox, then, inevitably, some or all control may be lost.

Attacks against online-based services have become increasingly prevalent, with inappropriate access through poor authentication controls, a lack of monitoring/logging, and unknown persons accessing online stored data. Insecure API and poor transport layer security (TLS) are a common man-in-the middle (MITM) target, as is token/credential hijacking. Mobile applications interact with APIs using well-known REST/Web Services or non-REST/Web Services proprietary protocols. Insecure implementation of APIs or services and not keeping the platform hardened/patched could allow attackers to compromise data on the mobile device when transferred to the platform, or to attack the platform through the mobile application. The importance of TLS to provide communication security should be considered as well.

Popular cloud storage services such as Dropbox and Google Drive can be manipulated and subsequently abused by malicious enterprises using phishing against data in a cloud account with poor authentication controls to prevent social engineering attacks. One well-publicized targeted attack involving data leakage of nude celebrity photos occurred recently and focused on user names, passwords, and security questions of user accounts.[17]

5 IDENTITY MANAGEMENT ISSUES

One of the most challenging aspects of mobile information security is that of identity management. The ability to swiftly and accurately identify an individual and manage that identity is an absolute necessity in this space, yet without detailed planning and governance, various identity management issues arise as highlighted in the following section.

- Emergence of what you have (mobile device) being an identity rather than a factor of authentication. For example:
  - your mobile phone is the identity in mobile payments
  - your mobile phone is the identity to access the extended corporate website
  - what you know PIN or password is still as used as an authentication factor
- Lack of federated identity at the operating system level due to tight integration with the application store is a common identity management issue. For example, can a user log in with an Apple ID on an Android device? If not, then the user has two identity credentials to manage.
- Collision of identities on a platform that was not designed for multiple identities. The following are different levels of identity at play in a mobile device:
  - Mobile number-based identity (e.g., IMSI)
  - OEM-supplied identity (e.g., Samsung Galaxy Apps)

---

[17] See the article "Apple blames 'targeted attack' for leaked nude celebrity photos" at http://www. computerworld.com/article/2600359/access-control/security-apple-blames-targeted-attack-for-leaked-nude-celebrity-photos.html.

- Application store-based identity (e.g., Apple iTunes, Google play)
- Social network-provided ID (LinkedIn, Facebook)
- Messaging services-based ID (Snapchat, WhatsApp)
- Corporate ID
- Personal Banking ID
- Payments-specific ID (e.g., PayPal)
- App-specific ID (the more apps you use, the greater the number of identities you have)

- How much personal information is stored within these respective identities and whose responsibility is it to protect them? Is it the responsibility of the person who stores it or the person that created it? Taking a WhatsApp identity as an example, one of the questions that needs to be considered in some detail is whose responsibility is it to protect my WhatsApp ID? The responsible parties could be:
  - WhatsApp as the application author
  - Google as the maker of the Android operating system
  - Samsung as the OEM, who may have modified Google's Android for their specific device
  - the individual who decided to use WhatsApp in the first place
  - all of the above
- Data stolen from mobile devices by apps with privileged access as outlined previously, such as identity data and credit card details, can be sold by an attacker on encrypted "dark net" sites or hidden forums. The inconvenience caused to the initial user involves recreating identity credentials or replacing credit cards and verifying any suspect online payments made.

The Jericho Forum produced an informative and enlightening paper on Identity[18] that distinguishes core identity, different personas, attributes, privacy, and trust.

The limiting of attributes in each persona minimizes the risk of other people connecting our different personas, which is a privacy-enhancing technique used to retain control over our personas and their related attributes. For example, the attributes assigned to your persona for a library or gym membership should be quite limited, whereas the attributes assigned to opening a bank account should be greater.

This is an especially effective technique to employ for users of mobile devices. In essence, it's about identity compartmentalization that complements app compartmentalization mentioned previously.

One group addressing these challenges is the Global Identity Foundation,[19] who is working on providing enhanced security and privacy for users and which is completely under their control. Human identities are fragmented, since we are different things in different communities, so to be able to control different personas is a step forward in an enabling an ecosystem of assured trust for digital transactions.

---

[18] Jericho Forum Identity Commandments: Key Concepts. Available from: https://www2.opengroup.org/ogsys/catalog/G128.

[19] Global Identity Foundation. Available from: http://www.globalidentityfoundation.org/index.html.

6 PRIVACY

6.1 The Need for Privacy

What are the issues relating to privacy, and why is there a need for privacy? Not everyone understands the privacy concept, but most understand the concept of secrets. Secrets are harder to keep in the information age. This is bad news for all who value their privacy! Long-lasting secrets, like the formula for Coca-Cola, are few and far between.

With few exceptions, our secrets are stored on computers, networks, and mobile devices, which may be vulnerable to hacking. Publishing someone's private information and communications is bad, because in a free and diverse society, people should have private space to think and act in ways that are different to how they think and act in public.

Users of mobile devices, particularly if they are using social media, need to be aware that they will be attractive targets to adversaries through their online presence. Users posting information about their travel plans, such as when someone is home and not home, is frequently used as a cue to perform breaking and entering. Involvement in high-profile or international events unknowingly provides people with information that can be used to elicit information from them or to tailor social engineering campaigns to compromise an organization's network. Users should assume everything posted on social networking websites is permanent and can be viewed by your enemies, the government, your competitors, and so on.

To prevent being the target of a privacy-exposing campaign, users should:

- Carefully consider the type and amount of information posted.
- Restrict the amount of personal information posted.
- Consider limiting access to posted personal data; for example, using the "Friends Only" option for posting on Facebook.
- Be aware of and be willing to learn about the conditions stipulated in the permissions of apps before allowing access.
- Be aware of location sharing of personal information such as tagging locations in posts on social networking sites. Location services are often used by apps to provide directions or "check in" to your local store, coffee shop, or other locations and share that information on various social networks. Not all apps need this data to function, and the ones that do should clearly explain how your location data will be used.
- Make an informed decision regarding geotagging on your mobile device for the camera and other apps that do not require your current location. For example, be aware of the risks and consequences, especially if you are sharing an image with this data still intact and don't want to reveal your true location.

Many apps collect information about the user for marketing purposes, diagnostics, or as part of the service they provide. This could include information such as your contact list, your SMS messages (or other instant messages), your physical location, and potentially even your photographs and Wi-Fi password. This information may be stored or distributed to third parties by the app developer, as well as stolen or intercepted by unauthorized users. Consequently, it is important to read the user agreement and consider the information an app can access.

One of the greater issues for privacy relates to continuing consumer trust in the digital economy. In the span of a few short years, social networking on the Internet has become the platform for communication among many mobile device users using apps like Twitter, Instagram, Facebook, or WhatsApp. Just because people are much more public in the nature and extent of information they share online does not mean privacy is dead. Crompton (2015), Australia's former Privacy Commissioner from 1999 to 2004, covers this in his book, *Privacy Incorporated: The Business of Trust in the Digital World.*

New apps, computing technologies, and channels are facilitating business processes that involve instantaneous streaming and linking of data from many networked sources. If organizations are going to use personal information in innovative ways, there is the question of who bears the risk when things go wrong. Organizations using personal data in this way contribute to people's sense of being out of control and the sense that things are going wrong and need to be fixed.

Individuals will be confident and trusting where they:

- Receive value and respect
- Feel in control and secure
- Find that use of personal information is based on expectations
- Are never surprised
- Receive quick, effective resolution of their issues

6.2 Privacy Implications

There are multiple implications, including legal ones, extending to the privacy of personal information held on mobile devices.

Some privacy implications include:

- Access to personal or corporate email.
- Access to SMS.
- Access to images.
- Access to network (personal, wireless, corporate, VPN).
- Access to corporate apps and data.
- Ability to send SMS to premium rated services (e.g., "Toll Fraud").
- Privacy threats may be caused by applications that are not necessarily malicious, but gather or use more sensitive information than is necessary to perform their function.
- Organizations that let employees use personal mobile devices should consider the BYOD privacy issues and other legal concerns that may arise.
- Use of location-based services technology such as a global positioning system (GPS).
- Outsourcing of MDM; that is, where staff from the outsourcer may act in an unethical way regarding access to privacy-related information.
- Legal compliance with privacy laws. This is often jurisdictionally bound, but for a multinational corporation, it can present some cross-border jurisdiction issues.
- The Internet never forgets. It's not just what is seen at the time, but also what is archived and recorded by countless services. Just because you delete a tweet doesn't mean it can't be used against you!

☞ Tip: Be aware of your social network privacy settings and know that if you are using social media and your post is public, anyone can see it!

With regard to jurisdiction based upon territoriality, even though individuals using IT systems have a specific physical location, the location of mobile devices can change during a usage session. For instance, a person with a mobile computing device (e.g., a tablet or smartphone) can initiate several database updates or queries for processing by a cloud-based service. As those updates and queries take place, the user may move to a different location. Any state from which the individual has operated enjoys jurisdiction because the individual and the devices involved were located on its territory when so used.

Furthermore, even with technology such as mobile cloud computing, the devices from which the human user is initiating requests can be geolocated; software services and applications may track the geocoordinates of the computing devices (e.g., Wi-Fi connection location or device GPS location). It is possible under certain circumstances for someone who does not wish to be tracked to spoof the geocoordinates advertised by their computing device. It is also possible that user location will not be made available by the infrastructure or service provider, or by the application or device itself. Actual physical presence is required and is sufficient for jurisdiction based on territoriality; spoofed presence does not suffice.[20]

Location is an important piece of personal information that should be managed. This personal information could be revealed by tagging locations in posts on a social networking site that advertises your current location or revealed by posts or in images through geotagging.

Organizations should have policies in place to manage mobile devices, including those owned by their employees, that are used in the workplace. Organizations should have the ability to access, recover, wipe, or protect data on mobile devices (e.g., when an employee ceases employment or a device is lost).

Mobile applications should ensure compliance with relevant data privacy laws, such as the Australian Privacy Principles.[21] In the European Union, it is mandatory to obtain user consent for the collection of personally identifiable information (PII).[22]

As mobile apps increase in popularity, many of them are seeking access to large amounts of personal information without adequately explaining how that information is being used. In 2014, the second annual Global Privacy Enforcement Network (GPEN) Privacy Sweep of more than 1200 mobile apps found that almost 70% of apps looked at failed to provide the user with a privacy policy or terms and conditions that addressed privacy prior to the app being downloaded.[23]

---

[20] Schmitt, M.N., et al., 2013. Tallinn Manual on the International Law Applicable to Cyber Warfare (see RULE 2—Jurisdiction section 5). The NATO Cooperative Cyber Defence Centre of Excellence, Cambridge University Press, Cambridge. Available from: http://www.cambridge.org/au/academic/subjects/law/humanitarian-law/tallinn-manual-international-law-applicable-cyber-warfare?format=HB).

[21] See the Australian Privacy resources. Available from: http://www.oaic.gov.au/privacy/privacy-resources/all/.

[22] See EU Data Protection Directive 95/46/EC of the European Parliament and of the Council. Available from: http://eur-lex.europa.eu/LexUriServ/LexUriServ.do?uri=CELEX:31995L0046:en:HTML.

[23] See the report "Mobile apps must put user privacy first" at http://www.oaic.gov.au/news-and-events/media-releases/privacy-media-releases/mob-apps-must-put-privacy-first.

7 VULNERABILITIES

Despite all the security improvements and architectural changes that have occurred within mobile applications, some categories of "classic" vulnerabilities show no sign of diminishing. The lesson is that we haven't learned our lesson. Despite many security flaws having been known about for decades, we're continuing to repeat those flaws in new platforms without having implemented the established fixes and improvements that have also been known about for some time. These include defects in business logic, failure to properly apply access controls, and other design issues. Another important point is that 20- to 30-year-old problems are not magically going away because users have gone mobile. If anything, they have become more prevalent due to accessibility to coding and lack of formalized security training and education. Even in a world of bolted-together application components and everything-as-a-service, these timeless issues are likely to remain widespread.

Vulnerabilities are commonly associated with applications that are installed on mobile devices. However, it is important to recognize that vulnerabilities can be exploited at all levels in the mobile device stack.

8 THREATS

Protecting mobile device data against today's threats is crucial (Whitlock et al., 2014). The recent growth in the use of mobile devices (smart phone, tablets, etc.) has greatly outpaced the ability to control the location and protection of information. The figures below explain why:

- In Australia at the end of Jun. 2014, there were more than 12.4 million Internet subscribers and almost 20.6 million subscribers to mobile services with an Internet connection.[24] Cybercrime affected 5 million Australians in 2013 and cost $1.06 billion.[25] The 2013 Norton Report from Symantec (2013) revealed that 57% of Australian mobile device users were not aware of security options for mobile devices, leaving their devices susceptible to attack.
- The average cost of a malware incident is $56,000 for a small-medium size business (SMB) and $649,000 for a large enterprise.[26]
- It is estimated 12,000 laptops will be stolen this week worldwide.
- Malware has increased year-over-year by 77%.

Given the sheer size of the figures above, it is clear that for both individuals and organizations, protecting mobile device data is important.

---

[24] Australian Bureau of Statistics 2013, Internet activity Australia, June 2014, Cat. no. 8153.0, ABS, Canberra at http://www.abs.gov.au/ausstats/abs@.nsf/mf/8153.0/.

[25] That figure is likely to be an underestimation because it is based on the cost to individuals only, not industry and government. Information from the Australian Crime Commission 2015 report on organized crime at https://www.crimecommission.gov.au/sites/default/files/FINAL-ACC-OCA2015-180515.pdf, ISSN: 2202-3925, May 2015.

[26] Figures published in Kaspersky Labs special 2015 report on Australia's mitigation strategies for advanced threats brochure "Preparing Australia Against Future Risks."

Market analysts predicted that smartphones would outnumber PCs by 2013 and that they would be the most common device for accessing the Internet. Today, there are 2.6 billion smartphone subscriptions globally[27] and are expected to reach 6.1 billion by 2020. Given that specific mobile threats exist, mobile threat testing should be conducted before a mobile app goes live.

As with most changes, these figures have included some new attacks and variations on existing attacks.

As Pete Singer and Allan Friedman point out in their book *Cybersecurity and Cyberwar, What Everyone Needs To Know* (Singer and Friedman, 2014), there are three basic factors needed to evaluate a threat: "The feasibility of adversaries being able to identify and exploit your vulnerabilities, the effect that would happen if they were able to take advantage of these vulnerabilities, and, finally, the likelihood that they will, in fact, be willing to do so."

Like viruses and spyware that can compromise your PC, there are a variety of security threats that can affect mobile devices. These mobile threats and risks can be divided into several categories: application-based, web-based, network-based, physical, overseas travel, and unintentional disclosure of data.

8.1 Application-Based Threats

Downloadable or preinstalled applications can present many types of security issues for mobile devices. Preinstalled applications are especially a problem in Android, where bloatware often includes insecure applications which present immediate "out-of-the-box" security and privacy risks. "Malicious apps" may look fine on a download site, but they are designed to do all sorts of things, such as capture passwords, retrieve information, collect personal information about the end-user without their knowledge, commit fraud, collect information for targeted advertising, or facilitate mischief (e.g., exploit a machine to become part of a botnet). Even some legitimate software can be exploited for fraudulent purposes. Application-based threats generally fit into one or more of the following categories:

8.1.1 Malware

- Malware is software that performs malicious actions while installed on your phone. Without your knowledge, malware can make charges to your phone bill, send unsolicited messages to your contact list, or give an attacker control over your device.

8.1.2 Electronic Tracking (Spyware or Adware)

- Spyware is designed to collect or use private data without your knowledge or approval. Data commonly targeted by spyware includes phone call history, text messages, user location, browser history, contact list, email, and private photos. This stolen information could be used for identity theft or financial fraud.
- Adware is typically installed unwittingly by the end-user and is a common component of free software such as file sharing applications. It collects information about the user that

---

[27] See "6.1B Smartphone Users Globally By 2020, Overtaking Basic Fixed Phone Subscriptions" at http://techcrunch.com/2015/06/02/6-1b-smartphone-users-globally-by-2020-overtaking-basic-fixed-phone-subscriptions/.

can be used for targeted advertisements in the form of banners, pop-ups, and privacy invasion through the tracking of cookies to correlate online behavior to identify a specific individual, which aids in targeted attacks.

8.1.3 *Vulnerable Applications*

- Vulnerable applications are apps that contain flaws that can be exploited for malicious purposes. Such vulnerabilities allow an attacker to access sensitive information, perform undesirable actions, stop a service from functioning correctly, or download apps to your device without your knowledge.
- Cybersecurity experts are expecting mobile payment security threats to grow over the next 12 months. Some 87% of the 900 experts interviewed for the industry body's 2015 Mobile Payment Security Study[28] claimed data breaches would increase over the coming year. In fact, just 23% said they thought mobile payments keep personal information safe, while 47 claimed mobile payments are definitely not secure. Interestingly, it seems that despite these security concerns, adoption of mobile payment is unlikely to be affected significantly. Users should consider how much sensitive information they store on a mobile device when making mobile payments using contactless enabled payment mechanisms. Some malware recently encountered includes Bitcoin-mining malware that targets Android devices.

8.1.4 *Ransomware*

- Another development is file-hting ransomware targeting mobile devices. Examples include Simplocker, CryptoLocker, and since Feb. 2016, Locky. Users will not be able to uninstall the malicious app by traditional uninstall means as one would normally do because the system or even the antivirus (AV) user interface is always "covered" by the malware's user interface.

To protect against these application-based threats, users should consider installing malware, spyware, and adware detection software on their mobile devices.

8.2 Internet-Based Threats

Since mobile devices are almost constantly connected to the Internet and frequently used to access Internet-based services, web-based threats pose persistent issues for mobile devices. Groups such as the Mobile Web Initiative's[29] mission includes ensuring that the web is available on as many kind of devices as possible. This includes ongoing work around mobile web best practices and mobile web application best practices. As Berners-Lee said "The Mobile Web Initiative is important. Information must be made seamlessly available on any device."[30]

Internet-based threats generally fit into one or more of the following categories:

---

[28] See the ISACA study at http://www.isaca.org/SiteCollectionDocuments/CSX-Mobile-Payment_whp_eng_0915.pdf.

[29] Mobile Web Initiative, Available from: http://www.w3.org/Mobile/.

[30] Berners-Lee, T. Available from: https://econsultancy.com/blog/65001-28-inspiring-mobile-marketing-quotes/.

8.2.1 *Denial of Service (DoS)/Distributed Denial of Service (DDoS) Threats*

- While actual DoS and DDoS attacks capture headlines, it is imperative that organizations also fully understand the impact of inadvertent, harmless outages for mobile devices. Up to now, most DoS attacks have been an infrequent and short-lived annoyance, one that most organizations are relatively well equipped to deal with. If the core of the Internet is impacted by a malicious attack or inadvertent outage, we all suffer because the Internet has become our lifeblood in terms of how we work, live, play, and learn. From a mobile device perspective, the focus may revolve around users' own networks and data, network, and data services that organizations provide to their customers, or a combination of both.

8.2.2 *Bots*

- Bots are one of the most sophisticated and popular types of cybercrime today. They allow hackers to take control of many mobile devices or computers at a time and turn them into "zombies," which operate as part of a powerful "botnet" to spread viruses, generate spam, and commit other types of online crime and fraud. Bots sneak onto a person's device in many ways. Bots often spread themselves across the Internet by searching for vulnerable, unprotected devices to infect. When they find an exposed device, they quickly infect it and then report back to their master. Their goal is to stay hidden until they are instructed to carry out a task.

The growth of mobile and other Internet-connected devices is allowing the bots to evolve. We are starting to see devices hijacked and turned into DDoS bots, creating a blended threat with the DoS/DDoS threat mentioned above, thereby increasing the barrier to detect and prevent DoS attempts.

8.2.3 *Advanced Persistent Threats (APTs)*

- Smartphones, tablets, and other mobile devices are getting hit by highly targeted attacks known as APTs intended to steal sensitive data. Mobile devices used in organizations are often the entry point for an APT-style attack aimed at specific individuals to gain access to corporate information. The types of technologies organizations need to invest in to protect against these threats include application control, data loss prevention, MDM, and device control.

8.2.4 *Phishing Scams*

- Phishing scams are about providing data of value to criminals. That can include usernames, passwords, other personally identifying information (PII), financial data, and more. In most cases, it's the lack of ability to validate the source of a message (no way to view full headers in email) and difficulty in viewing full links on the small form factor of a mobile device. Plus, the on-over hovering is tough to replicate on mobile devices.

8.2.5 *Social Engineering*

- Social engineering threats for mobile devices can occur through mobile malicious advertising (or malvertising), which is the promotion of malicious apps that look like legitimate apps or apps that claim to be for "security." As Lacey points out in his book, social engineering can be much safer and easier when the attacker is operating across a network.[31]

Unlike ads displayed inside PC web browsers, ads displayed within mobile apps are delivered by code that is part of the applications themselves. This could represent a backdoor into the device. There are examples of malware from the Google Play store, and Trojanised Android apps through third-party stores, some even installing and executing adware on the device.

8.2.6 Drive-By Downloads

- Drive-by downloads prompt for an application package to be installed, usually under the guise of a security certificate update, but sometimes something as straightforward as a MMS message. For example, the Stagefright Android hack opened the possibility of silent execution of malicious code. The exploit happened when a hacker sent an MMS message containing a video that included malware code. What's most alarming about it is that the victim did not have to open the message or watch the video in order to activate it. As such, a hacker could gain control of the device before the victim even knew about the text message, and even if the phone owner found the message right away, there was nothing to be done to prevent the malware from taking over the device. The hacker would have access to all data and the ability to copy or delete it, as well as have access to the microphone, the camera and all pictures on the device, and Bluetooth.

8.2.7 Browser Exploits

- Browser exploits take advantage of vulnerabilities in your mobile web browser or software launched by the browser such as a Flash player, PDF reader, or image viewer. Simply by visiting an unsafe web page, you can trigger a browser exploit that can install malware or perform other actions on your device.

8.3 Network Threats

Avoid or limit the use of open, public 802.11 wireless networks. Additionally, ensure that you are using the later, stricter security protocols such as WPA2 and avoid the earlier flawed protocols such as WEP and WPA. Where possible, use a virtual private network (VPN) to connect to your organization's secure network. However, a poor VPN technology that doesn't use "pinning" or a similar technology to validate an encrypted authentication session may not do you any good if you're using a fully insecure, crypto-less Wi-Fi network; as cyber adversaries may be able to access your username, password, or passphrase, as well as other private information by a MITM attack tracking your keystrokes. Mobile devices typically support cellular networks, as well as local wireless networks (Wi-Fi) and Bluetooth. Each of these types of networks can host different classes of threats:

---

[31] Lacey, D., 2009. Managing the Human Factor in Information Security, John Wiley & Sons, pp 144, ISBN: 978-0-470-72199-5.

8.3.1 Network Exploits

- Network exploits take advantage of flaws in the mobile operating system or other software that operates on local or cellular networks, such as an International Mobile Subscriber Identity (IMSI) catcher. Once connected, they can intercept your data connections and find a way to inject malicious software on your phone without your knowledge.

8.3.2 Electronic Eavesdropping Such as Wi-Fi Sniffing and Bluetooth/Bluejacking

- Wi-Fi sniffing intercepts data as it is traveling through the air between the device and the Wi-Fi access point. Many applications do not use proper security measures, sending unencrypted data across the network that can be easily read by someone who is grabbing data as it travels. Shared encryption is just as bad. Public sites such as coffee shops, restaurants, and bookstores may have WPA2, but it is likely that anyone with the password can decrypt your packets.
- Bluetooth threats are serious. People who leave BT on all the time leave themselves vulnerable to pairing from nefarious devices and the uploading of spyware. Bluejacking is an older-style attack where someone will use another person's Bluetooth-enabled device. Bluejacking refers to sending of unsolicited data (vCards, etc.) to open Bluetooth listeners in the area. It has more recently been used for marketing, but many more modern smartphones are less vulnerable to Bluetooth stack exploits. This can lead to phishing attempts and the spread of malware or viruses.

8.3.3 Location Detection

- Location tracking, through user-controlled location push apps, where someone checks in and intentionally shares their location. Apps such as Facebook, Foursquare, Swarm, Tinder, Twitter, Uber, and similar hold and share information about where you are exactly at what moment, not to mention a history of where you were.
- Location detection, through bypassing enhanced LTE (4G) security measures with IMSI attacks, also known as IMSI catchers. The thought of a cyber adversary triangulating someone's mobile device to determine their location is a threat that could be used for many purposes such as criminals targeting high-profile individuals and professionals. Using an IMSI catcher to track someone, who has not intentionally used user-controlled location sharing apps, is quite a different threat than the threat above.

8.3.4 Hotel or Conference Facility Networks

- Savvy cyber intruders have been known to exploit hotel or conference facility networks to gain access to mobile devices. Avoid communicating any sensitive information on devices that are not connected to a secure network. Where possible, try to avoid using hotel Internet kiosks or Internet cafes to send or receive important data. Do not connect to open, public Wi-Fi networks for business purposes. Only wireless communications that are needed and can be secured should be enabled.

8.4 Physical Threats

Mobile devices are small, valuable, and we carry them everywhere with us, so their physical security is also an important consideration.

8.4.1 Stolen Data Due to Loss, Theft, or Disposal of Devices

- Lost or stolen mobile devices are a significant risk to the security and privacy of data. The mobile device is valuable not only because the hardware itself can be resold to third parties on the black market, but more importantly because of the sensitive personal and corporate data it may contain. Mobile/smartphone/tablet data leakage is a possible consequence, which may have legal implications, data breach implications, and so on.
- Data can also be stolen via attacks on decommissioned mobiles, smartphones, or tablets. In these cases, the attacker has the potential to recover the information over a longer time frame, as the previous owner or user of the device is typically no longer expecting an attempt to exploit their information. Selling a used device on eBay or Gumtree, for example, without a proper device wipe that has been verified, can leave personal information on the device that may be recovered by the next owner and used for attacks against the previous owner. Indeed, it's been shown that many Android/MDM device wipes don't actually securely wipe data from devices. iOS does, but this means there's a continued risk of data access by third parties if the wipe has not been properly validated.

8.4.2 Unauthorized Access

- Many smartphone users do not have a password lock on their phones when they turn them on or wake them from sleep mode. That widespread lack of security makes any mobile device a tempting target for unauthorized access, which can subsequently lead to data leakage and system infection. Some of the consequences of this include, in iOS, the passphrase or PIN is used to encrypt the filesystem, and having a password permits advanced features such as automatic-wipe on bad password entries.

8.4.3 Gifting

- It is common to receive USB thumb drives as a gift when attending industry events. The area of concern is people with malicious intent may use these opportunities to gift electronic devices that are preloaded with malicious software. A gift of a mobile phone or tablet, rather than a mouse with a microphone powered by USB, is more an area of concern as they have very different threat profiles. When these devices are used or connected to an organization's network or personal device, malicious software may install and run.

8.5 Travel Threats

- If traveling with an electronic device while at high-profile or international events, consider that the compromise of a company-issued mobile device could have an impact on your organization, its information, and its reputation. In most countries, you should have no expectation of privacy in hotels, Internet cafes, offices, or public places. The implications of any compromise are different depending on the use of the device; for example, corporate devices have different implications than personal devices.

8.6 Unintentional Disclosure of Data Threats

• Poorly implemented applications usage of device information and authentication credentials by a developer can expose sensitive data to third parties, including location, owner identification (such as name, number, and device ID), authentication credentials, and authorization tokens. Smartphone apps can give automatic access to NFC payments, premium rate phone calls, roaming data, SMS, etc. Apps with privileged access to such APIs can allow cyber adversaries to take advantage of this, among other things, to abuse the user's financial resources with subsequent financial impact.

What should be generally evident is that outside of malicious insiders, configuration management failure, or DoS attacks, the likelihood of accomplishing a compromise requires very few steps and little complexity.

☞ Individual implications

- o Social engineering and phishing scams
- o Unpatched device implications
- o Awareness of mobile malware
- o Credential harvesting
- o Privacy threats such as location tracking
- o Security considerations when using apps that require financial details
- o Wi-Fi network settings

☞ Organizational implications

- o Data loss
- o Supply chain threats
- o Network-based threats such as network exploits and DoS threats

---

9 RISKS

A lot of security terms are being used in an improperly interchangeable way. Three security terms, in particular—risk, threat, and vulnerability—are explained here for clarity. The term "risk" refers to the likelihood of being targeted by a given attack, of an attack being successful, and general exposure to a given threat. The likelihood of the risk materializing also needs to be taken into consideration. Likelihood can be expressed in terms such as Rare, Unlikely, Possible, Likely, and Almost Certain, with each category increasing in magnitude of likelihood. The term "threat" refers to the source and means of a particular type of attack. The term "vulnerability" refers to the security flaws in a system that allows an attack to be successful.

There is a common formula, $R = TV$ (or Risk = Threat × Vulnerability). As an example, using this formula to address risk for illustrative purposes, if there is a vulnerability but no threat, then there is no risk; alternatively, if there is a threat but no vulnerability, there is also no risk.

If there is both threat and a vulnerability and the likelihood of the risk materializing is likely or almost certain, then the risk is high.

As information technology advances, more powerful and diverse functionality can be found in smartphones, tablets, and other types of mobile devices. While tailoring guidance may support allocating particular security controls to a specific technology or device whilst leaving out other controls, any residual risk associated with the absence of those missing controls must be addressed in risk assessments to adequately protect organizational operations and assets, individuals, and other organizations.

Despite offering much of the functionality of full computers, smartphones, and tablets do not have the same control models or security controls as computers; therefore, attempting to apply a computer's security policies and procedures to such devices will not work. Mobile devices have their own security models, and some may even be more secure than laptops. For example, iOS having full filesystem encryption for several years is way ahead of most corporate laptops and their endpoint encryption. MDM technology often provides far greater granularity of controls, as well as flexibility, than standard PC antimalware. Plus, mobile devices try to make more use of sandboxing technologies by default, something that is still rare at the desktop level (other than OS X and their app store sandboxes). Even within each class of device, there is immense variety; iPhones have a different risk profile than Android phones and, to further complicate the matter, different versions of the same device can have different risk profiles.

The threat and attack vectors for mobile devices are often composed of overlapping versions of attacks aimed at other endpoint devices, mixed with significantly different motivations and goals by the attackers. For example, one attack vector might be social engineering or phishing to gain the identity or credentials to a mobile phone, which can be used by someone else to access the phone as if they were the phone's owner, with the intent to extract other information (e.g., banking credentials stored on the mobile phone) in order to obtain a financial reward at a later time.

A number of lists exist that cover the risks for mobile devices; each has a slightly different focus and identifies different risks. Various organizations like ENISA,[32] NIST,[33] the Open Web Application Security Project (OWASP),[34] and Veracode[35] all publish mobile risk lists. However, it is wise to avoid checklist-based security models only. Mobile risk is a complex field and there are many ways of evaluating the risk; therefore determining what is best and most appropriate for individuals and organizations may take some shopping around of the various lists that have been highlighted above and that exist elsewhere.

Instead, the goal of understanding mobile risk should be to focus on how an organization or an individual can identify the security gaps they have regarding threats, as well as the real-world problems faced in large numbers every day, which will translate to their

---

[32] ENISA, Top ten smartphone risks. Available from: http://www.enisa.europa.eu/act/application-security/smartphone-security-1/top-ten-risks.

[33] National Institute of Standards and Technology, 2013. Guidelines for Managing the Security of Mobile Devices in the Enterprise. Available from: http://nvlpubs.nist.gov/nistpubs/SpecialPublications/NIST.SP.800-124r1.pdf.

[34] OWASP, Top 10 mobile risks. Available from: https://www.owasp.org/index.php/OWASP_Mobile_Security_Project#tab=Top_Ten_Mobile_Risks.

[35] Veracode, Mobile app top 10 list. Available from: http://www.veracode.com/directory/mobileapp-top-10.

risk profile. Consequently, there should be more awareness of risk points, rather than specific steps to take. There are actually some very secure ways to store incredibly sensitive data on a mobile device, which is something that is improving all the time.

☞ Individual implications

- o Understanding the risks that are most relevant to individuals
- o Understanding and acting on best practices about mobile devices
- o Only using trusted sources for downloading apps
- o Understanding the risks when using open, public Wi-Fi networks

☞ Organizational implications

- o Understanding the risks that are most relevant to organizations
- o Managing malicious functionality and vulnerabilities in mobile devices
- o Working within business risk appetite for mobile devices
- o Data loss and organizational reputation management

---

10 MOBILE SECURITY STRATEGY FOR ORGANIZATIONS THAT DEVELOP MOBILE APPLICATIONS

A typical company isn't going to do code review or developer training since they're not developing apps. However, for any organization that develops mobile applications, a mobile security strategy should be developed prior to any actual corporate mobile access deployment. The items listed below provide a high-level framework of key areas for consideration:

10.1 Architecture

The architecture should be flexible and robust enough to support devices, apps, and any back-end infrastructure and associated networks. The mobility revolution puts incredible power in the hands of the end-user, but that power depends on-access to back-end information systems. This means that for the existing systems, a new mobile application architecture needs to be built around them.

10.2 Basic Device Management

Where the organization issues mobile devices, the devices should be exclusively used for work, and no work at all should be allowed on personal devices.

10.3 Secure Software Development Life Cycles (SDLC)

Mobile apps should be subject to regular source code reviews throughout the secure software development lifecycle to detect and remove any code vulnerabilities as early and as often as possible.

10.4 Data Validation

Develop and enforce sound app security processes to prevent unauthorized code manipulation.

10.4.1 Developer Training

If developing mobile apps, developers should undertake mobile security awareness training.

Code analysis through a combined approach of static and automated software analysis and expert review by trained professionals. The network-centric position of mobile application development requires specialized understanding and expertise.

10.4.2 Session Management

Implement appropriate session management as the form factor for mobile often means applications use long-lasting tokens for authentication/authorization, as well as session management.

10.4.3 Cryptography

Minimum cryptography settings for mobile devices should be defined and enforced.

Make sure that device encryption is enabled on the device. While some device manufacturers enable encryption by default, others require that encryption is enabled in the device settings. If the device is owned by an individual, then individual device encryption should be used. If the device is owned and managed by an organization, then enterprise encryption is recommended.

10.4.4 Data Confidentiality

Consider what the default data confidentiality setting should be for mobile device apps.

10.4.5 Environmental and Biometric Sensors

Environmental and biometric sensors in the device (such as acceleration, ambient temperature, fingerprint or iris scan, geolocation, humidity, motion, orientation, proximity, sound, video/still image capture, etc.) should comply with the organization's data capture policies, and their use should be selectively controlled by MDM.

10.4.6 App Penetration Testing

Mobile apps should be subject to a multilevel approach. Test the application to ensure it complies with policies and best practices, but since it is a mobile app, also test the network functionality and any APIs or servers the application may connect to. Furthermore, the mobile apps should be subject to application penetration testing before being loaded to an app store and before going live.

10.4.7 Handle Identity Management

USER AUTHENTICATION

Require confirmation of the user's identity as described in a corporate directory service before giving access to secured data or software.

Two-factor authentication is recommended for confidential data, such as a user name/ password combination plus a successfully answered challenge question or positive finger-print identification.

N.B. It's worth calling out the three forms of authentication in general use:

- Single-factor authentication (e.g., password or PIN).
- Multifactor authentication (e.g., single-factor plus a software- or hardware-generated token code, or a smart card).
- Multistep authentication (e.g., single-factor plus a code sent to the user out-of-band).

Usually, the second step in multistep authentication involves the user receiving a code via SMS or an app such as Duo and entering it alongside (or after) their PIN/password. The phone could be considered as "something you have," thus qualifying this as two-factor authentication. However, the code that is actually used, as well as the credentials used to access the account/ device which receives the code, in the second step is still a "something you know."

Two-factor authentication refers specifically and exclusively to authentication mechanisms where the two authentication elements fall under different categories with respect to "something you know," "something you have," and "something you are."

An example of "something you know" is a password. This is the most common kind of authentication used for humans. We use passwords every day to access our systems. Unfortunately, something that you know can become something you just forgot. And if you write it down, other people might find it. An example of "something you have" is a smart card. This form of authentication removes the problem of forgetting something you know, but some object now must be accessible by you any time you want to be authenticated. Such an object might be stolen and then become something the attacker has. An example of "something you are" is a fingerprint, which is something intrinsic to the user being authenticated. After all, it's much harder to lose a fingerprint than a wallet.

Multistep authentication that requires two physical keys, two passwords, or two forms of biometric identification is not two-factor, but the two steps are still valuable.

DEVICE AUTHENTICATION

Confirm the unique identity of the physical device; it must meet security and configuration requirements, independent of any of its users.

DEVICE ACCESS CONTROL

Protect physical access to the device by requiring successful recognition of a policy-defined password, pattern swipe, biometric scan, voice, or facial recognition.

10.4.8 *Bring Your Own Device (BYOD)*

If BYOD is allowed, organizations should consider limiting users to certain types of devices and not others in order to support a limited fleet of devices, rather than a vast array of different devices that will consume a significant amount of time, effort, and support resources.

10.4.9 *Mobile Device Management*

A well-thought-out MDM strategy is a key ingredient for any successful mobility deployment.

Ideally, the organization's IT section should be at least aware of every smartphone and tablet used in an organization, from activation to retirement. Accomplishing this requires a cohesive plan for MDM. It is advised that assets are defined and how mobile apps use these assets.

Include capability for over-the-air device wipe (i.e., erase all applications and data on the device), device lock (i.e., block device access), and remote device configuration.

10.4.10 Mobile Application Management

Decide on relevant acceptable use policies to help set expectations. Make sure employees are clear on which applications are blacklisted and which they're allowed to access.

Consider an enterprise app store, which provides a central online location for distributing, downloading, and tracking policy-compliant mobile apps for use by employees.

Use mobile application management (MAM) tools to transparently install and configure business or security apps, especially if you allow BYOD; you can't always count on employees to do it correctly on their own.

Establish a way to track app downloads and ongoing usage, monitor to detect outdated or disabled apps, and enforce the removal of blacklisted apps.

10.4.11 Decommissioning

A process should be in place to decommission legacy or end-of-life mobile devices to avoid leaving vulnerable devices in use. This will help reduce the technical debt of the organization and reduce the attack surface.

10.4.12 Auditing

Regular auditing should be carried out to ensure the strategy is effective and that no gaps have been introduced into the organization.

☞ Individual implications

- o Managing enrollment in MDM solutions
- o Ensuring data stored on mobile devices is secure
- o Managing strong passwords or passphrases to secure the mobile device
- o BYOD privacy issues and other legal concerns

☞ Organizational implications

- o Maintaining digital trust with customers.
- o Managing malicious functionality and vulnerabilities in mobile devices.
- o Managing end-of-life or decommissioned mobile devices.
- o An end-to-end security strategy is the goal, which focuses on security capabilities that reach from the mobile device endpoint to its apps and data to the core of the data center and/or cloud.

11 MITIGATIONS

With the increased penetration of mobile devices into the enterprise, the need for mobile device security has also grown. This section aims to show users how to do it correctly and see some of the wins possible. Each individual and/or organization needs to independently assess the risks that are salient for their use cases and environment and consider mitigations as appropriate.

Some mitigations that will assist individuals in addressing mobile device security issues include:

- Maintain up-to-date software through normal lifecycle management
- Ensure strong passphrases are used, where possible. A passphrase should never be written down and stored with the device.
- Sync or back up your mobile device to avoid the risk of lost/stolen devices, as well as ensuring that it is part of an overall resilience strategy for the individual.
- Educate yourself on best practices regarding mobile devices. There are a lot of bad ideas and bad suggestions out there, so verifying the advice you read is a fundamental step. Use as many of the best practices as practically possible to ensure you are not relying on a single control to protect yourself.
- Limit personal attributes stored on the device.
- Review privacy settings.
- Restrict apps and resources, such as denying access to specific device features or data sources on iOS for camera, browser, Google play, YouTube, music, and photo-sharing apps such as Instagram and Snapchat, etc. *N.B.* On Android, there are fewer ways to restrict apps and resources and to limit what these applications can do.
- Disable your device's ability to install apps from sources outside of the standard app stores, such as Google Play, and double check the developer of the app you want to download and be very meticulous of the app reviews to verify any apps' legitimacy.
- Configure device security such as encryption of data at rest.
- Overall device and account hygiene is important, so delete any social media accounts that you no longer use as the terms and conditions may change.
- Disable Bluetooth and wireless capabilities and the ability to "auto-join" a network if possible. This will prevent your device from inadvertently connecting to untrusted networks.
- If wireless capabilities are required, ensure the use of the most secure wireless authentication that your device can support, rather than using older, less secure protocols. For example, use WPA2 for wireless authentication.
- Disable premium calls and in-app purchases.
- Use a search engine to research your digital shadow to see if unexpected content about you is available online that may have originated from a mobile device and manage what is sent digitally. *N.B.* This activity is not trivial to accomplish and may involve changing the settings for various apps to restrict content, as well as following up with web site owners to remove unexpected and unwanted content.
- Only attach your mobile device to a trusted computer. In some cases, by inserting your devices into an unknown computer, you are exposing your mobile devices to unknown risks, and great care should be taken before doing so. Attaching your mobile device to an untrusted computer is not just a malware concern, but also a rooting/jailbreaking one,

as physical access is often required for many of these exploits. You also have to consider data access such as backups and replication in order to protect your data.

- When charging mobile devices, you should only use a trusted computer to connect to the device charger, or go directly into the wall. You can also use a USB charger which removes the data pins and only provides charging pins.

In addition to the above mitigations for individuals, some further mitigations will assist organizations in addressing mobile device security issues.

Mobile device mitigations that are of specific focus for organizations include:

- Whitelist specific applications (or blacklist applications as a second preference) similar to the way firewalls work, where it is best by default to block all and allow only known good sites rather than by default to allow all and block only known bad sites.
- Educate your users on best practices regarding mobile devices.
- Creating a balanced approach for corporate and employee-owned phones, which respects the needs of both sides. If the devices are owned by the employees, there are many restrictions about what an employer can and cannot do. Location tracking, for example, may contravene the workplace surveillance act. It is also a privacy invasion.
- When connecting to enterprise resources, only connect through secure technologies, such as corporate-secured Wi-Fi and VPN services.
- Enforce security policies to protect corporate data.
- Enforce secure BYOD policies if you allow staff to use their devices inside the network.
- Keep highly sensitive organizational data off mobile devices, or as a secondary measure, identify and protect sensitive organizational data on the mobile device.
- Disallow removable media, such as SD cards, in corporate mobile devices by logging the devices in a mobile device inventory solution, then blocking unwanted memory cards. For example, a USB card may be allowed by the policy, while an SD card may be blocked.
- Block attachment execution or downloading to media by blocking unwanted memory cards as above.
- Detect and prevent use of jailbroken or rooted devices by maintaining baseline device information, through both MDM and MAM solutions, managed by the organization.
- Internal segregation controls on what access mobile devices have inside the network, for example, VLAN separation or network filtering.
- Expedite handling of secure lost, stolen, or retired smartphones through full and selective wipe.
- Provide rogue app protection, as well as inventories of installed apps.
- Ensure secure distribution/provisioning of mobile applications.
- Define and enforce allowed device types, operating systems, and patch levels.
- Keep back-end APIs (services) and platforms (servers) secure by implementing, for example, the latest TLS to provide communication security, the right ciphers, DDoS protection, and regular security assessments.
- Secure data interaction with third-party applications and services.
- Comply with the requirements of the Privacy Act in relation to the concept of consent. For example, pay specific attention to the collection and storage of consent that has been given by a user for the collection and use of that user's data.

☞ Individual implications

- o Acting on best practices regarding mobile devices
- o Managing credentials
- o Managing data securely
- o Privacy
- o Device and data loss
- o Wiping the mobile device before disposal

☞ Organizational implications

- o Enforcing security policies to protect corporate data
- o Managing BYOD assets, if used in the organization
- o Maintaining and managing MDM and MAM solutions
- o Mobile device education for staff and mobile app developers
- o Complying with legal and regulatory requirements
- o Keeping back-end services and platforms secure
- o Comply with relevant Privacy Act requirements

In addressing the mitigations, it should be recognized that there are shared/overlapping concerns for individuals and organizations. With the increased use of BYOD policies, there is a trend to connect these two worlds anyway, which means there is overlap that blurs the distinction between the two.

11.1 Exploit Mitigation

Exploit mitigation technologies attempt to prevent the abuse of vulnerabilities. They typically achieve this by making the execution of unauthorized code difficult or impossible while not affecting legitimate programs such as address space layout randomization (ASLR) and similar techniques.

Recent versions of smartphone and tablet operating systems have seen significant improvements in exploit mitigation technologies. Vendors are strongly motivated to implement and develop such technologies, not only because they can help to protect users, but they can also make jailbreaking less likely, as jailbreaks rely on abuse of security vulnerabilities.

N.B. There is very little that an organization or an individual can do about vendor-provided exploit mitigation technologies—short of ensuring that your platform is updated to the most recent version of hardware and software available. You can't enable these technologies yourself (the vendor has to do it for you), and you need to procure the software/hardware that is compatible.

11.2 Travel Mitigation

For corporate-issued devices, prior to departure, consult your IT security team. They can confirm that your device's configuration is correct and that all updates, patches, encryption, and AV software have been installed and baseline the device prior to departure and again on return to look for any signs of compromise.

Remove all nonessential data from the device. In particular, reconsider the need to take sensitive information overseas.

Maintain physical control over mobile devices (whether they are your own or company-issued), not only to minimize the risk of theft or loss, but also to protect the confidentiality of information stored on the device. It is advisable to keep your device in your possession at all times and not trust hotels, room safes, or other services to provide physical protection of equipment. When traveling, never check your device in as luggage; devices should be taken on board as hand luggage.

Avoid connecting to unsecured Wi-Fi networks for business purposes when traveling overseas. Only wireless communications, such as a password-protected business Wi-Fi or a trusted Wi-Fi network, should be utilized. Where possible, connect back to your organization's VPN to use the Internet. *N.B.* You may not be able to do this without using Wi-Fi, and there is still an issue of trust with the VPN process because of what happens prior to the VPN being established. For example, a lot of devices still leak information after joining a network.

Finally, when you return, advise your IT security staff if the device was taken out of your possession for any reason, particularly if you have traveled to a high-risk country. Also advise them if you left your device in your hotel room for an extended period of time. IT security staff should be able to check the device for any malicious software or evidence of compromise.

12 MOBILE SECURITY TECHNICAL CONTROLS

This section contains suggestions for a number of technical controls covered under mobile device security. There are a multitude of technical controls that can be used to mitigate the risks that arise from the use of mobile devices; however, not all apply to all types of mobile device.

In order to help mitigate the risk of lost, stolen, or misplaced devices, below are some actions that can be taken to protect your own data and that of others.

12.1 Passwords, Passphrases, and Biometrics

Passwords are a key control, as a weak password can enable the bypass or deactivation of many other controls. As mentioned earlier, a key bypass risk is having a simple PIN as a protection and the lost/stolen device being attached to a computer to conduct a brute force attack and mount the filesystem.

Laptop passwords can be long and complex without adversely affecting users, as laptops typically have full keyboards, allowing easy entry of the password.

It can be particularly challenging to ensure that users select secure passwords for smartphones and tablets, as they are typically accessed frequently throughout the day, with users regularly checking information in brief spurts rather than engaging in extended work periods.

Password or passphrase protect your device and enable auto-lock. Handle password credentials securely on the device, such as choosing the strongest alphanumeric passcode or passphrase that your device can support.

Users often think making good passphrases is harder than it really is. It is worth the effort, as a strong passphrase is harder to detect than for a password that may be fairly easily subjected to a dictionary attack.

Examples of good passphrases that are also mobile friendly are "scratchybrownvinyl420" which uses random common words and some numbers that includes 21 characters, or "Back2dafewture!" which is a short, easily remembered 15-character phrase that includes a capital letter, a number, a substituted word, a misspelt word, and a special character—although there is the hassle of typing them all in. Other example passphrases could be "x-Ray vision Is g00d," or using a foreign word mixed with a different language—say an English phrase with a Malaysian word in the middle.

It should also be noted that some modern mobile devices have biometric locks, which typically provide more secure access control and are a supplementary or alternate control.

12.2 Encryption

Although encryption has been a staple of IT systems for decades, their implementation in mobile devices has its obvious limitations with the ever-growing number of devices to be managed, hence the use of automated enterprise systems. There is a reason that certain phone brand costs are prohibitively high for certain economies, paving the way for the proliferation of Android or Windows phones that do not include this special chip, making them three to four times cheaper. As stated by Auguste Kerckhoffs, even in mobile devices, everything about the encryption can be public knowledge other than the key. This stresses the importance of secure generation of key material either for link encryption or data protection.

12.2.1 Code Encryption

There are multiple reasons for a developer or an organization to encrypt the code used in their mobile application. From an operating system perspective, it helps in maintaining system integrity by providing a facility to detect code integrity violation. From a user perspective, this protects them from information theft or privacy violation.

Code encryption is not implemented by default by all mobile operating system providers. iOS, for example, does binary encryption by default; however, this is not necessarily the case with Android-based devices. It has to be noted that code signing is not the same as code encryption, as both the major mobile application curators require the apps to be signed to varying degrees. We will discuss this further later on.

Code encryption may help in preventing reverse engineering or code modification; however, the effectiveness of this control has been contested by many practitioners. While poor key management practices and implementation of insecure algorithms heavily degrade the effectiveness of code encryption, the question being raised by these practitioners is what is the point in encrypting code when it must be decrypted on the device before loading it into the processor for execution. At this point in runtime, taking a snapshot of the decrypted code in memory is trivial at best.

Identity-based code execution utilizing code signing techniques may very well be addressing most of the security and privacy concerns and could overcome many of the limitations not fully addressed by code encryption alone. As with any technical control, it is imperative that the intent is not lost during implementation. Certificates and key management techniques should cover appropriate process and technical controls to realize benefits of implementing code signing. Self-signed certificates and poorly managed private keys offer no real benefit of code signing.

12.2.2 *Data Encryption*

Data encryption deals with protecting user/consumer data and privacy. Although application code is also data for all practical purposes, the delineation can be drawn at the prime control objectives for each data type. The delineation is more easily seen in defining "whose data is it"—is it from me and based on things I know and do, or is it from the application, based on the intellectual property of the developers, their infrastructure, and architecture? When it comes to code, the prime control objective, in our justifiable view, should be integrity. This doesn't mean that code confidentiality is unimportant, but there is little point in protecting intellectual property when its integrity cannot be assured. For example, how can you be sure the information out there is what you actually released if you can't assure integrity? One would expect that the user-generated content in a mobile device is stored locally in a device. However, there are cases where data is not local, and that has implications not just for security/privacy, but for resilience and business continuity. User data is stored both locally and in the cloud. Let's look at the security controls offered in both environments below:

LOCAL

With the growing concern over privacy and the quest to make the mobile OS suitable for Enterprise IT, almost all mobile operating systems are providing some form of a full-disk encryption solution in their recent releases. In this context, full-disk encryption only refers to the process where data is encrypted before committing to the disk and decrypted before supplying data back to the calling process. This does not mean the entire disk is encrypted; as a matter of fact, some mobile device providers allow only encrypting certain volumes, but still call it full-disk encryption.

CLOUD

Cloud storage is offered by mobile application curators, and mobile developers themselves in some instances, as a means to back up your data and provide multiple-device support and synchronization, as is the fact that they want to mine your personal data to sell it to third parties and generate ads.

Below are some of the types of data that are frequently stored in the cloud, as well as existing security controls offered by some of these storage providers.

Types of data that are potentially stored in the cloud:

- Contacts list
- Browser bookmarks
- Chat logs
- System and application specific settings and logs
- Downloaded free and paid content including apps
- Passwords (such as saved passwords like those of your Wi-Fi network)
- Photos
- Game progress

Actually, nearly any function that is available on a mobile application that involves data could potentially be transmitted/stored on servers online. The downside of online servers is that they require a full-time data connection.

It is safe to assume that the data at rest that is leaving your device can be read by others unless it is encrypted locally within the mobile device with a key generated in the mobile device by user-supplied input.

☞ Callout: Maybe it is worthwhile to think about the number of applications or platforms that asked for your input to generate a key for backup encryption before storing it in the cloud. There aren't too many, you say? We are not surprised!

There is also a difference between application PINs/passwords and specific encryption of application data. A lot of applications have an additional PIN option required prior to their launch, but that does not mean the data is encrypted; it will be up to the user to read the developer notes to determine this.

Quite often we see companies claim that their product is secure because they use protocols such as TLS. While it is true that they address transport level security issues, they have no effect on the security of data at rest in cloud storage. Protection of data at rest can be best assured if the solution seeks user input for encryption and decryption of data.

The following implementation can offer some level of protection for your data that is stored in the cloud:

- The key generation process happens on your device.
- This key is encrypted using user-supplied input.
- The personal data is encrypted using this key.
- Only the encrypted data encryption key and the encrypted data are ever stored in the cloud.
- The data is only decrypted after bringing it back to the device.

Any other implementation of key management design is questionable. For example, Hardware Security Modules (HSMs) are not built to handle millions of keys. There is a theoretical limit on all of them, including those that are attached to cloud resources but behave pretty much the traditional way. You can have HSM-like features in the device, like Trusted Platform Module (TPM) and Apple's crypto processors, which bring it back to the device as the approach suggests here. It is never a good design to put millions of keys in a solution even if it supports it theoretically, as your solution will likely become a bottleneck due to the overhead.

KEY MANAGEMENT DESIGN

Key management design describes how cryptographic keys are protected, managed, and distributed. At the core, any key management design follows quite a similar approach. While device or platform specific implementation may vary, the following are the main components:

CHAIN OF TRUST   This is the starting point of the key hierarchy, the seed. This seed in most cases is the unique device identifier (UID) of your mobile device. There are multiple claims from different sources that this UID cannot be seen or extracted by anyone including the device manufacturer, which is equally being challenged, too. For the purpose of this book and for a general understanding of the concept, unless this seed is generated by the user of the device within the device only, we cannot be certain about the ability, or lack thereof, of a device manufacturer to gain access to your data. Having said that, we would like to reiterate that cryptography is the science of delaying access to the data, not preventing it.

MASTER KEY The master key can be created utilizing the UID, or in the devices where UID is not used, some cryptographic library functions are utilized to generate this master key. These functions may utilize environment variables to generate this key. Some manufacturers make claims that they only use a kernel-level key derivation function. The intent of such deep-rooted functions is to be able to encrypt the media at the block level, rather than any real security benefit. This master key is used to encrypt key stores or other keys including the data-encrypting key.

USER-SUPPLIED PIN/PASSPHRASE In most cases, this user-supplied variable (referred only as PIN hereafter) is utilized to encrypt the master key only. Designwise, there is a good reason for not including it in the actual key generation process of the data encryption key. By design, the user-supplied PIN is expected to change frequently. When a user changes a PIN, unless the key that is encrypting the data is intact, the entire volume would need to be decrypted and then reencrypted with the new key. While we don't see any major design constraint in utilizing this user-supplied variable for generating the master key, such an implementation is not common, for reasons not known to us. This should be one of the most important items, given that nobody else is talking about it. It is only covered here at a high level, but it is a topic that needs to be covered in depth elsewhere, as it does not align with the intention or the tone of the book to go into that detail here.

KEY STORES Also called key bags in certain implementations, these are software constructs for storing the encryption keys. These key stores reside in your device and are also utilized to transport the keys over to other systems, like the device you authorize for backup/sync, and management servers.

Even with such a complex implementation, the data is only protected until you boot up or unlock your device after boot up (depending upon implementation), by which point the media is decrypted and the data is available in the clear. This is not a terrible thing because that is where the control cycle of a solution like full-disk encryption ends. This is the case with any implementation of a full-disk encryption solution on any type of device, including laptops and workstations. The key observation to note here is that the data should not be decrypted after boot up until the user authenticates themselves during the unlock process. It pays to reiterate that when a system has been unlocked after a reboot, the only protection that is available to safeguard your data on the device is your PIN. Fig. 2 from NIST Special Publication 800-63 shows the difficulty in guessing a password (expressed as entropy) in relation to its length.

While the design described above is common, it is not universal. We encourage readers to learn more and ask questions of their vendors and solution providers. This is the only way to have detailed assurances as to the security of a solution.

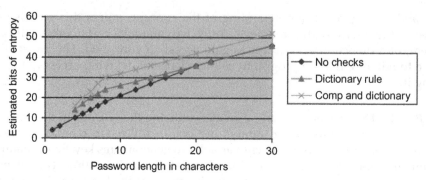

FIG. 2   Difficulty in guessing a password.

12.2.3 Key Management

Key management usually lies at the foundation of any other security activity, as most protection mechanisms rely on cryptographic keys one way or another. There are just too many keys with varying degrees of complexity (some perceived) with inadequate key management infrastructure. The figure below represents the global perception in terms of the relevant complexity in managing each key type. It has been realized that there are opportunities for some quick wins in this area with clear definition of the requirements and some perception management, with relatively little investment in technology.

Having said that, we acknowledge the challenge in managing the ever-growing number of keys utilized in public key infrastructure and persistent data protection. The key management systems, if any, have not scaled up to manage the proliferation of keys and the applicable requirements in protecting those keys. Further, some of the technologies utilized as key management systems were not intended for that purpose. For example, in the figure below, we can observe a strong notion globally that a Certificate Authority (CA) is a key management system, although it was not designed to be one (Fig. 3).

In our view, a key management system/solution is an integrated approach for generating, distributing, and managing cryptographic keys, not certificates, for devices and applications. The effectiveness of cryptographic techniques is highly dependent on the effectiveness of the systems and processes that are protecting the keys. If the integrity of the key cannot be assured, the integrity of the encrypted data cannot be assured either. Encryption only, without proper key management defeats the purpose of the control. Key lifecycle management covers keys through their lifecycle starting from creation, initiation, distribution, activation, deactivation, and termination.

12.3 VPN

VPNs are frequently used by mobile workers who are unable to guarantee a secure connection, yet might need to access an organization's resources. If properly configured, a VPN prevents attackers from intercepting and modifying traffic, while allowing approved access to internal resources. However, a VPN does not offer security if the attacker has a presence on the mobile device or the network to which it is connected, such as the network at a coffee shop operator, hotel, the ISP/Telco, or even the VPN endpoint operator. Poorly configured

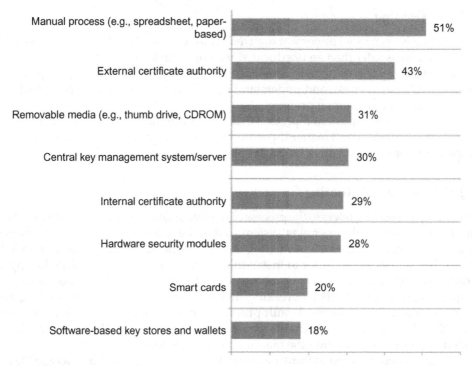

FIG. 3   Technologies used as key management systems.   *Global Encryption and Key Management Trends Study (Apr. 20, 2015).*

and secured VPNs can pose a risk, as they could expose sensitive assets and potentially give an attacker access to the organization's internal network, information systems, or credentials, enabling them to gain a foothold within the organization as the first step to a subsequent attack. One method to enhance the VPN's security utility is to deploy multistep authentication or multifactor authentication to strengthen the VPNs security posture.

Three main types of VPN are available:

- IPsec VPNs, which are useful for point-to-point connections when the network endpoints are known and remain fixed.
- SSL VPNs, which provide for access through a web browser and are commonly used by remote workers (telecommuting workers or business travelers).
- Mobile VPNs, which provide mobile devices with access to network resources and software applications on a network, when they connect via other wireless or wired networks. Mobile VPNs are used in environments where workers need to keep application sessions open at all times throughout the working day, as they connect via various wireless networks, encounter gaps in coverage, or suspend and resume their devices to preserve battery life. A conventional VPN cannot survive such events because the network tunnel is disrupted, causing applications to disconnect, time out, fail, or even the computing device itself to crash. Mobile VPNs are being adopted more and more by mobile professionals and white-collar workers. They are commonly used in public safety, home care, hospital settings, field service management, utilities, and other industries.

12.4 User Training

User training is even more important than technical controls. An educated user on a device with poor security is safer than an uneducated user on a device with "strong" security.

The importance of how to actually use all of the security controls that are in place, information asset value awareness, and understanding the big picture are hugely important and should be a focus of any training program.

N.B. This is a hugely important topic that deserves additional consideration. All the technical controls in the world won't matter if you don't have the right knowledge and understanding by the users, or for that matter, mobile application developers.

12.5 Jailbreaking and Rooting

Jailbreaking and rooting refers to the process of removing limitations put in place by a device's manufacturer, modifying the operating system so that the native operating system restrictions are removed and modifications can be made to any part of the operating system and underlying filesystem. This allows the end-user to install third-party software from outside the app store. Essentially, jailbreaking allows you to use software of which the manufacturer does not approve.

Companies don't want users jailbreaking their devices to get past the operating system limitations so you can change the default programs or run third-party applications. To perform a jailbreak, someone has to find a security vulnerability that allows the device to be "exploited" in order to get around the manufacturer's safeguards.

Android allows users to install third-party applications from outside the Google Play Store right out of the box, so Android doesn't need to be jailbroken. This is both a great feature and a threat to the security of the operating system. Users need to balance this and understand the trade-off if they install such third-party applications.

Rooting is the process of gaining "root access" to a device, which refers to gaining privileged control or administrative access to a device and getting around Android's security architecture that is designed so that the user does not have full administrative access for good reasons; in the vast majority of cases, users won't ever need it.

N.B. This is generally performed on Android devices, giving the user the ability to perform operations that are otherwise inaccessible to a normal user, but rooting can also occur on other devices.

On some devices, rooting may need to be accomplished via a security exploit. Just like jailbreaking, manufacturers generally don't want you rooting, since it can affect device performance and behavior and potentially lead to support issues. If you make changes to the underlying operating system and applications, then things can behave erratically, which drives up customer complaints and could lead to a poor user experience.

It should be noted, that jailbroken, rooted, nonmanufacturer devices may not respond to the wipe command to pose risks to users' sensitive information if a device is lost stolen or misplaced.

☞ Tip: Removing hardware restrictions (e.g., rooting on Android, and jailbreaking on Apple) on your mobile device in order to install unapproved third-party apps or features can weaken built-in security protections, leaving your phone susceptible to malware.

12.6 Patching

Patching is the process by which software flaws are fixed and features improved. Smartphones and tablets require patching as vulnerabilities are discovered. However, since apps are restricted in terms of what they can do if properly coded in the right modern mobile operating system, the significant attack surface is the operating system itself. It should be noted, however, that jailbreaking/rooting destroys this protection. As such, many attackers, security professionals, and jailbreakers attempt to find security issues in mobile OS, or more frequently, in vendor-distributed applications that serve as a gateway to OS exploits. As an example, Apple's iOS 9 upgrade improved/fixed about 100 security issues from the last release of iOS 8.

12.7 Asset Management

Asset management is an important control for organizations in deciding policy and monitoring its implementation, as well as allowing an effective response to breaches or security issues.

MDM software is available from many vendors, each offering a range of features, in addition to simple asset lists. However, MDM software rarely adds controls to a smartphone or tablet operating system; instead, it simply provides convenient access to built-in controls on the device itself. The level of control that an MDM solution can offer is therefore dependent on the device and, occasionally, on the version and even the manufacturer of the device.

12.8 Mobile Device Management

MDM solutions provide features such as secure access to corporate email, automatic device configuration, certificate-based security, and selective wipe of enterprise data for both corporate and user-owned devices.

MDM software can often indicate whether a device has been jailbroken. Jailbreaking deactivates or bypasses many crucial security controls and it is therefore recommended to track it and deprovision any jailbroken devices, which should be prevented from accessing the organization's resources.

The following sections cover some specific MDM areas for organizations:

12.8.1 Inventory

An organization's MDM should maintain a list of devices to be managed; that is, a mobile asset inventory.

The MDM inventory may include:

DEVICE INVENTORY

Beyond the basics (e.g., device ID, hardware model, firmware version), an MDM can help record and report on related assets like wireless adapters and removable memory.

INVENTORY CLASSIFICATION

An MDM might autoclassify devices by mobile OS/version or state (e.g., unknown, authorized, provisioned, decommissioned).

INVENTORY MAINTENANCE

An MDM might be used to periodically poll devices, check for changes at network connect, or carry out administration-initiated audits.

PHYSICAL TRACKING

With many smartphones now supporting GPS, location-based MDM features are possible.

DATABASE INTEGRATION

An MDM may be able to integrate managed mobile device records into a common database using inventory exports or reports.

12.8.2 Device Eligibility

Device eligibility depends on many characteristics, including operating system and vendor/model/version that the organization is prepared to support. The organization needs to decide what platforms (e.g., Apple iOS, BlackBerry OS, Google Android, Microsoft Windows Phone) and minimum models/versions (e.g., Samsung SAFE devices running Android 4+) to support. Device-independent management choices should be made wherever possible and practical while establishing baseline acceptance criteria for specific business uses (e.g., hardware-encrypted devices with remote find/wipe capability).

12.8.3 Device Registration/User Enrolment

MDMs can help administrators register organization-issued mobile devices, or let users register their own devices (e.g., through enrollment portals), or some combination thereof.

With good MDM, users can quickly self-enroll their mobile devices.

12.8.4 Lockout screen

If a mobile device is found to be out of policy, lost, or stolen, or if an employee leaves the organization, an MDM server can take action to protect corporate information in a number of ways.

To permanently delete all media and data on the device and restore it to factory settings, MDM can remotely wipe the device. If a user is still looking for the device, the IT section can also choose to send a remote lock command to the device. This locks the screen and requires the user's passcode to unlock it.

12.8.5 Policy

To gain user acceptance, organizational policies might need to balance a user's desire for access and the organization's desire for security. Policy should be developed with an understanding of business and user requirements, as experience indicates that users will attempt to bypass or otherwise render ineffective controls that they feel are overly restrictive. Users should therefore be educated as to the reason for the restrictions and the implications of bypassing them.

☞ Tip: Regardless of the phone you use, it is vital to keep your operating system and apps up-to-date by enabling automatic updates. Old versions of software can have security issues and fraudsters can exploit these to access your data.

12.8.6 BYOD vs. Choose Your Own Device (CYOD)

If BYOD personal smartphones and tablets are used for business purposes, it is recommended that they be managed using MDM software, as this can ensure that organizational policies are followed.

An alternative to BYOD is CYOD. Offering employees a choice of approved devices provides more control for IT, compared to allowing them to bring any smartphone or tablet they want.

However, CYOD strategies also mean less freedom for employees and may not provide as high a satisfaction as BYOD.

Businesses can let employees choose from devices that they are sure can be managed and secured to the required extent. This is useful for dealing with Android fragmentation, meaning the multitude of different Android versions on different phones on the market. CYOD ensures that only the most up-to-date and secure versions of the OS are supported.

12.8.7 Remote Wiping BYOD Devices

Many configurations will allow a corporate administrator to wipe a personal device that has been enabled for BYOD usage. A capable MDM solution that actually can per-app-wipe and only touch organizational data i.e., a "selective wipe" that only removes corporate information, shouldn't need a full device wipe. However, in some cases, an administrator will need to wipe the entire device; for example, if there aren't containers around corporate data it can increase this requirement, meaning that personal data will be lost in the process. An entirely possible use case involves the loss of an employee's phone that contains family photos not saved on any other device. An administrator might wish to wipe the device to ensure the safety of the organization's data, while an employee might prefer to wait in the hope that the device is recovered. Wiping the device could potentially present the organization with legal issues.

Policy and user education is therefore vitally important, so organizations supporting personal devices are strongly encouraged to design a policy that takes remote wipe into account and to ensure that users are aware of the implications. Likewise, users need to do their homework as to what their MDM solution provides and to take into account what their organizational policies may require.

12.9 Mobile Application Management

Successful enterprise mobility management requires a MAM solution that has an enterprise app storefront, as well as the ability to secure mobile applications on the device, authenticate end-users, separate business and personal apps, monitor application performance and usage, remotely wipe data from managed applications, and retire apps when necessary.

MAM focuses on application management and differs from MDM. It provides a lower degree of control over the device, but a higher level of control over applications. MDM solutions manage the device by saying what major operating system is required, the configuration settings and can include management of all applications and application data, and crucially, things like accounts (e.g., email accounts), network connections (VPNs, Wi-Fi), etc.

12.10 Remote Track and Wipe

Remote track and wipe is slightly different from remote wiping, as described in the previous section. Remote track and wipe aims to mitigate the risk of device theft or loss. For many, this is about the end-user having a self-service and "native" capability under their control. iOS has this built-in, and recent Android devices may support it as well. It works by having the device maintain or regularly establish a connection over the Internet to check for updates or to phone "home."

Most modern smartphone and tablet platforms have remote wiping and tracking built into the operating system. As tablets may not always have a mobile Internet connection, it may be more difficult to track or wipe a tablet until it is connected to a data network and is once again reachable for review and potential wiping.

12.11 Antivirus/Antimalware

AV solutions are helpful controls against common malware types. The flaw in older AV solutions is that a sample of malware has to be detected and analyzed before it can be identified by an AV product, but this style of AV is not that common anymore. Many newer mobile solutions use behavioral analytics and signaling back to a remote cloud server to analyze malware; signatures are still used, but other approaches are growing.

Regardless of ownership, where corporate systems are using Windows, having an AV solution in place is of higher value, given that is also where the threat is. Furthermore, since AV is dependent upon updates in order to work effectively, policies should ensure that the AV is able to update.

AV solutions for iOS and Windows devices, such as the iPhone, iPad, and Windows Phone devices, offer security "controls" built into the operating system, which contain the security risk. Consequently, AV on these devices is typically limited to scanning specific files rather than offering background, on-access scanning of files. If AV could operate freely on the platform that would imply that malware could as well. However, this is a trade-off that is worth encouraging. You don't want any software to have full and unrestricted access to the operating system/device—only the operating system kernel and tightly restricted APIs.

Android is a different matter, though, as the operating system is more permissive, which is also the problem. Permissiveness comes at a cost, and if the user is willing to accept that cost, it may mean they also have to bring on board additional controls and protections. Malware has been found on Android devices, hence an AV product could potentially provide a useful function in the same way it does on a laptop.

12.12 Transmission Security

Since the majority of smartphones are capable of using multiple network mechanisms including Wi-Fi, provider network (3G, 4G, CDMA, GSM, LTE, and others), Bluetooth, etc., sensitive data passing through insecure channels could be intercepted if the user explicitly runs applications to permit this. Therefore, it is advisable that where the device is the receiver of data to disable wireless access, such as Wi-Fi or Bluetooth, when not in use so as to prevent unauthorized wireless access to the device.

Tip: Cyber adversaries have ways of capturing information being sent over free public Wi-Fi networks.

Using public Wi-Fi when performing sensitive online transactions such as shopping or banking can be risky and should be avoided. You can be far more confident performing these activities when connected to a trusted Wi-Fi network, such as in your home.

12.13 Mobile Usage Controls

Mobile phone telecommunication service providers have various options for controlling mobile devices including controls for privacy and usage, filtering content, and location and monitoring settings.

12.13.1 Usage Controls

Most companies will allow users to turn off features, such as downloading videos or images, texting, premium call numbers, overseas calls, and Internet access. These controls can also be used to limit the number of calls or texts and set time restrictions.

12.13.2 Content Filtering

These controls can block certain websites to allow for safer mobile browsing on the Internet. Some filters can also limit videos and other multimedia.

12.13.3 Location and Monitoring Settings

These controls allow users to track their mobile device's whereabouts using GPS systems that are built into the phone.

Tip: Location services on mobile devices are great to help you find your way or locate nearby services. It can also be used to share details of your location. But sharing this information publicly could place the user at risk.

12.14 Memory

Most modern mobile devices contain a combination of SIM cards and removable storage, such as an SD card, and most devices have some amount of internal storage. If you are intending to replace your mobile device with a new device, before disposing an old mobile device, it is important to consider deleting all of your personal information, photos, messages, and contacts from the SIM, removable storage, and internal storage. However, it is worth noting, some information may still be stored on the device in locations you missed or are restricted by the manufacturer.

12.15 Cross-Border Data Theft

Mobile devices as a vector for data to leave the organization is nothing new, as the inherent mobility beginning with laptops has always made it impossible to rely on a strong perimeter for adequate protection. The cloud computing revolution and the myriad of hosted application services that are not geographically fixed has made it easier for data to cross national borders. With the increased use of mobile, the applications and data stored in mobile devices used locally and globally may put both users and organizations at risk. In addition, data traveling on the mobile devices is typically subject to laws and regulations that will vary from one jurisdiction to another. There are many legal/jurisdictional issues with this architecture, and organizations are just now starting to work through them.

The cross-border nature of cybercrime means that organizations should ensure good document protection practices by improving digital document security techniques. A second aspect is for organizations that have international offices, where cross-border document exchange is known, should establish proactive relationships with colleagues in international locations to identify and minimize barriers to swift and effective international cooperation in response to cross-border data theft.

12.16 Regulatory Retention

The amount of data that can be stored and processed in mobile devices has grown dramatically.

The increased use of the inherent storage and computing capacity of mobile devices has created a new data retention risk. As an example, one trend is the popularity of iPads for use by company board members to access confidential corporate data and board reports. While the electronic copies of board papers made available on a device may be secure, annotations made to/for a document on the device itself, which constitute legal documents, are not captured or stored under corporate ownership. This is important for complying with statutory recordkeeping requirements and for preventing legal risks, such as Income Tax Assessment Acts, which require entities to keep records that note and explain all transactions and other acts relevant to the Act for a number of years. The same goes for Corporations Acts, which require companies to retain documents that disclose the company's transactions, financial position, and performance for a number of years after the transactions covered by the records are completed. The period of retention for these and similar Acts may vary, depending on the country involved.

☞ Individual implications

o Managing credentials
o Managing data securely
o Keeping mobile devices up-to-date
o Locking mobile devices when not in use
o Privacy
o Device and data loss

☞ Organizational implications

o Managing the comprehensive set of technical controls covered above
o Handling issues related to jailbreaking and rooting

13 FORENSICS

Mobile device forensics relates to the recovery of digital evidence or data from a mobile device under sound conditions due to the necessity to preserve "evidence" when it comes to legal proceedings.

With the ubiquity of mobile devices, forensic evidence extracted from mobile as well as other electronic devices can be an invaluable source of evidence for investigators in both civil and criminal prosecution cases. Smarter, more powerful mobile devices hide a potential treasure trove of evidence for investigators and prosecutors alike. Mobile device data can be extracted and then used to generate reports on a range of data including an individual's communication, location, and travel habits. For example, in a criminal investigation, the data, which includes transaction information such as calendar events, call history, emails, messages (SMS/MMS/emails), and photos, are often able to be supplied to an investigating official in a report format. For the evidence to be admissible in a court of law, relevant forensic procedures must be followed.

A number of frameworks exist to provide guidance for the conduct of digital forensics that form the basis of these procedures. Digital forensics frameworks have been published (Kent et al., 2006; McKemmish, 1999; Martini and Choo, 2012), as have mobile forensic procedures and tools (Me and Rossi, 2008; Owen and Thomas, 2011; Savoldi and Gubian, 2008). This has enabled practitioners to make sound decisions in the development of high-level forensic procedures, as well as in specific cases using specific tools (Guo et al., 2009).

One of the key strategic challenges presented to digital forensic practitioners, particularly those in law enforcement, is maintaining capability in an environment of rapid development of communication and information technologies and its ready adoption by the public and offenders (Adams, 2008; Choo, 2011). Smart mobile devices, for example, are much more complex than traditional mobile phones and with a range of personal data management facilities, these mobile devices more resemble personal computers than they do phones. By holding a significant amount of data that could be of interest to a forensic investigator, it makes smart mobile devices particularly interesting for analysis. The 2016 lawsuit of FBI v. Apple wanting to unlock the San Bernardino shooter's phone received widespread media coverage, but was far from an isolated case.[36] As Nate Smith of URX.COM says, "The future of mobile means a more intricately connected ecosystem of applications! The "walled gardens" will be torn down and roads and bridges between apps will be constructed. The relationships between the apps that a user has installed on their phone will become exponentially more important, to both the consumer and the businesses themselves." However, the method of collecting evidence for mobile devices is quite different when compared with traditional forensic computer hard disks.

☞ Individual implications

- Storing unnecessary data on mobile devices can expose personal habits

☞ Organizational implications

- Maintaining forensic capability in a rapidly developing mobile environment
- Admissibility of evidence must follow legal requirements

---

[36] Ongoing phone-unlocking cases in the U.S. See http://techcrunch.com/2016/03/30/aclu-map-shows-locations-of-63-ongoing-phone-unlocking-cases/.

14 SUMMARY

This chapter provides information on awareness of mobile device risks for individuals, as well as items to consider for organizations.

It suggests 10 steps to secure mobile devices for the digital age, which were mentioned near the start of this chapter.

Application builders, mobile device manufacturers, and telecommunications providers all need to provide assurance for users that they are acting responsibly in protecting mobile device information and thereby building trust for the digital economy. This means applications responsibly accessing data, the secure storage of data on the mobile device, and the secure transmission of data by telecommunication providers. When all three of these act responsibly together, trust will be built-in line with the individual's expectations.

Some of the key risks for individuals to be aware of are:

- Information exposure. Be aware of the risks of keeping highly sensitive or confidential personal data on mobile devices.
- Privacy implications that come along with the technological capabilities that mobile devices provide.
- If the device is lost or stolen, the information goes with it and can potentially be viewed by unauthorized individuals.
- Every person who has or will have a mobile device means that every mobile device is a target that can be exploited.
- Lack of protection of data through not implementing encryption can lead to straightforward data exposure. For example, inclination to trust default mobile device settings will result in continued exposure.
- The scope and risk of mobile device information exposure is extended by the remote-control capability to spy.

Some of the key concerns for organizations are:

- It is essential that organizations have suitable strategies in place for securing mobile devices.[37]
- That there are implications in place for the confidentiality of information for business.
- Organizations must shift their focus to data-centric models rather than system or device-centric models, to ensure they have appropriate security coverage because the risks have already shifted.
- MDM controls can help with general security. However, it isn't a universal cure-all, and products vary significantly with respect to functionality and approach.
- Protection of data through encryption.
- Mobile testing before a mobile application, or app, goes live.
- Privacy concerns.
- Identity management.
- Security awareness training for mobile devices for staff.

---

[37] See Mobile device security information for IT Managers from the Trusted Information Sharing Network at http://www.tisn.gov.au/documents/mobiledevicesecurityinformationforitmanagers.pdf.

– Maintaining digital trust with customers.
– Consideration of BYOD programs and the implications for organizational policy and security relating to integration within the organization.

This can be summarized in the following diagram, showing the overlap between individuals and organizations (Fig. 4):

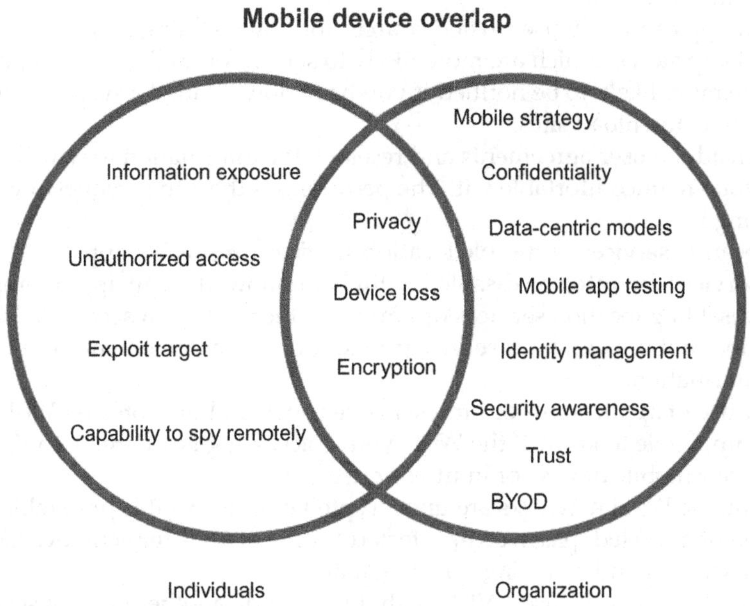

Mobile device overlap

Information exposure	Mobile strategy
	Confidentiality
	Privacy
Unauthorized access	Data-centric models
	Device loss
	Mobile app testing
Exploit target	Identity management
	Encryption
	Security awareness
Capability to spy remotely	Trust
	BYOD
Individuals	Organization

FIG. 4   Mobile device overlap.

Below are 10 steps to share in the quest of realizing a safe, private life in the digital age and to make sure that your mobile devices—and everything that's on them—stays safe:

1. Lock your mobile device when you're not using it.
   Be sure to use a strong and unique passphrase, pattern sequence, or biometrics. It's a lot harder for people to gain access to your valuable information if the device is secured with a strong password or "passphrase" (a series of three of four words and some numbers together).
2. Consider encrypting your data to prevent unauthorized access.
   Make sure that device encryption is enabled on your device. While some device manufacturers enable encryption by default, others require that you enable this in the device settings. If your device is lost or stolen, contact your mobile device manufacturer/operating system maker as soon as possible. Your manufacturer/operating system maker may have the native functionality capability to remotely wipe or disable the device to prevent unauthorized access or remove the data stored on the device. Additionally, contact your telecommunications service provider, who has

the ability to manage charges due to unsolicited messages sent from your device by malware, and can disable the device from being able to register on the mobile network. In the case of theft, contact your local police agency as they may be able to work with your service provider to track and recover your device if reported promptly.

3. Update your device.
   Install updates for both the operating system and the apps running on your device. These updates often provide functionality improvements and security enhancements to prevent malicious attacks.

4. Know your apps and only use trusted sources for downloading them.
   Use official app stores, which are more likely to screen for malicious or counterfeit apps, and you are more likely to be notified if you have downloaded a suspect app than if you use alternative download sites.
   Be sure to read the user agreements and research the information to which an app has access. If you are uncomfortable with the permissions the app is requesting, consider not installing it.

5. Turn off location services or disable location services for specific apps.
   Location services can often be disabled entirely or allowed on an app-by-app basis. Consider disabling location services or limiting which apps can access location services. Doing so does not prevent your service provider or law enforcement from using your location information.

6. Limit your use of applications or browsers over open and unprotected Wi-Fi.
   It's often impossible to know if the Wi-Fi you're accessing is secure. If you're not sure, don't use your mobile device, or limit your use of it.
   Most free public Wi-Fi networks are unencrypted or open, so it is preferable to use your mobile data or a trusted, password-protected Wi-Fi network for activities like Internet banking or sending and receiving sensitive materials.
   If you have a smartphone, use a VPN with it to provide another layer of security and protection, especially when you send sensitive information. A VPN encrypts data while in transit, both through regular and wireless networks.

7. Turn off Bluetooth when not using it.
   Disable Bluetooth-enabled services when not required to help prevent phishing attempts and the spread of malware or viruses.

8. Don't root or jailbreak your device.
   Not only does rooting or jailbreaking violate the terms of service of most device manufacturers, it potentially exposes your device to greater harm from malicious apps.

9. Back up your device.
   Sync or back up your mobile device. Many mobile devices have the ability to be synced and backed up to your personal computer or the cloud. Loss, damage, and even software updates can cause you to lose all of your data. If you don't have a backup, your important phone numbers, favorite photos, and other data could be lost forever.

10. Be sure to wipe your device prior to trading it in, selling, donating or otherwise disposing of it.
    Delete all your personal information, photos, messages, and contacts from all SIM cards, removable memory, and internal memory.

Consider taking your device to your service provider or dealer to be wiped and reset to factory defaults in order to remove information that may still be stored on the device in locations you missed or are restricted from accessing by the manufacturer.

15 MOBILE DEVICE SECURITY RESOURCES

A multitude of security resources exist for mobile device users, developers, and enterprises. Some useful security resources include:

ENISA Smartphone secure development guidelines at http://www.enisa.europa.eu/activities/application-security/smartphone-security-1/smartphone-secure-development-guidelines

Google Identity Platform Mobile App Best Practices at https://developers.google.com/identity/work/saas-mobile-apps

Mobile device security information for IT Managers from the Trusted Information Sharing Network at http://www.tisn.gov.au/documents/mobiledevicesecurityinformationforit-managers.pdf

NIST Mobile Device Security Project with best practices for mobile security at https://nccoe.nist.gov/projects/building_blocks/mobile_device_security

NIST Computer Security at http://csrc.nist.gov/publications/nistpubs/800-57/sp800-57_PART3_key-management_Dec2009.pdf

OWASP Mobile Security Project at https://www.owasp.org/index.php/Mobile

OWASP Top 10 Mobile Controls at https://www.owasp.org/index.php/Mobile#Top_10_Mobile_Controls

OWASP Top 10 Mobile Risks at https://www.owasp.org/index.php/Projects/OWASP_Mobile_Security_Project_-_Top_Ten_Mobile_Risks

Security Tips and Tricks for the iPhone 6s/6s Plus at https://blog.malwarebytes.org/mobile-2/2015/10/security-tips-tricks-for-the-iphone-6s6s-plus/

Stay Safe Online mobile safety information at https://www.staysafeonline.org/stay-safe-online/mobile-and-on-the-go/mobile-devices

The Mobile Web Initiative at http://www.w3.org/Mobile/

Acknowledgments

Our warmest thanks goes to Scott McIntyre for his devil's advocacy and to Catherine Brown for her emerging technology and sociological insights; also to Dr Kim-Kwang Raymond Choo from the University of South Australia for his kind invitation to contribute a chapter.

References

Adams, C.W., 2008. Legal issues pertaining to the development of digital forensic tools. In: Proceedings of the SADFE Third International Workshop on Systematic Approaches to Digital Forensic Engineering. pp. 123–132.

Choo, K.-K.R., 2011. Harnessing information and communications technologies in community policing. In: Putt, J. (Ed.), Community Policing in Australia. Research and Public Policy Series No. 111, Australian Institute of Criminology, Canberra. Available from http://www.aic.gov.au/publications/current%20series/rpp/100-120/rpp111.html.

Crompton, M., 2015. Privacy Incorporated: The business of trust in the digital world. Information Integrity Solutions, Sydney, NSW, ISBN: 978-1-942-52670-4.

Guo, Y.H., Slay, J., Beckett, J., 2009. Validation and verification of computer forensic software tools-searching function. Digit. Investig. 6 (3–4), 12–22.

ISACA, n.d., Securing mobile devices using COBIT® 5 for information security. Available from http://www.isaca.org/knowledge-center/research/researchdeliverables/pages/securing-mobile-devices-using-cobit-5-for-information-security.aspx.

Kent, K., Chevalier, S., Grance, T., Dang, H., 2006. Guide to Integrating Forensic Techniques into Incident Response. SP800-86. US Department of Commerce, Gaithersburg, MD. Available from http://csrc.nist.gov/publications/nistpubs/800-86/SP800-86.pdf.

Martini, B., Choo, K.-K.R., 2012. An integrated conceptual digital forensic framework for cloud computing. Available from https://fenix.tecnico.ulisboa.pt/downloadFile/563568428736506/Martini2012.pdf.

McKemmish, R., 1999. What is Forensic Computing? Trends & Issues in Crime and Criminal Justice No. 118. Australian Institute of Criminology, Canberra. Available from http://www.aic.gov.au/media_library/publications/tandi_pdf/tandi118.pdf.

Me, G., Rossi, M., 2008. Internal forensic acquisition for mobile equipments. In: Proceedings of IEEE International Symposium on Parallel and Distributed Processing. pp. 1–7.

Owen, P., Thomas, P., 2011. An analysis of digital forensic examinations: mobile devices versus hard disk drives utilising ACPO & NIST guidelines. Digit. Investig. 8 (2), 135–140.

Savoldi, A., Gubian, P., 2008. Data recovery from windows CE based handheld devices. Adv. Digit. Foren. IV (285), 219–230.

Singer, P.W., Friedman, A., 2014. Cybersecurity and Cyberwar, What Everyone Needs To Know. Oxford University Press, Oxford, ISBN: 978-0-19-991809-6.

Soulodre, L., 2015. Reinventing Enterprise Architecture for the Digital Age. Available from https://www.linkedin.com/pulse/reinventing-enterprise-application-strategy-digital-age-soulodre. May 5, 2015.

Symantec, 2013. 2013 Norton report: total cost of cybercrime in Australia amounts to AU$1.06 billion'. Available from: http://www.symantec.com/en/au/about/news/release/article.jsp?prid=20131015_01. October, 2013.

Toffler, A., 1970. Future Shock. Pan Books, London. p. 195.

Whitlock, S., et al., 2014. W-142 Protecting Information: Steps for a Secure Data Future. The Open Group, San Francisco, USA.

GLOSSARY

Definitions in this glossary are based on a variety of web-based sources such as Google, Webopedia, and Wikipedia, as well as from specific vendor sites like Cisco, Intel, Lookout, Norton, and Trend. They are included here for informational purposes.

Address space layout randomization (ASLR) This is a memory-protection process for operating systems (OSs) that guards against buffer overflow attacks by randomizing the location where system executables are loaded into memory.

Android Android is a mobile operating system (OS) currently developed by Google, based on the Linux kernel and designed primarily for touchscreen mobile devices such as smartphones and tablets.

Antivirus (AV) Antivirus solutions aim to detect, remove, and prevent malware from a system. As malware is detected and analysed by vendors, signatures are created to identify it.

Application programming interface (API) This refers to a set of routines, protocols, and tools for building software applications.

Asset management The act of cataloging and controlling devices (assets) that access corporate resources.

Asymmetric cryptography The practice of securing data using a public key that is shared with everyone and a private key that remains secret. Data encrypted with the public key can only be decrypted with the private key and vice versa. This allows secure communications without a shared secret.

Biometrics Biometrics refers to authentication techniques that rely on measurable physical characteristics that can be automatically checked such as the analysis of an individual's unique fingerprint, which is starting to be used on some mobile phones, or alternatively, the analysis of the tone, pitch, cadence, and frequency of a person's voice. There are other types of biometric identification schemes as well, such as face, retina, iris, signature, and vein and hand geometry, but these are not in common use for mobile devices.

Bluejacking The sending of unsolicited messages over Bluetooth to another Bluetooth-enabled device, such as sending a vCard that typically contains a message in the name field (i.e., for Bluedating or Bluechat).

Bring your own device (BYOD) An IT policy in which employees are allowed to use their personal mobile devices to access organizational data and systems.

Certificate authority (CA) A trusted organization that produces signed digital "certificates" that explicitly tie an entity to a public key. This allows asymmetric cryptography users to trust that they are communicating with the right party.

Choose your own device (CYOD) Offers employees a choice of approved devices and provides more control for IT, compared to allowing employees to bring any smartphone or tablet they want.

Code encryption Code encryption is the process of encrypting source code by a developer or vendor organization to protect its intellectual property or business logic. Code encryption is one of the approaches taken to prevent unauthorized access to source code written in certain programming languages, in addition to watermarking or code obfuscation.

Cryptography The art of protecting information by transforming (encrypting) it into an unreadable format, called cipher text. Only those who possess a secret key can decipher (decrypt) the message into plain text to read or process the information.

Data loss prevention (DLP) A control designed to identify and prevent critical and sensitive data from "leaving" or being "leaked" from private confines.

Drive-by downloads Drive-by downloads can automatically download an application when a user visits a web page. In some cases, users must take action to open the downloaded application, while in other cases the application can start automatically.

Geotagging This is the process by which global positioning system (GPS) coordinates are embedded in information shared online such as photos and comments. This occurs via the GPS functionality on smartphones and other mobile devices, which could end up revealing your home address and other sensitive location information.

Hardware Security Module (HSM) Hardware devices that are dedicated to creating cryptographic keys while storing and protecting them are referred to as HSMs. They're utilized in an effort to lock away important cryptographic information, thus increasing the security of data encryption.

Identity management This refers to a broad administrative area that deals with identifying individuals in a system (such as a computer, a network, or an enterprise) and controlling their access to resources within that system by associating user rights and restrictions with the established identity.

iOS Apple's Unix-based operating system that runs on iPhones and iPads.

Key In cryptography, a string of data used to encrypt text or to decrypt text. Longer keys are harder to guess by trial and error, so key length is almost directly correlated with greater security within an algorithm (e.g., 128-bit AES vs. 192-bit AES). An exception is that elliptical curve cryptography (ECC) proves a smaller key length can have the same benefits of a non-ECC and longer key. This has a real impact on the computational power and actual power that is required. *N.B.* Key length has no comparative meaning across algorithms such as when trying to compare, for example, a 128-bit AES key to a 1024-bit RSA key.

Malware Malevolent software with malicious intent and function, such as spyware, Trojan horses, viruses and worms, that is programmed to attack, disrupt, and/or compromise other computers and networks.

Mobile application management (MAM) Describes software and services responsible for provisioning and controlling access to internally developed and commercially available mobile apps used in business settings on both company-provided and BYOD smartphones and tablet computers.

Mobile device management (MDM) Software that allows management of mobile assets.

Near-field communication (NFC) The set of protocols and hardware that enable electronic devices to establish communication with each other via radio by touching the devices together or bringing them into close proximity (typically within a distance of 10 cm or less).

OS Operating system. Some common examples are Android, iOS, Windows, BlackBerry, Firefox OS, and Ubuntu Touch OS.

Portable applications A program (e.g., script, macro, or other portable instruction) that can be shipped unchanged to a heterogeneous collection of platforms and executed with identical semantics.

Ransomware Ransomware is a type of malware that locks a device or encrypts the data on it and then demands a ransom payment to unlock the device or to decrypt the data.

Sideloading Refers to the process of transferring data between two local devices, in particular between a computer and a mobile device such as a mobile phone, smartphone, PDA, tablet, portable media player, or e-reader. Its purpose is to install and run applications on mobile devices that haven't been authorized and are available through an official app store.

Smartphone A mobile phone that can do more than simply phone and message/SMS. For example, it can be a phone, send/receive SMS messages, and run third-party apps, as well as act as a camera, GPS device, and music player.

Social engineering An attack method taking advantage of human nature by manipulating people into revealing information, providing access, or otherwise being conned into performing actions that are not authentic in nature.

Software watermarking Software watermarking involves embedding a unique identifier within a piece of software.

Trojan horse Any software program containing a covert malicious function.

TPM (Trusted Platform Module) An integrated security module that provides protection of sensitive data.

UID User identifier; used with other access control criteria to determine which system resources a user can access.

Virus A malicious piece of software that may attach to a legitimate program or file and cause harm.

Virtual private networks (VPN) A technology that allows computers to establish trusted connections over untrusted communication channels.

Wired equivalency privacy (WEP) This refers to a security algorithm for 802.11 wireless networks, introduced as part of the original 802.11 standard. Its intention was to provide data confidentiality comparable to that of a traditional wired network; it has been superseded by WPA2.

Wi-Fi protected access (WPA) This refers to an older, less secure security protocol and security certification program that secured wireless computer networks; it has been superseded by WPA2.

Wi-Fi protected access II (WPA2) This refers to a newer, more secure security protocol and security certification program to secure wireless computer networks.

Worm A stand-alone malicious program that is capable of automated self-replication that can spread automatically over a network. The network traffic from rapid replication and spread can cripple networks even when the malware does not have a malicious payload.

ABOUT THE AUTHORS

Shane Tully is an enterprise security architect with experience in Australian state government agencies, transport and financial services industries. His interest is in the security of international businesses.

Shane was the founder of the Oneworld® airline alliance IT Security Forum; a founding member of the board of management of the global security thought leadership group, The Jericho Forum; an invited attendee at the APEC 2007 data privacy seminars; and an invited SCADA representative to the Australian Government IT Security Expert Advisory Group (ITSEAG) from August 2009 to June 2013. He has contributed to the Cloud Security Alliance, SABSA-TOGAF integration; Australian Government Trusted Information Sharing network (TISN), Australian Law Reform Commission, NIST, and various other security initiatives. He also was the Transport Sector Lead for Australia in the Department of Homeland Security's Cyberstorm III exercise that involved government and industry from Australia, New Zealand, Canada, the UK, and the US in 2010.

Recent achievements include being made the first Fellow of the Institute of Information Security Professionals (IISP) outside the UK and receiving an award by The Open Group for his outstanding contribution to the Information Security Decade of De-perimeterisation 2004–13, which was awarded to 11 recipients worldwide for contributions to information security.

In his spare time, Shane is currently working with various global stakeholders on development of a Security Services catalogue for The SABSA Institute (TSI); and is an assessor for membership of the Institute of Information Security Professionals (IISP).

Yuvaraj Mohanraj is a business-oriented IT security professional with a payments industry background. He is acknowledged for his solid track record in developing and producing comprehensive service offerings that detail, analyze, and forecast market trends and customer requirements.

Yuvaraj has more than 13 years of experience in IT and IT security at large multinational corporations in both Australia and India that cover the financial services and transport sector.

Recent achievements include developing cryptographic services from a certificate management service to a full-fledged security infrastructure service, as well as further facilitating expansion of the service both vertically and horizontally.

He has certifications from SABSA, holds a CISSP, and is a qualified PCI-ISA and an ISO 27001 Lead Auditor.

3

Mobile Security: End Users are the Weakest Link in the System

L. Lau

Asia Pacific Association of Technology and Society (APATAS), Hong Kong Special Administrative Region

1 DEFINITION: SECURITY "INTERNETWORK"

There are various definitions of computer system security. According to the Oxford dictionary, "security" generally means any system that is consistently free from danger or threat. For example, if we strictly follow this definition, the "internetwork" system must be designed to provide maximum security against any "malicious" attack or "uninvited access" into the system; that is, it must be a practically air-tight system that nobody can penetrate or access. Other definitions for internetwork security include a more traditional definition made up of three criteria to protect the physical machine, even though the data inside the machine are worth more than the machine itself. These criteria are: (i) to prevent others stealing or damaging the computer hardware, (ii) to prevent others stealing or damaging the computer data, and (iii) to minimize or prevent disruption of computer service. Another definition is more specifically related to Internet security, of which, broadly speaking, there are two levels. These are: (i) security for the Internet browser, and (ii) security for the operating system as a whole (i.e., "network security"). Internet browser security is the first layer of Internet defense, protecting the network data and computer systems from uninvited attacks, as the browser is basically a software application for retrieving, presenting, and traversing information resources on the World Wide Web (WWW). Whenever a browser communicates with a website, as part of that communication the website collects some information about the browser to be able to process the formatting of the page to be delivered and made readable for the human user. Therefore, the browser security methodology typically used is called "perimeter defense." This involves a firewall and a filtering proxy server, which block unsavory websites and perform antivirus scans of any file data downloaded, thereby blocking malicious network data before they reach the browser.

However, network security is far more complex than browser security because it involves the core function of the Internet; that is, the "heart and mind of the Internet" in the operating system, or the "engine" of the Internet. Typically, this involves a different layer or "suite" of security protocols. Mainly these are: a network layer security protocol, which largely consists of two additional types of protocol, the Transmission Control Protocol (TCP) and the Internet Protocol (IP). Both provide end-to-end connectivity and format how data should be packetized, addressed, and transmitted until it is received at the destination. TCP and IP are secured through cryptographic methods and security protocols. Internet Protocol Security (IPSec) is specifically designed to protect TCP/IP communication in a secure manner using encryption and consists of two protocols, the Encapsulating Security Payload (ESP) and the Authentication Header (AH) protocols. These two protocols provide data integrity, data origin authentication, and an antireplay service. They can be used alone or in combination to provide the desired set of security services for the IP layer.

As discussed, there is no single definition for computer system security, but instead a range of definitions that make up information technology (IT) security. For convenience, the definition of Internet security is adopted in this chapter. Technically speaking, today's smartphone largely functions as a PC that is smaller and more mobile than the traditional PC. This brings the smartphone within the ambit of computer security.

2 GROWTH OF SMARTPHONE BREACHES

With the commercialization of the Internet and the proliferation of its usage over the past three decades, it has been estimated that by Jun. 2014, 39% of the world population was surfing the internet daily, which included both the developed economies (global North) and the less-developed economies (global South).

With such a vast number of individuals now using the Internet, particularly in recent years, there has been a growing adoption rate of mobile devices, even in the developing economies (global South). As a result, mobile security has increasingly become a concern, as more and more commercial activities migrate from the traditional PC-based platform to the mobile phone platform.

Smartphone ownership is no longer confined to the privileged few who can afford high-priced technology, as increasingly cheaper devices are being introduced into the consumer market by manufacturers in Asia. For example, purchasing an Xiaomi[1] smartmobile can be as cheap as $140 per device in mainland China. As a result, according to the Pew Research Center Technology Ownership Survey of Oct. 2015,[2] 68% of American adults owned a smartphone, compared with only 35% in 2011. In the 18–29 age group, almost 90% had a smartphone, while ownership among those aged 30–49 stood at 83%.

Similarly, smartphone ownership in Asia is also high; for example, as the BBC reported in Sept. 2015, there were 2.5 billion mobile smartphone users in Asia, a high number of whom were addicted to their smartphones. The *BBC News* explained:

[1] See the Xiaomi Mobile official website. Available from: http://www.mi.com/hk/ (accessed 09.11.15).

[2] See Pew Research Center Technology Device Ownership Survey, October 2015. Available from: http://www.pewinternet.org/2015/10/29/technology-device-ownership-2015/ (accessed 09.11.15).

Asia and its *2.5bn smartphone users* provides a stream of phone-related 'mishap news', such as the Taiwanese tourist who had to be rescued after she *walked off a pier* while checking Facebook on her phone. Or the woman from China's Sichuan province rescued by fire fighters after *falling into a drain* while looking at her [smart-] phone.[3]

Fig. 1[4] highlights the number of smartphone users and the penetration rate in the Asia Pacific region. As indicated in the table, the percentage of smartphone users is high and has led the way for the mobile phone revolution, especially in Mainland China.

As *Mobile Marketing* reported on Sept. 1, 2015, the smartphone adoption rate in Asia has risen year over year:

Demand for smartphones in Southeast Asia has hit new heights in the first half of 2015, with sales up nine per cent year-on-year and almost 40 million units shipped in the first six months of the year alone. Consumers across seven of the region's key markets (Singapore, Malaysia, Thailand, Indonesia, Vietnam, Philippines and Cambodia) have generated more than $8bn (£5.2bn) in sales value so far this year, with 3.2m more smartphones sold between January and June 2015 compared to the same period last year.[5]

According to Statista,[6] the two market leaders in smartphones are Samsung and Apple.

So far, this has all been positive news for both smartphone manufacturers and end users alike. End users are spoiled for choice and enjoy lower prices, too, as most smartphones are manufactured in Asia, such as Samsung, Huawei, and Xiaomi; even the Apple iPhone is produced in Asia.

However, along with the new benefits that every new technology delivers, there come new risks, too. The smartphone is no exception, especially regarding the security risk to smartmobile data. For example, according to the *Mobile Industry Review*,[7] there are a number of risks with smartphones. These include nation state-sponsored "license to kill" spyware, with the Communist party in Mainland China known to plant a hidden spyware app on smartphones in order to seek out individual user information, especially on Xiaomi's phones, as widely reported in the media. Likewise, both the US and British governments are known to be setting up mobile towers to eavesdrop on people and monitor their conversations.

Another example concerns smartphone security and privacy in regard to adware and Trojan horse malware. This involves sending a text message that contains Trojan horse malware that captures the unknowing smartphone user's financial details, such as credit card information.

---

[3] *BBC News* report on 7 September 2015: "Asia's Smartphone Addiction." Available from: http://www.bbc.com/news/world-asia-33130567 (accessed 10.11.15).

[4] eMarketer, September 16, 2015. Available from: http://www.emarketer.com/Article/Asia-Pacific-Boasts-More-Than-1-Billion-Smartphone-Users/1012984 (accessed 11.11.15).

[5] See Mobile Marketing. Available from: http://mobilemarketingmagazine.com/smartphone-market-in-southeast-asia-h1-2015/ (accessed 10.11.15).

[6] See Statista. Available from: http://www.statista.com/statistics/271490/quarterly-global-smartphone-shipments-by-vendor/ (accessed 23.11.15).

[7] See Mobile Industry Review: "Smartphone security—what's the risk?" Available: http://www.mobileindustryreview.com/2014/10/smartphone-security.html (accessed 23.11.15).

Smartphone Users and Penetration in Asia-Pacific, by Country, 2014–19 (eMarketer, July 2005)

Millions and % of mobile phone users

	2014	2015	2016	2017	2018	2019
Smartphone users (millions)						
China[a]	482.7	525.8	563.3	599.3	640.5	687.7
India	123.3	167.9	204.1	243.8	279.2	317.1
Indonesia	44.7	55.4	65.2	74.9	83.5	92.0
Japan	46.2	51.8	55.8	58.9	60.9	62.6
South Korea	32.2	33.6	34.6	35.6	36.5	37.0
Philippines	21.8	26.2	29.9	33.3	36.5	39.2
Vietnam	16.6	20.7	24.6	28.6	32.0	35.2
Thailand	15.4	17.9	20.0	21.9	23.4	24.8
Australia	13.5	14.6	15.4	16.0	16.5	16.8
Malaysia	8.9	10.1	11.0	11.8	12.7	13.7
Hong Kong	4.4	4.8	5.0	5.2	5.3	5.4
Singapore	3.8	4.0	4.2	4.3	4.4	4.6
Other	74.5	91.1	106.7	121.3	134.7	147.2
Asia-Pacific	**888.0**	**1023.9**	**1139.8**	**1254.7**	**1366.3**	**1483.4**
Smartphone user penetration (% of mobile phone users)						
Singapore	83.1%	85.2%	86.3%	87.2%	88.0%	88.9%
South Korea	79.5%	82.3%	84.3%	86.0%	87.6%	88.4%
Hong Kong	76.6%	80.7%	84.0%	85.9%	87.2%	88.3%
Australia	74.3%	78.4%	81.0%	82.6%	83.6%	84.3%
China[a]	48.1%	50.9%	53.3%	56.0%	59.3%	63.3%
Japan	44.0%	48.9%	52.4%	55.1%	56.9%	58.4%
Malaysia	42.6%	46.6%	49.2%	51.3%	54.3%	57.3%
Thailand	34.9%	39.2%	42.8%	45.8%	48.1%	50.0%
Indonesia	32.6%	37.1%	40.4%	43.2%	45.4%	47.6%
Philippines	32.0%	36.6%	40.0%	43.1%	46.1%	48.4%
Vietnam	30.4%	36.2%	41.5%	46.8%	50.9%	54.6%
India	21.2%	26.3%	29.8%	33.4%	36.0%	39.0%
Other	25.1%	29.0%	32.1%	34.5%	36.4%	37.8%
Asia-Pacific	**37.3%**	**40.8%**	**43.6%**	**46.2%**	**48.7%**	**51.5%**

[a]Excludes Hong Kong.
Note: Individuals of any age who own at least one smartphone and use the smartphone(s) at least once per month.

193860   www.eMarketer.com

FIG. 1   Smart-phone Users and Penetration Rates in Asia Pacific (2014–19).

According to *PC World*, individual end users are still the weakest link to security:

> You can implement rock solid network security; enforce strong, complex passwords; and install the best anti-malware tools available. Most security experts agree, however, that there is no security in the world that can guard against human error ...[8]

A similar comment from *Science Nordic* (*"You (individuals) are the weakest link in IT security"*) went on to say that:

> Hackers often gain access to IT systems by exploiting the weakest link in IT security—the users. New social IT security system aims to weed out the human factor. Why bother to hack into complex security systems when it's so much easier to hack into people, by using social engineering technique ...[9]

For example, spear phishing is the technique often used to exploit individual users' smartphone and information technology devices. *Bloomberg Businessweek* reported that "the U.S. Justice Department told the source that a common spear phishing attack was used by hackers to gain access to several companies after malicious individuals obtained usernames and passwords from users themselves. In 2013 alone, there were 450,000 reported phishing attacks, which resulted in $5.9 billion in losses."[10]

In another instance, individual mobile apps with weak passwords were the problem. As widely reported in the news, phantom thieves withdrew money from individual Starbucks app accounts in the United States:

> Maria Nistri, 48, was a victim this week. Criminals stole the Orlando wom[a]n's $34.77 in value she had loaded onto her Starbucks app, then another $25 after it was auto-loaded into her card because her balance hit 0. Then, the criminals upped the ante, changing her auto reload amount to $75, and stealing that amount, too. All within 7 minutes. ... The trouble started at 7:11 a.m. on Wednesday when she received an automated email saying her username and password had been changed, and if she hadn't authorized the change, she should call customer service. She tried, but the number she called notified her an operator couldn't answer until 8 a.m. Whoever did this knew the right time to do it, she said. When Nistri launched her phone's Starbucks app, she could actually see the thieves stealing first the $25, then $75, in real-time as it happened—and other Starbucks app users report suffering similar thefts, too.[11]

The examples cited above provide only a snapshot of potential security issues, but they reinforce the truth that the individual end user is likely to be the weakest point in the cyber-security chain. According to various reports, over 70% of cyber-related incidents, including smartphone attack incidents, pointed to human error, and, even though the corporation itself

---

[8] See *PC World*. Available from: http://www.pcworld.com/article/260453/users_are_still_the_weakest_link.html (accessed 02.12.15).

[9] See Science Nordic. Available from: http://sciencenordic.com/you-are-weakest-link-it-security (accessed 02.12.15).

[10] Cited in Cloud Entr. Available from: http://www.cloudentr.com/latest-resources/industry-news/2014/6/10/top-security-weakness-users-fall-for-password-phishing-scams (accessed 02.12.15).

[11] See Consumer Affairs. Available from: http://www.consumeraffairs.com/news/hackers-steal-money-from-starbucks-apps-accounts-presumably-those-with-weak-passwords-051815.html (accessed 02.12.15).

and its information technology system is relatively secure, it is the individual who brings the cyber system down. One reason for this vulnerability in individuals lies in how we define information technology (IT) security itself, and there are many ways we can define, promote, or project what computer security is.

3 ORGANIZATION INTERNETWORK SECURITY

The main objective of a commercial corporation is to pursue profit for its shareholders. Therefore, a commercial organization's internetwork system is designed to focus on business growth. In general, an internetwork system security is designed at an acceptable or standard level that meets regulatory requirements at home and abroad. As a result, it is fair to say that organizations' computer networks are not designed with security as their most important goal; in fact, only military-classified computer systems are designed with security as their most important objective.

Nevertheless, multinational corporations, for a number of reasons, have worked to improve their internetwork security. First, there is compliance with national legislation, as most countries have been updating their existing legislation or have passed new laws on cyber-related issues; in particular, legislation has addressed data protection and individual clients' personal details as related to privacy protocols or protection. Furthermore, panregional trading blocs and global institutions have been active in this area. For example, the European Union (EU) Parliament has passed cyber legislation and regional conventions that set the standard on cybersecurity for organizations that are based in the EU, such as the Council of Europe Convention on CyberCrime. Moreover, the United Nations has written a guideline treaty for itself and its member countries to follow the best practices set forth by the United Nations Convention or Protocol on Cybersecurity and Cybercrime. All of these new cyber-related laws, conventions, and treaties, both at home and aboard, have forced multinational organizations to seriously beef up their provisions on data protection and security so they can satisfy and meet the required trading standards.

Second, political groups and parties have put pressure on multinational organizations to shore up their cyber security due to pressure from their respective voters and members. Third, nongovernmental organizations (NGOs), such as consumer rights groups, have also been very actively lobbying on behalf of consumers to pressure governments to legislate and regulate multinational organizations on cybersecurity. Finally, the public and the consumers themselves are actively putting pressure on multinational organizations by way of boycotting organizations whose e-commerce websites do not meet the standards required by law or the industrial conventions on cybersecurity. For all of these reasons, multinational organizations must patch up their cybersecurity. More importantly, multinational organizations have the financial means to do so, including the human resources required to maintain the requisite cybersecurity. This is especially so with global banks and financial investment organizations. As a result, the security measures on multinational organizations' network systems are largely mature.

In theory, small-medium enterprises (SMEs) and their internetwork security are subject to the same regulatory oversight as multinational organizations because SMEs play a major role in the economies of most countries, particularly in providing employment and alleviating poverty. In practice, however, there is likely to be a gap between SMEs and multinational organizations in cybersecurity practice. This is because SMEs are inherently constrained by a number of characteristics. First, SMEs' financial and human resources are much more limited than those of multinational organizations. For instance, if the business environment changes, especially regarding the ever-present technology changes coming onto the market, SMEs may not have readily available resources to respond to change as efficiently as multinational organizations because their resources for acquiring information about the market are limited. Second, as single-business firms, SMEs largely operate locally, although some may operate at a regional level within their respective country or trading bloc. This means that if the business environment changes, the options for SMEs are limited by the firm's resources, location, and industry, whereas multinational organizations can respond by exiting from one of its business areas. Third, SMEs tend to be at different developmental stages; the developmental stage of one SME is not necessarily representative of other SMEs.

While SMEs are subject to the same regulatory controls on cybersecurity, they are not likely to receive the same degree of attention from politicians and the public as multinational organizations, and they are also likely to be treated more leniently. One probable reason for this is when an SME fails, the effect on society is not as far-reaching as when a multinational organization fails because the number of people affected (in terms of the number of customers and the geographical coverage of the operation) is much smaller. When a multinational organization fails, the effect on society is far greater, with sometimes millions of customers being affected; therefore the public's expectations are much higher and oversight from the regulatory authority is stricter. Nevertheless, in recent years, even SMEs are moving towards investing more of their limited resources in cybersecurity because having a recognized, secure website improves sales figure and retains customers who can be confident of the internetwork system. Moreover, in recent years, internetwork safety awareness has increased within the business community, as a number of high-profile, global online breaches reported in the news media has increased interest in cybercrime prevention at management and even executive levels. In turn, SMEs have increased their budgets for cybersecurity. However, the survival of any business depends on how well it satisfies its customers' needs, which includes the expectation that a business website is easy to access with minimal barriers, such as lengthy online authentication procedures. Given that it is human nature to turn away when confronted by a barrier, an enterprise is likely to have made strategic business decisions so that it can provide its customers with ease of access to its online store, which in some cases involves scaling down website safety measures by removing or limiting strict authentication processes.

4 INDIVIDUAL INTERNET SECURITY

As discussed, nobody likes barriers, and they will go to great lengths to avoid them. However, there is no law in place to coerce individuals to install antivirus software to protect them from falling victim to smartphone crime, or to be their first line of defense against spyware or Trojan horse malware being installed on their devices, including their smartphone. It is completely at the discretion of individuals whether they purchase and install antivirus software for their smartphone, even if it means suffering psychological and or financial losses should an individual become the victim of a smartphone crime. Statistically speaking, the potential for falling victim to smartphone crime is not that remote; with active Facebook users numbering 1.6 billion globally (as of Nov. 2015[12]) and email users sending almost 300 million messages a day, there is a large pool of personal data that can be stolen. For example, perpetrators can obtain valid names and other personal data through phishing on social network sites, as Yachi Chiang explained:

> [T]he privacy setting options of Facebook are difficult for users to understand. While users need to learn about user privacy options, under pressure from the privacy protection movement, Facebook has changed its privacy option models on a frequent basis, which has made the relationship between Facebook and privacy even more complicated … It seems, therefore, that there are many privacy traps on Facebook that users often ignore.[13] *Chiang, 2015, p. 230.*

It is not clear why users ignore social networking sites' stronger privacy protection options, but there are a number of possible explanations. First, as discussed earlier, there is the rapid growth in modern technology owners and users, particularly of mobile devices and smartphones that we have witnessed in recent years, especially in Asia. Now, newer technology devices are no longer confined to being used by technology geeks in advanced science laboratories or universities; instead, it is members of the ordinary general public who purchase and use them. The late 20th century has seen hyperconsumerism combined with a clever marketing drive for modern technological devices, such as the smartphone, making these devices not only a tool for verbal communications, but also a commodity and lifestyle product. Mobile devices have become fashion trends with a very short product lifecycle with ever-extending add-on accessories, such as Bluetooth headsets. Second, as more and more new technology devices flood the marketplace, competition inevitably reduces the price of these products with each newer generation. This is especially so in Asia, not only are most of these technological devices manufactured in here, but also because this is where the majority of the world population lives. Further, as more and more consumers purchase these products, they do not necessarily understand fully what is required to protect their privacy from uninvited third parties. This problem will only grow and multiply as the number of consumers buying smart devices continues grows. The third reason is directly linked to the second one, as Nick Sulvited of Symentec outlined:

> Individual [consumers of technological devices] lack of awareness of security … well over 70 percent of smart-phone breaches were largely due to lack of awareness of the individual end-users, this problem would only grow as more and more users migrate to smart-phones …[14]

Individual end users' lack of awareness of their smartphone security and privacy can result in a bitter aftertaste. Here is a real-life example: On Nov. 5, 2015 it was reported by Eurosport[15] that a woman from Perth, Australia, expressed her delight in scooping AU$900 after backing

[12] See Statista. Available from: http://www.statista.com/statistics/272014/global-social-networks-ranked-by-number-of-users/ (accessed 07.12.15).
[13] Chiang, Y.-C., 2015. When privacy meets social networking sites-with special reference to Facebook. In: Smith, R.G., Cheung, R.C.-C., Lau, L.Y.-C. (Eds.), Cybercrime Risks and Responses: Eastern and Western Perspectives. Palgrave Macmillan, London, p. 230.
[14] The researcher watched this live TV interview on December 1, 2015, on *Singapore Tonight*, Channel News Asia, Singapore.
[15] See Eurosport. Available from: https://uk.sports.yahoo.com/news/esp-horse-racing-woman-fumes-selfie-allows-facebook-friend-110425012--rah.html (accessed 06.11.15).

100-to-1 shot Prince of Penzance in the Melbourne Cup horse race by taking selfies of herself flashing the winning betting slip, which she then posted on Facebook. Her post was accompanied with the message: "Winner winner chicken dinner!!" However, her delight was short-lived, as someone soon poached the barcode from her photo on the smartphone, then cashed out the winnings at an automated machine through another smartphone.

This smartphone user did not realize that the digital photo on her Facebook is basically a 0-and-1 binary code, and that the barcode on her betting slip is valid on any smartphone. This lack of knowledge may come down to several factors. First, individual end users are currently too dependent on others laying down internetwork security for them; particularly, as discussed, end users rely on the organizations they access to provide cybersecurity, and organizations must provide this if they want individual end users to use their online shopping services. Additionally, organizations are coerced by law to do so, whereas individuals are not. However, even when individual end users want to equip their smartphones with security software, the standards of the many different products on the market are various and fragmented.

As a result, individual end users are probably not adequately armed with sufficient knowledge to choose one security product over another. Moreover, reliable security products tend to involve personal expenditure, and with the reliance on organizations providing cybersecurity, an inertia has developed, with end users tending not to purchase antivirus software for their smartphones. Second, most countries do not automatically provide public smartphone security protection awareness campaigns or education, especially in the developed economies in the West, because there is a strong belief that users should be the ones who pay, not the public. This is the sentiment, despite the fact that when smartphone breaches do occur, society as whole also pays for it in some way, whether by the cost of the police investigation or in taking measures to prevent the same breach happening again. However, in addition to the ethical and moral issues, the costs of cybercrime, including smartphone crime for individuals, organizations, and governments, are expected to increase year over year. As we have seen, there is a combination of causes for this. Not enough attention is given to cybercrime, with governments assigning it only limited resources and seeing it as a low political priority. It depends on the individual end users; the mindset they have acquired for their desktop PCs needs to change for their mobile devices, but such a skill set is slow to pick up because the knowledge isn't the same for desktop as it is for mobile. Additionally, individual smartphone users need to realize that they themselves have to take responsibility for personal security on their mobile devices, such as by purchasing reliable antivirus software.

5 CONCLUSION

As shown in this chapter, the multinational corporations have invested large financial and human resources to beef up their cyber and mobile security. Although a small number may not be up there yet, overall multinationals are relatively mature on cyber and mobile security, especially regarding their internal network. However, SMEs are fragmented in terms of investment in their cyber and mobile security, due to inherent financial constraints. The evidence of cyber and mobile security for individual smartphone end users is dire; as indicated by the example of the horse race winner in Perth, there is little awareness or knowledge of issues regarding smartphone mobile security and privacy. However, with the proliferation of individual and personalized portable devices, these problems will only grow and multiply. Furthermore, there is evidence to suggest that individuals are reluctant to invest money in equipping their different devices with security software, or that they are unaware of their vulnerability to uninvited third parties accessing their devices. As a result, there is clear evidence that smartphone end users are the weakest link in the mobile security chain.

Finally, the ease of access to and the affordability of developing mobile devices will inevitably fuel an explosion of new products, including the Internet of Things (IoT). In the not-too-distant future, the installed bases of these systems will reach critical mass and will offer enough penetration levels that they will attract attackers. To ensure that security and privacy are not playing catch-up to technological innovation, the cybercrime theorist, practitioner, technology vendors and manufacturers, and vertical solution providers should work to educate end users and establish best practices for using smart devices, such as ISO 27001 Information Technology Management. Alternatively, security controls should be built into the mobile device architecture by default, where appropriate, thereby reducing smart device breaches and crime, thus reducing the costs borne by society as a whole and those sustained by individual end users.

Reference

Chiang, Y.-C., 2015. When privacy meets social networking sites-with special reference to Facebook. In: Smith, R.G., Cheung, R.C.-C., Lau, L.Y.-C. (Eds.), Cybercrime Risks and Responses: Eastern and Western Perspectives. Palgrave Macmillan, London.

How Cyber-Savvy are Older Mobile Device Users?

C. Chia*, K.-K.R. Choo[†,‡], D. Fehrenbacher[§]

*University of Melbourne, Melbourne, VIC, Australia †University of Texas at San Antonio, San Antonio, TX, United States ‡University of South Australia, Adelaide, SA, Australia §Monash University, Melbourne, VIC, Australia

1 INTRODUCTION

Digital literacy can be defined as the "practices involved in reading, writing, and exchanging information in online environments" (Selfe and Hawisher, 2004, p. 2), such as smart mobile devices (e.g., smartphones and tablets). Singapore has one of the highest smart mobile device penetration rates in Asia, where the ratio of mobile devices to residents was 1.48 to 1 in the calendar year 2014 (Infocomm Development of Singapore, 2015). However, older users are likely to be less digitally literate compared to the younger groups for a variety of reasons. The older age group (defined as age 45 and above in this chapter) grew up in an era when mobile devices and later smart mobile device technology was still nonexistent or developing at a slow pace. These people are sometimes known as "digital immigrants." It is even regarded as an "aging infrastructure" because digital immigrants refuse or are reluctant to incorporate technology in their everyday lives. By contrast, "digital natives" grew up in an era when computers and later smart mobile devices "are not technology, they are part of life" (Fieldhouse and Nicholas, 2008).

In the past, the digital divide between digital natives and digital immigrants may be more physical; that is, the ownership of digital gadgets by the former while there is little or no ownership of such gadgets by the latter. However, given the high smart mobile device ownership of digital immigrants, the current and possibly future digital divide may exist in terms of perception and awareness of digital literacy. Hence, there is a need to enhance the digital literacy of digital immigrants.

It is hoped that this study can provide some useful suggestions to digital immigrants in other societies that have a prominent aging population and are increasingly digitized.

Even though there are comparable similarities with increasingly digitized societies as mentioned earlier, it is important to know some characteristics in Singapore that may have an impact on the digital literacy of digital immigrants. English is the official language in multiethnic Singapore. However, the wide usage of English does not mean that everyone is literate in the language. Considering the relatively large proportion of ethnic Chinese population in Singapore of 74.2%, there is still a considerable number of people who are literate only in a single non-English language. In 2010, 20.6% of the population was literate in Chinese only, with the highest proportion coming from those aged between 45 and 64 years. This has served one of the main reasons for setting the age criteria of our participants; that is, 45 years and above. The literacy in Chinese only among the population in Singapore is also most concentrated among those who have never received any qualification numbering a total of 199,063. This is followed by those who received primary education numbering a total of 94,279 (Singapore Department of Statistics, 2010). (Note: the Census of Population is conducted once every 10 years.)

Given that the official working language is in English, this may indicate that those who are literate in Chinese only may have difficulty accessing official documents that are mostly available in English only. With the lack of command in English among some Singaporeans, they may not be able to understand the cybersecurity issues covered on this website.

1.1 Contributions

In this chapter, we build on the work of Imgraben et al. (2014) and seek to contribute to a better understanding of the security and privacy risks faced by elderly Singaporean Chinese smart mobile device users, particularly those who are literate in Chinese only. More specifically, we provide a snapshot of the following:

1. Prevalence and types of smart mobile device usage by these elderly users
2. Prevalence, nature, costs, and impacts of smart mobile device-related security incidents.

This survey provides a good indication of the risks associated with smart mobile device usage and also serves as the basis for an extended study of this population.

This survey focuses on examining the level of literacy as a variable to find out if users have difficulty using their smart mobile devices due to their lack of ability to read English. This is, to the best of our knowledge, the first (academic) study to examine how the lack of English literacy among the elderly will affect the ease of smart mobile device usage and their awareness of cyberthreats. Previous studies such as those of Kurniawan (2008) and Elliot et al. (2013) focus on the digital literacy and technology uptake of the elderly.

We then explain how the Situational Crime Prevention Theory can be used to mitigate risks by reducing the opportunities for criminal activities targeting mobile device users to occur, making cybercrime more difficult to commit by increasing perceived effort, increasing perceived risks, reducing rewards, removing excuses, and reducing provocations.

1.2 Chapter Outline

The rest of this chapter is organized as follows: We document the survey design in Section 2. In Section 3, we discuss our findings and outline four recommendations. Educational programs are important components when dealing with the risks of cybercrime. Therefore, in Section 4, we explain the role of criminological theories, and more specifically, the Situational

Crime Prevention Theory that can help to inform and enhance cybercrime prevention strategies. Section 5 concludes the chapter and looks at future work to take forward this chapter/survey's analysis and conclusions.

2 SURVEY DESIGN

The survey comprises five main sections, each representing the main threats that users of mobile devices are generally exposed to: (1) general security, (2) malware, (3) unauthorized access, (4) Wi-Fi and Bluetooth security, and (5) phishing. The questions relate to the 2012–13 financial year (i.e., Jul. 1, 2012 to Jun. 30, 2013), unless otherwise specified.

This study is based on convenient sampling because it allows us to obtain basic data and trends, particularly on how literacy in Chinese affects cybersecurity awareness, which has not been studied in the past. We will follow up with randomized sample comprising a wider group in the future.

Initial contacts with participants were made through email, Facebook, and WhatsApp. Some of the contacts were also made through friends who would relate the survey to their parents and/or seniors with whom they have contact. A typical limitation of this approach is self-selection bias, as the participants are unlikely to represent the entire target population.

Participants were selected based on their age and smart mobile device ownership. The selection process had to go through a number of factors, including willingness to participate in the survey (both online versions and hard copies of the survey form were made available), whether participants use smart mobile devices as a feature phone (for calling and text-messaging only), and the request to participate in surveys was set in Chinese, as some participants were unable to do them in English.

The initial intention to include Singaporeans of all ethnic groups had to be dropped because of the request to provide surveys conducted in non-English mediums due to the inability of the researchers to draft the survey in mediums (i.e., Tamil and Malay) other than Chinese and English. This inability to read English was also one of the motivating factors in this study to further examine how users who read little or no English respond to their use of smart mobile devices.

Analysis of data is based on 55 participants comprised of 28 males and 27 females. The age of participants are 45 years and above, with the highest number coming from the age group 51 to 55; see Fig. 1.

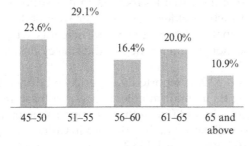

FIG. 1   Age group of participants ($n = 55$).

The educational level of participants ranges from primary to university level, with the exception of one who had never received any education. The literacy level of participants ranges from being literate in English only, Chinese only, both Chinese and English, and English but prefer Chinese; see Fig. 2.

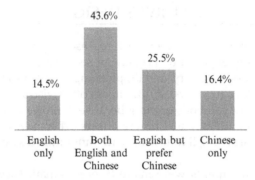

FIG. 2   Literacy of participants ($n = 55$).

In addition to the survey, the study also includes feedback through phone interviews and emails from participants during the process of collecting survey responses. There were also those who explained why they could not do the survey. This feedback can serve as an additional source of reference in understanding the attitude of users towards smart mobile devices.

This study had gathered 23 participants who either know little or no English or prefer to access their smart mobile devices in Chinese. Findings from this study indicate that the lack of literacy in English is directly related to the ease of usage and the user's awareness of cyberthreats.

To test on the ease of usage, a few factors were considered during the design of the survey. This includes asking participants whether they experience difficulty using their smart mobile devices with or without the change of language settings and their awareness of phishing.

3 FINDINGS AND DISCUSSION

Although literacy is one of the variables focused in this study, we will also present findings on the main threats to which elderly users of smart mobile devices are generally exposed. These findings are analyzed from the 55 participants who had participated in the survey, which cover five sections as mentioned in the survey design. This will be presented in Tables 1 and 2.

18 of the 55 participants (~32.7%) reportedly experienced difficulty in understanding the information while accessing their smart mobile devices. Of these 18 participants, 15 participants are literate in Chinese only, and five of the participants are literate in both Chinese and English but prefer to access their smart mobile devices in Chinese (e.g., changed the language settings of their devices to Chinese); see Table 3.

TABLE 1 Participants' Responses on General Security ($n = 55$)

Questions on General Security	Participants' Responses
Do you use the "Remember me" feature to save your passwords, login credentials, or credit card information? (Select all that are applicable)	Of the seven participants who reportedly saved the passwords, two also saved login credentials.
Do you use any encryption software to protect information on your mobile device?	Although four responded "yes," it is doubtful if participants knew what encryption software is and more likely that they were referring to the password on their devices.
Have you "jail broken" or "rooted" your mobile device (s) before?	Only one responded "yes."

TABLE 2 Participants' Responses on Loss/Theft ($n = 55$)

Questions on Loss/Theft	Participants' Responses
In the past calendar year (01/01/2013 to 31/12/2013) has/have your mobile device(s) been lost or stolen?	Only two responded "yes."

TABLE 3 Participants' Responses on Unauthorized Access ($n = 55$)

Questions on Unauthorized Access	Participants' Responses
How likely are you to read up on information before you download an application?	See Fig. 3.
Have you installed any applications from nonreputable or unknown application providers?	Four responded "yes" and five responded "not sure"
In the past calendar year (01/01/2013 to 31/12/2013) has your mobile device(s) been accessed without your permission?	Three responded "do not know" ($n = 54$).

The lack of English literacy, or that the level of comfort lies more with the Chinese language, indicates that the users may not be able to either understand all or most of the features available on smart mobile devices, such as instant messaging, emails, and information on websites or social networking sites. Such information is usually not translated into Chinese even if the user sets language settings to Chinese.

65.5% (36) of the participants are literate in both English and Chinese, but nine of them preferred to do the survey in Chinese (a total of 15 participants completed the survey in Chinese). This reflects that their level of comfort in reading lies more with Chinese. Users also responded that they have had difficulty accessing their smart mobile devices even after changing language settings.

First, we look at the 23 users who are either literate in mainly Chinese or regard Chinese as their preferred medium. Of those, 69.6% (16) have changed their language settings to Chinese.

Among these 16 users, 68.8% (11) still experience difficulty in understanding information on their devices, and 9 out of these 11 users still experience difficulty understanding information after changing language settings.

Among these difficulties that the 11 users experience, the highest response came from understanding instructions while downloading mobile applications (81%). One user also reported having difficulty understanding messages prompted while playing online games and accessing social networking sites and requests to play games and join social network by friends and unknown contacts, as well as having a fear of leaking sensitive and personal identifiable information (PII) data such as bank account, credit card details, or personal photos/videos.

The two remaining users, who did not have problems understanding instructions while downloading apps, reported to have experienced difficulty in understanding advertisements and requests to play games and join social networks by friends and unknown contacts, as well as a fear of leaking sensitive data and PII.

The problem of understanding the information on their mobile devices is not unique to users who are mainly literate or feel more comfortable accessing in Chinese only.

However, the problem lies less with understanding and probably more with not being sure how to respond, as well as the possible consequences of responding. This is an indication that as features of smart mobile devices increase in function and variety in the form of new apps and device functions, digital immigrants who make use of these features may experience more difficulty in accessing their devices.

> *Recommendation* 1: There is a need for smart mobile device and app designers to consider the ease of usage in the design of the devices and apps, particularly among first-time users and elderly users who are not familiar with dynamically changing digital context.

Understanding the information of the various features on their smart mobile devices may be difficult for those who are not accustomed to reading in English. It may also deter them from reading up before downloading an app. More importantly, participants may be unaware of the retrieval of sensitive data and PII upon downloading an app. 38.2% (21) of the participants responded that they are unlikely to read up on information before downloading an app. Of these 21 participants, 52.4% (11) responded "very unlikely" and nine participants responded "somewhat unlikely" (Fig. 3). Eight other participants responded "neutral" to reading up before an app is downloaded.

Other than the lack of awareness that downloading apps may retrieve sensitive data and PII from the user, four participants reportedly installed apps from nonreputable or unknown application providers (e.g., third-party app stores). There are five other participants who were "not sure" whether their apps were installed from nonreputable or unknown providers.

A study conducted by Hewlett Packard Security Research (2013), for example, revealed that 90% of the 2107 mobile apps examined were vulnerable to attacks, 97% accessed sensitive data and PII, and 86% had privacy-related risks. Lack of binary code protection was identified

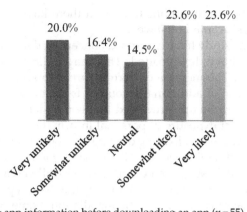

FIG. 3 Likelihood of reading app information before downloading an app ($n = 55$).

as a potential vulnerability affecting 86% of the apps examined. Another major vulnerability was weak or inappropriate implementation of cryptographic schemes to secure sensitive data stored by the apps on mobile devices, which was revealed in 75% of the apps examined. A study by D'Orazio and Choo (2015) revealed that due to the inappropriate implementation of cryptographic algorithm and the storage of sensitive data and PII in an unencrypted database in a widely used Australian government health care app, users' sensitive data and PII stored on the device could be compromised by an attacker. In another related work, the authors also revealed vulnerabilities in four video on-demand apps, one live TV app, and a security DRM protection module (D'Orazio and Choo, 2016).

Recommendation 2: Considering that older mobile device users may not be accustomed to reading very wordy information, easy-to-read manuals (both in hard/soft copies and audio/video formats) available in different languages (other than English) can be attached to the smart mobile device package upon purchase or made easily available online to inform users of possible cybercrime risks and to heighten their awareness of possible risky activities related to the use of their device or app.

The lack of understanding app information, coupled with a low likelihood of reading up on information before downloading and installing apps from nonreputable or unknown app providers, may put these users at risk of revealing their personal information. This is an indication that awareness needs to be increased in these areas.

Linking the above concerns about the lack of understanding of app information and the low likelihood of reading up on information before downloading an app, we also draw our attention to the type of smart mobile device the participants own.

Thirty-five out of the 55 (63.6%) participants own an Android device. The permission-based method utilized by Android to determine an app's legitimacy has been shown to be insufficient at classifying malicious apps reliably. On the other hand, the review process used by Apple is more restrictive for developers, as each app is thoroughly analyzed for security issues before being released to the public (although there have been reports of potentially malicious apps getting past Apple's reviewers).

Some participants in our study have expressed concern with encountering advertisements while using the app they have downloaded. This may indicate in-app advertising, which is commonly seen in apps. The increase of permissions is predicted to be related to in-app advertising that requires use of additional resources for data mining (Shekhar et al., 2012). A 2012 study of 100,000 Android apps revealed that some mobile advertising libraries used by apps resulted in the direct exposure of personal information, and some advertisement libraries result in unsafe fetching and loading of dynamic code from the Internet. For example, five out of the 100 identified ad libraries had the unsafe practice of downloading suspicious payloads, which allowed the host app to be remotely controlled (Grace et al., 2012).

In addition, an Android device user must choose either to accept all permissions required by the app in order to download or cancel the installation. Some of these permissions may not be necessary, and granting all permissions may pose a privacy risk to Android users. For example, in a 2014 study, seven Android social networking apps were examined (Do et al., 2014). It was discovered that the Facebook app requires the "read contacts" permission, which means retrieving users' contact data including contact numbers, contact addresses, and email addresses, regarded as unnecessary. Both Facebook and Tango require permission to "read phone state" that includes allowing the app to access the device's phone number, the international mobile equipment identifier (IMEI) of the device. As the IMEI serves as a unique identifier that is often used to locate the device, providing such information may be disadvantageous to the user.

56.4% (31) of the participants in our study reported using the Facebook app and 20 out of the 31 participants (64.5%) have used the app on their Android devices. Nine out of the 20 participants who used the Facebook app on their Android devices are mainly literate in Chinese. Given their lack of understanding the information when downloading an app, these participants may be put at risk of granting more than the necessary permissions.

If this need for permissions when downloading apps in Android devices is linked to a lack of understanding of information (in English) on apps and the low likelihood of reading up on information before downloading an app, as seen with our participants, people may be exposed to a higher risk of revealing their sensitive data and PII without being aware of doing so.

> *Recommendation* 3: While studies such as that of Do et al. (2014) suggested that permissions removal in Android devices can be used to enhance user's privacy, we further suggest that incorporating the flexibility of language settings will help users who have little or no literacy in English to be able to remove permissions.

Leaving your belongings unattended in a public place or work environment that may be temporarily out of your sight may be a risky thing to do, especially when the smart mobile device contains a lot of sensitive data and PII about the user, such as photos, login details for the apps installed, corporate and personal emails, and other messages with people you know.

Even though most participants responded "very unlikely" and "somewhat unlikely," there are still 10.9% of the participants who responded "very likely" (3) and "somewhat likely" (3). The likelihood of half of these participants leaving their smart mobile devices unattended in a public place or work environment may be related to the nature of their work, such as working in an outdoor environment that requires them to travel from place to place, and so the tendency of leaving their belongings unattended is high. Three of these participants, for example, are in the theatrical trade.

Users working in such environments have to be more wary of leaving their smart mobile devices unattended. If leaving a smart mobile device unattended is risky, not having password protection for your device or not knowing if your device has been accessed without your permission may further increase the risk. Among the six participants who are likely to leave their smart mobile devices unattended, half of them do not use a password or PIN to lock their devices. Although most of the other participants responded that their likelihood of leaving their devices unattended is low, 43.6% (24) of them do not lock their mobile devices. Three participants reported that they are "not sure" if their devices have been accessed without their permission.

Unauthorized access of smart mobile devices is a serious threat for any organization whose employees store sensitive data and/or credentials on their smart mobile devices. It should by now be common knowledge that leaving a device unattended, especially if no locking mechanism is in place, exposes any personal and corporate data stored on the device. Even if data has been deleted from the device, it could still potentially be retrieved using open-source and commercial forensic software (e.g. Micro Systemation XRY and CelleBrite UFED Kit) (Tassone et al., 2013; Quick et al., 2013).

While Internet access via smart mobile devices is easily accessible today, connecting to public Wi-Fi networks may put the user at risk of revealing sensitive data and PII. Using Wi-Fi hotspots, a hacker in the local area network may steal such information by replicating the legitimate provider's login or registration webpage. Four of our participants responded "yes" and 10 responded "depends" when asked if they would connect to unknown Wi-Fi networks (see Table 4).

This study also aims to test participant's awareness of phishing. Our findings suggested that a high proportion of the participants are unaware of phishing; see Fig. 4.

This trend stretches across all age groups and educational levels. However, the sample may be biased in finding out if literacy mainly in Chinese may affect users' perception of phishing due to the difficulty in gathering such participants.

TABLE 4 Participants' Responses on Wifi and Bluetooth Security ($n = 55$)

Questions on Wifi and Bluetooth Security	Participants' Responses
Do you keep your mobile device(s)'s Wi-Fi switched on at all times?	27 (49.1%) responded "yes"
Would you connect to unknown Wi-Fi networks?	Four responded "yes" and 10 responded "depends"
Do you keep your mobile device(s)'s Bluetooth switched on at all times?	Five responded "yes"
Would you accept a Bluetooth pairing request from unknown sources?	Three responded "depends"

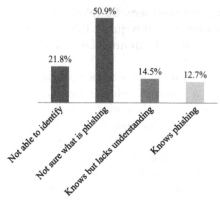

FIG. 4   Understanding of phishing (*n* = 55).

87.3% (48) of the participants are either unaware or do not have a sufficient understanding of phishing. Eight of the fifteen participants who said that they know what phishing is fail to identify some of the phishing examples set out in the survey, and 23 participants will perform one or more of the following actions:

- Open SMS from unknown contact (20)
- Open email (7)
- Access instant messaging request (Facebook, MSN) (2)

Table 5 illustrates the questions on phishing, and Tables 6 and 7 illustrate the 10 phishing examples set out in the survey and the participants' responses. There are five examples set in Chinese for participants who are literate mainly in Chinese, while the remaining five examples are the same with the English survey. This is to test the responses of participants who are mainly literate in Chinese on whether they will access without asking for advice, ignore it, or ask for advice from family/friends. Figures marked in bold indicate the number of participants who are aware of what phishing is.

We tested the correlation of phishing with variables like age and educational level. Out of the seven participants who are able to recognize all the phishing examples, six have university education and one graduated with college education. The age group is also more concentrated in the 45–50 age group (4), followed by 51–55 (2) and 56–60 (1). One participant prefers to read in Chinese. However, as the number of participants who are able to identify phishing is small, more tests will need to be conducted on a larger scale for more conclusive results.

TABLE 5   Participants' Responses on Phishing (*n* = 55)

Questions on Phishing	Participants' Responses
Will you access the following from an unknown contact?	23 participants will access one or more of the following: Open SMS from unknown contact, open email, or access instant messaging request (Facebook, MSN)
Will you be able to detect phishing scams received on your mobile device?	See Fig. 4.

TABLE 6 Responses on Phishing for English Survey

Phishing Examples	Responses		
	P	L	N
Local bank phishing email ($n=39$)	18	5	16
Bank update SMS phishing ($n=39$)	21	3	15
Permission allowing app to messages, personal information, network ($n=38$)[a]	17	8	13
eBay phishing email ($n=39$)[b]	20	4	15
Facebook phishing email ($n=40$)	16	4	20
Amazon phishing email ($n=40$)	19	1	20
PayPal phishing email ($n=40$)	21	5	14
Facebook request ($n=40$)	34	0	6
Facebook phishing email ($n=40$)	16	4	19
Bank phishing email ($n=40$)	21	5	14

P, phishing; *L*, legitimate; *N*, not sure.

[a]*The example here pertains to app permission. Participants will reply "yes," "no," or "not sure" to whether they feel this permission is necessary. The "no" option is counted under the "phishing/yes" column to imply participants' awareness that this requirement is unnecessary.*

[b]*The example question asks whether the email is legitimate, hence the "no" option will be categorized under the "phishing/yes" column to imply participants' awareness that this email is not legitimate.*

TABLE 7 Responses on Phishing for Chinese Survey

Phishing Examples ($n=15$)	Responses		
	P	L	N
QQ phishing email	9	1	5
Reply to WeChat SMS phishing	14	0	1
Phishing email requesting login	14	1	0
Permission allowing app to messages, personal information, network	12	1	2
Phishing alert on downloading free antivirus software	12	0	3
English phishing examples	I	W	S
Local bank phishing email	8	0	7
PayPal phishing email	11	0	4
eBay phishing email	12	0	3
Facebook request	14	0	1
Facebook phishing email	11	1	3

P, phishing; *L*, legitimate; *N*, not sure; *I*, ignore; *W*, will access; *S*, seek advice.

A recent research indicates that by 2017, over 1 billion users globally will use their smart mobile devices for banking purposes. Cybercrime is heading towards the "post-PC" era, which is the era of smart mobile devices. It is important to note that the term "phishing" may be unfamiliar to some but other users may have some understanding of the concept of phishing; that is, emails or websites that pretend to be from a trustworthy entity.

> *Recommendation* 4: Given the findings from this survey and the increasing risk of cybercrime targeted at mobile devices, there is an urgent need to increase (elderly) users' awareness about phishing; see Section 4.

Other than responses from the survey, this study has also compiled some feedback from participants and other elderly smart mobile device users whom we have approached but did not participate in the survey.

One user, who did not participate in the survey, responded that he has "technology phobia" and he only knows a few features on the phone such as calling, messaging, and photos, which are mainly the functions of a feature phone. The user occasionally accesses Facebook using both his mobile device and computer.

Most of the users are unsure of how to use features, such as surfing the Internet, playing online games, and social networking. An important factor that obstructed their use of smart mobile devices is the use of the touch-screen feature, as they often face the difficulty of motor and sensory motions like the synthesis of timing to swipe or touch features of the smart mobile device.

As digital immigrants, these seniors may have a longer contact with feature phones than smartphones, so they need time to use the latter more effectively. It is worth noting that a Singapore company manufactures iNo Mobile, an elderly-friendly mobile phone with some models that support smart mobile device features (Dyeo et al., 2010). However, none of our participants own such a mobile device.

4 A SITUATIONAL CRIME PREVENTION APPROACH

A typical crime prevention intervention is to create conditions that are unfavorable for crime. For example, the routine activity theory is a popular theory used to explain criminal events. The theory proposes that crime occurs when a suitable target is in the presence of a motivated offender and is without a capable guardian (Cohen and Felson, 1979). Offender motivation is a crucial element in the theory, which draws on rational exploitation of "opportunity" in the context of the regularity of human conduct to design prevention strategies, especially where terrestrial interventions are possible. Criminals are assumed to be rational and appropriately resourced actors operating in the context of high-value, attractive targets protected by weak guardians (Felson, 1998; Yar, 2005), and that victimization risk is a function of how one victim patterns their behavior and lifestyle (Imgraben et al., 2014). For example, a password-protected device may be of little use to an opportunistic thief.

The interaction between smart mobile device users, cybercriminals who are financially motivated, and situational conditions e.g., opportunities and weak guardianship has great influence on the situation. For example, how easy is it to design malware and phishing websites targeting older smart mobile device users who may not be as IT literate and cyber-savvy and what is the risk of getting caught and prosecuted in a court of law?

Therefore we should examine ways of creating conditions unfavorable for crime. For example, according to the Situational Crime Prevention Theory (Clarke, 1997; Cornish and Clarke, 2003), the five broad categories (comprising 25 techniques) to reduce crime targeting mobile users are:

1. *Increasing perceived effort*: Target hardening, controlling access to facilities, screen exits, deflecting offenders, and controlling tools/weapons
2. *Increasing perceived risks*: Extending guardianship, assisting natural surveillance, reducing anonymity, utilizing place managers, and strengthening formal surveillance
3. *Reducing rewards*: Concealing targets, removing targets, identifying properties, disrupting markets, and denying benefits
4. *Removing excuses*: Reducing frustrations and stress, avoiding disputes, reducing emotional arousal, neutralizing peer pressure, and discouraging imitation
5. *Reducing provocations*: Setting rules, posting instructions, alerting conscience, assisting compliance, and controlling drugs and alcohol (which we will replace with "provocation factors")

Measures that users, mobile device and app designers, app store operators, and government agencies can undertake to ensure a secure mobile environment are outlined in Table 8.

The findings from this survey, as well as those in previous studies such as Imgraben et al. (2014), suggested that many elderly (and young university-educated, respectively) smart mobile device users are generally unaware of the risks that they may expose themselves to every day. More concerning, however, is that mobile device users do not appear to be sufficiently informed regarding their smart devices' usage and security. As pointed out in previous studies as well as our own study, the participants were generally unaware of the risks they subjected themselves to; for example, by leaving their Wi-Fi and Bluetooth turned on at all times, particularly those who were also likely to perform online banking (four of our participants do so) and other activities (two participants shop online) that could expose personal information to an attacker.

There is, arguably, a need for an integrated, coordinated, and concerted effort by government agencies, mobile device and app providers, and community and educational organizations (e.g., University of the Third Age; see http://www.u3aonline.org.au/) to combat the cybercriminal activities that victimize mobile device users, which can help to ensure that the most effective cybercrime prevention advice is provided to the users (Australian Government House of Representatives Standing Committee on Communications, 2010).

The success of cybercrime education programs can be mediated by a range of individual, contextual, and cultural factors. It should also be noted that education is not the only solution or the most reliable method. The broad aim of the ongoing cybercrime education should be to bring about behavioral change and increase user awareness.

Although there are various cybercrime educational initiatives in countries such as Singapore, there has been limited evaluation of these educational initiatives. The evaluation and study of such educational initiatives is important (e.g., to develop a good understanding of what works, what does not work, and why), as a badly implemented educational initiative may not result in any of the hoped-for benefits, regardless of how well-conceived the educational initiative may be.

TABLE 8 Cybersafety Practices Based on Situational Crime Prevention Theory

Increase Perceived Effort	Increase Perceived Risks	Reduce Rewards	Remove Excuses	Reduce Provocations
Target hardening such as installing antivirus software and software updates on a regular basis	*Extending guardianship* by not collecting device-unique identifiers and/or personal information not related to the functions or activities of the device or app	*Concealing targets* by securing mobile devices when not in use, using a different email address for suspicious app signup, etc.	*Reducing frustrations and stress* by providing a transparent online reporting system where users can report malicious apps to app stores for remediation action, etc.	*Setting rules* such as best practices for design of mobile apps and devices that ensure the security and privacy of user data, and regulating third-party app stores
Access control such as securing mobile devices when not in use	*Assisting natural surveillance* such as reporting lost or stolen devices and cyber victimization to appropriate authorities	*Removing targets* such as avoiding websites of dubious repute or downloading apps from third-party app stores	*Avoiding disputes* between app designers and users by allowing users to opt in or out from the collection or use of their personal information, and by identifying third parties and including links to information in the privacy policy about how users can modify or delete the data used by those parties, etc.	*Posting instructions* such as limiting dissemination of sensitive and personally identifiable information on public forums such as social networking sites
Screen exits such as deleting personal information from mobile device or app before disposing of the mobile device	*Reducing anonymity* by registering app providers or individuals who upload apps to app stores	*Identifying properties* such as physical marking of mobile devices or use of remote wiping and locating apps	*Reducing emotional arousal* by the banning or removal of apps that encourage violence or facilitate criminal behavior	*Alert conscience* by providing regular user education to train them on how to be vigilant and for device and app providers to conduct due diligence on third-party libraries and code, etc.

Deflecting offenders by reducing their possibility or incentive to commit a crime, such as prompt installation of patches to software and hardware	*Utilizing place managers* that will be responsible for vetting devices and apps before they are approved for public release, securing the data collected from users, etc.	*Disrupting markets* by criminalizing the sale of lost or stolen devices and development of malicious apps	*Neutralizing peer pressure* to avoid creating situations that could lead to collusion between malicious perpetrators to target mobile device users	*Assisting compliance* by encouraging users to report cyber victimization, by revoking the ability of a malicious or noncompliant app or device provider, and by discouraging device or app providers to collect and store personal information unnecessarily
Controlling tools such as using privacy enhancing apps or opting out of sharing personal information with third parties	*Strengthening formal surveillance* such as monitoring of app activities (e.g., are a user's movements and activities collected through the use of integrated location and movement sensors without informed consent?)	*Denying benefits* such as using encryption and an alphanumeric and nonguessable password, as well as prosecution of offenders	*Discouraging imitation* such as fake or misleading apps	*Controlling provocation factors* using measures such as setting rules to discourage noncompliant behaviors without compromising usability

In addition, we suggest that any educational materials developed for smart mobile device users be tailored specifically to the user group (e.g., Generation X, Generation Y, and baby boomers; as well as end users from diverse cultural and linguistic backgrounds) and end users with varying technical and literacy backgrounds.

5 CONCLUSION

In our study, we have discovered that some participants who know little or no English have difficulty understanding instructions of the applications installed on their smart mobile devices. Other than the language settings of the smart mobile device, which is already available in most devices, our findings have concluded that there is also a need to have flexibility in the language settings for their features. There is an urgent need to increase users' awareness about cybersafety measures.

Possible future extensions of this survey include surveying other populations of elderly users in different countries, who are literate in English or only in a single non-English language, and undertaking a targeted approach to help develop cybersafety educational materials, where small groups of older mobile device users are selected to participate in face-to-face interviews and are presented with the survey multiple times with educational materials specific to their results given after each round. The overall results can be used to show the effect that the materials have, and feedback from the participating user groups can be used to further refine the educational materials.

Acknowledgments

We would like to thank Mr. Zhuang Haining, who had approached the participants about their responses on smart mobile devices on our behalf, and Mr. Seet Chong Boon for helping to recruit participants for this survey.

References

Australian Government House of Representatives Standing Committee on Communications, 2010. Hackers, Fraudsters and Botnets: Tackling the Problem of Cyber Crime. Commonwealth of Australia, Canberra.

Clarke, R., 1997. Situational Crime Prevention: Successful Case Studies, vol. 2. Harrow and Heston, New York, NY.

Cohen, L.E., Felson, M., 1979. Social change and crime rate trends: a routine activity approach. Am. Sociol. Rev. 44 (4), 588–608.

Cornish, D.B., Clarke, R., 2003. Opportunities, precipitators and criminal decisions: a reply to Wortley's critique of situational crime prevention. In: Smith, M.J., Cornish, D.B. (Eds.), Theory for Practice in Situational Crime Prevention. Crime Prevention Studies, vol. 16. Criminal Justice Press, Monsey, NY, pp. 41–96.

D'Orazio, C., Choo, K.-K.R., 2015. A generic process to identify vulnerabilities and design weaknesses in iOS Healthcare apps. In: Hawaii International Conference on System Sciences 2015, pp. 5175–5184.

D'Orazio, C., Choo, K.-K.R., 2016. An adversary model to evaluate DRM protection of video contents on iOS devices. Comput. Secur. 56, 94–110. http://dx.doi.org/10.1016/j.cose.2015.06.009.

Do, Q., Martini, B., Choo, K.-K.R., 2014. Enhancing user privacy on android mobile devices via permissions removal. In: Hawaii International Conference on System Sciences, pp. 5070–5079.

Dyeo, C., Lee, T.M., Abdul Rahman, N.B., 2010. An exploratory study on the emotional, cognitive and behavioural inclinations of the Singapore elderly towards mobile phones. Wee Kim Wee School of Communication and Information (WKWSCI) Student Report (FYP), Nanyang Technological University, Singapore. pp. 1–49.

Elliot, A.J., Mooney, C.J., Douthit, K.Z., Lynch, M.F., 2013. Predictors of older adults' technology use and its relationship to depressive symptoms and well-being. J. Gerontol. B Psychol. Sci. Soc. Sci. 69 (5), 667–677.

Felson, M., 1998. Crime and Everyday Life. Pine Forge Press, New York, NY.

Fieldhouse, M., Nicholas, D., 2008. Digital literacy as information savvy: the road to information literacy. In: Lankshear, C., Knobel, M. (Eds.), Digital Literacies: Concepts, Policies and Practices. Peter Lang, New York, NY, pp. 47–90.

Grace, M.C., Zhou, W., Jiang, X., Sadeghi, A.-R., 2012. Unsafe exposure analysis of mobile in-app advertisements. In: ACM Conference on Security and Privacy in Wireless and Mobile Networks, pp. 101–112.

Hewlett Packard Security Research, 2013. Hewlett Packard press release. http://www8.hp.com/us/en/hp-news/press-release.html?id=1528865 (accessed 01.08.15).

Imgraben, J., Engelbrecht, A., Choo, K.-K.R., 2014. Always connected, but are smart mobile users getting more security savvy? A survey of smart mobile device users. Behav. Inform. Technol. 33 (12), 1347–1360.

Infocomm Development of Singapore, 2015. Facts and figures, telecommunications. http://www.ida.gov.sg/Infocomm-Landscape/Facts-and-Figures/Telecommunications#1 (accessed 03.08.15).

Kurniawan, S., 2008. Older people and mobile phones: a multi-method investigation. Int. J. Hum. Comput. Stud. 66 (12), 889–901.

Quick, D., Martini, B., Choo, K.-K.R., 2013. Cloud Storage Forensics. Syngress/Elsevier, Amsterdam.

Selfe, C., Hawisher, G., 2004. Introduction: literate lives in the information age. In: Selfe, C., Hawisher, G. (Eds.), Literate Lives in the Information Age: Narratives of Literacy From the United States. Lawrence Erlbaum Associates, Mahwah, NJ, pp. 1–28.

Shekhar, S., Dietz, M., Wallach, D., 2012. Adsplit: separating smartphone advertising from application. In: Proceedings of the 21st USENIX Security Symposium, pp. 1–15.

Singapore Department of Statistics, 2010. Census of population 2010. http://www.singstat.gov.sg/publications/publications-and-papers/population#census_of_population_2010 (accessed 03.08.15).

Tassone, C., Martini, B., Choo, K.-K.R., Slay, J., 2013. Mobile device forensics: a snapshot. Trends Issues Crime Crim. Justice 460, 1–7.

Yar, M., 2005. The novelty of 'cybercrime': an assessment in light of routine activity theory. Eur. J. Criminol. 2 (4), 407–427.

5

The Role of Mobile Devices in Enhancing the Policing System to Improve Efficiency and Effectiveness: A Practitioner's Perspective

F. Schiliro*, K.-K.R. Choo*,†

*University of South Australia, Adelaide, SA, Australia
†University of Texas at San Antonio, San Antonio, TX, United States

1 INTRODUCTION

Information and communications technology (ICT) is an umbrella term that includes any communication device or application encompassing mobile phones, computer and network hardware, software, the Internet, satellite systems, and so on. ICT also refers to the various services and applications associated with them, such as videoconferencing and distance learning.

Police organizations within Australia, like other police organizations throughout the world, are dependent on ICT to operate. This need grows as ICT develops.

Poor ICT systems prevent police officers from getting on with their jobs. A better ICT system will raise police productivity so that the same amount of work could be done by fewer officers, or more work could be done by the current number of officers.

Over the years, technological innovations such as the telephone, mobile radio, and tape recorder have been introduced into policing to improve effectiveness. They have had a major influence on how police organizations function and how police do their work (Choo, 2011; Ready and Young, 2015; Tanner and Meyer, 2015; Koper et al., 2015).

When it was introduced into policing over three decades ago, mainframe computer technology also had a profound influence on how police agencies functioned, although it was not well recognized at the time. It allowed the collection, storage, and retrieval of large amounts of data and, as a consequence, police information systems became a reality. However, numerous forms had to be designed to capture the data, and officers were required to report the data by completing the forms. Then people had to be hired to code and feed the data into the computers, while others were made responsible for retrieving and distributing data in different combinations to still others who analyzed the results. In essence, mainframe computer technology created more employment, bureaucracy, and, for the police officer, more paperwork.

Now client/server computer technology has replaced or enhanced mainframe functions and has revolutionized some basic organizational functions and paper systems. Ordering of police supplies, payment of bills and salaries, and keeping of inventory can all be done electronically through much shorter and faster processes executed by fewer people. For example, operational police can take laptop computers into their patrol cars and into investigative interviews to collect data directly. Internal electronic mail systems and the Internet are also giving police access to unlimited information to help them perform their jobs more efficiently. Internal information systems are also more accessible to the police officer. Some police training can also be automated and pursued individually at times convenient to the officer and the organization, thus reducing training costs and eliminating the difficulty of taking a number of officers out of the field at the same time. The trend in information technology during that period has had an appreciable impact on police work. Police agencies are even exploring the integration of all justice information systems to allow justice practitioners and agencies to electronically access and share information between systems and/or across jurisdictional lines. Some agencies have already partially implemented this into their system. Police-related websites and list servs are also enabling officers to consult and share information with colleagues all over the world via the Internet.

However, the phablet, a new network computer technology linked to telecommunications systems, has even more potential to transform police work. The phablet has evolved, too, as smartphones stretched in size to compete for the convenience and capability of tablets. Phablets have screens that measure diagonally 135–178 mm (5.3–6.99 in.), a size that complements screen-intensive activity such as mobile web browsing and multimedia viewing. Phablets may also include software optimized for an integral self-storing stylus to facilitate sketching and annotation. It was perhaps these character traits, the screen size and stylus that distinguished itself with policing?

While Samsung's Galaxy Note is largely credited with pioneering the worldwide phablet market when launched in 2011, examples of early devices with similar form factors date to 1993. By the time the Galaxy Note 3 came to market, policing agencies such as the Australian Federal Police were already conceptualizing how a policing organization's capabilities could be delivered from the IT backend to the frontline officer, thanks in part to the benefits of phablet usage. Will the phablet become the dominant computing device for police of the future?

ICT has an important role to play in the success of criminal investigations, but police competence and management are also important. For ICT to play a significant role it must be adopted, not adapted, into police work as part of a solid base alongside management, competent police officers, and well-organized investigations.

2 INTERACTIVE CONSTABLE ON PATROL SYSTEM

The police officer's typical duties relate to the response to, the detection of, and the prevention of crime. Officers are expected to respond to a variety of situations that may arise while they are on duty. The law and an organization's policies and procedures dictate how an officer should behave within the community.

In response to the variety of situations that may arise while they are on duty, the officer is required to think critically in a situation and to make sound decisions. But what is critical thinking? There are many ways to initially define it. Unfortunately, internal debate in the field of critical thinking often centers on disagreements between theoreticians (Hale, 2008). Hale convincingly argues that while theoreticians often emphasize different aspects of critical thinking, virtually all agree that it entails the analysis and evaluation of thinking with a view towards improving it; that it includes the development of intellectual traits, which should be applied to one's own thinking; and the thinking of others and thinking within subject disciplines.

Therefore in keeping with this literature, we can divide critical thinking into the following broad dimensions:

- *Skilled intellectual analysis*: the ability to divide important intellectual constructs into constituent parts so as to internalize and evaluate them
- *Skilled intellectual evaluation*: the ability to determine the quality of intellectual constructs and their parts
- Intellectual improvement: the ability to creatively devise strategies aimed at correcting weaknesses and improving strengths that have been identified through analysis and evaluation
- *Intellectual traits*: characteristics of mind necessary for developing fair-minded critical thinkers, such as: perseverance, integrity, courage, empathy, and autonomy. It is argued that such traits guard against the development of sophistic or self-deceptive thinking.
- *Knowledge of the problems of thinking*: including intrinsic tendencies such as egocentrism and sociometrist, which trap the mind in oversimplified and prejudiced mental states.

Furthermore, these dimensions need be applied to various contexts:

- To thinking generally (one's own thinking, the thinking of a professor, colleague, friend, parent, spouse/partner …)
- To subject disciplines (each of which have specific and sometimes unique forms of analysis and evaluation)
- To personal life, both with regard to significant decisions (e.g., buying a car or house, making career decisions) as well as day-to-day activities (e.g., diet and exercise, parenting, voting and politics, managing finances)

However, when identifying areas of investigation within which to develop a means of making police officers more efficient and effective at the frontline, it is necessary to have some idea of the broad and noncontroversial framework of critical thinking into which these individual understandings can be placed. There is an intimate interrelation between knowledge and thinking; therefore an important capability for policing is knowledge.

Interactive Constable on Patrol System (ICOPS), as seen in Fig. 1, is a mobile application downloaded on a phablet or, where convenient, a tablet. The application itself is a framework delivering a policing organization's capabilities sitting on a platform to the frontline officer. Two examples of those capabilities are: knowledge exchange and communications, which can augment a police officer's knowledge and experience whilst performing his duties. It provides critical information at the time of an incident, improving the police officers options and decision making ability.

FIG. 1   An example of eight capabilities being presented.

The purpose of the framework is to make police officers more efficient in carrying out their duties.

For example, at the end of a shift, a police officer is typically required to return to a station to enter data into systems, which includes completing and faxing hardcopy documentation to a centralized area for retyping into the database. Around 50 percent of a police officer's time on each shift is spent in the station, with a significant proportion attributed to administrative tasks associated with information capture and reporting. Increasingly, police find that their paperwork burden requires them to commence shifts early and finish them late in order to complete documentation. Delays in processing information and making it available for operational members present difficulties for police in responding to service delivery calls and increase safety risks for both police and the public (Victoria Police, 2014).

3 CAPABILITIES

3.1 Information Management and Knowledge Exchange

In terms of technology, despite the availability of sophisticated recorders and computers, the police notebook remains one of the simplest, most economical, and most basic of investigative tools used to record all facts observed and learned during an investigation.

Therefore, the ICOPS framework sitting on a phablet represents a new technological advancement for police to adopt in order to fulfill a well-overdue function in the area of criminal investigation.

For "knowledge workers" (a term coined by Peter Drucker in 1959), a role which police play, technology becomes a vital enabler of communication, collaboration, and access to rising volumes of information.

ICOPS takes a structured provision of knowledge approach, delivering a range of functions. The most important is workflow technology that controls how the frontline police get information and job tasks. The system also links them to a platform supporting technologies that include information portals, business rules or algorithms to automate decisions, document or content management systems, business process management and monitoring systems, and collaboration tools. Such technologies are often called case management systems because they allow workers to complete an entire case or unit of work. Case management can create value whenever some degree of structure or process can be imposed upon information-intensive work. Until recently, structured provision approaches have been applied mostly to lower-level information tasks that are repetitive, predictable, and thus easier to automate.

Productivity is the major benefit as measured by the completion of key tasks per unit of work time, productivity often rises by 50 percent when organizations implement these technologies. The reason for the improvement was that workers had few distractions and spent no time searching for information.

Adding to the efficiencies, in most cases organizations can route tasks to any worker with the time and expertise to undertake them. For example, if a police officer is away on leave, the system knows and sends cases to another for approval instead. Work processes become more transparent, and it becomes easier to manage them, to exercise approval authority, and to monitor improvements. The structured model also facilitates collaboration and the coordination of tasks. Many implementations help organizations to engage multiple workers and groups to process incidents. These systems also often incorporate business rules or algorithms, determined by an organization's best experts, which help organizations decide the best course of action. For managers, these systems can therefore improve the quality and consistency of decision making, while also speeding it up through automation or semi automation.

By providing smart forms linked to automated workflows as in Figs. 2 and 3, police can complete an incident report at the scene. This will reduce delays in processing information and make it available for operational members, resulting in a reduction of time spent at the station completing paperwork.

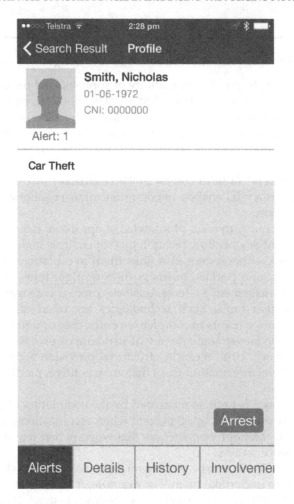

FIG. 2   A search result.

3.2 Intelligent Personal Assistant—Bobby

A new technological advancement on the horizon for the law enforcement community are web service applications known as intelligent personal assistants (IPA). Apple's Siri, Google's Google Now, and Microsoft's Cortana represent a class of emerging IPAs. An IPA is an application that uses inputs such as the user's voice, vision (images), and contextual information to provide assistance by answering questions (using natural language), making recommendations, and performing actions. These IPAs have emerged as one of the fastest-growing Internet services after having been deployed on well-known platforms such as iOS, Android, and Windows Phone, making them ubiquitous on mobile devices worldwide.

Three decades ago, a young officer graduating from the police academy would have been buddied up with a senior officer such as a senior constable or sergeant. This senior officer was an experienced officer with over 10 years of accumulated experience and knowledge. Today an emerging trend exists that a police officer is less likely to make policing a career and is

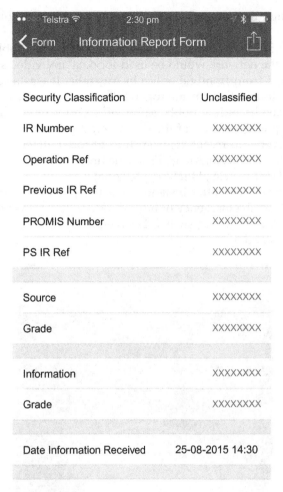

FIG. 3 An information report form.

only expected to stay in policing for 5–9 years, decaying the traditional method of knowledge transfer from veteran officers to rookies.

Integrating ICOPS to an unlimited number of public and private databases, employing data mining technology, and communicating with existing law enforcement communications systems (e.g., computer-aided dispatch, GPS-guided locator systems, and mobile data computers) could create a powerful and efficient information management system. A police officer using such a tool in the field could accomplish many tasks simultaneously by simply conversing with the device and issuing verbal commands.

3.3 Communications

One of the key aspects of effective workforce management is the clear, unambiguous communication of instructions, responses, and information. A key benefit of ICOPS will be the reduced demand on traditional police radio communications as information traditionally sought via radio through the communications centers can now be obtained via the mobile device using ICOPS.

When long-term evolution (LTE) technology was chosen by the public safety community, it was envisioned that the network would be used for data and video services and designed to provide access to and from frontline police in Australia. It was also envisioned that the network would be the foundation for interoperability on a nationwide basis, helping to fix the issues that have been hounding public safety officials for more than 30 years, but only became known to the public because of the communications failures experienced during a spate of catastrophic events in recent years such as terrorist attacks (e.g., Sep. 11, London, Madrid, Mumbai), factory explosions (e.g., Enschede fireworks disaster, Toulouse warehouse explosion), floods, and storms (e.g., Hurricane Katrina).

Push-to-talk communications offer instant connectivity with the press of a button. This feature becomes crucial in an emergency or hazardous environments where instructions and information must be relayed quickly, such as between the command center and frontline officers in the field (Figs. 4 and 5).

FIG. 4   Of push-to-talk.

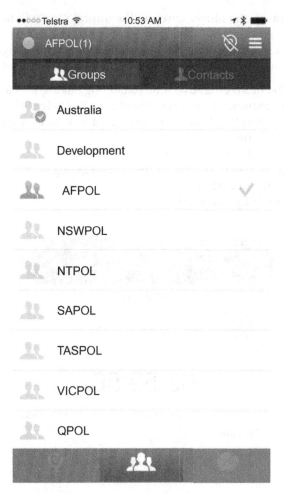

FIG. 5   Of interoperability between groups.

3.4 Custody Management

In Australia, all detained persons must be placed into custody when:

- detained as part of an investigative procedure, or
- detained as not a subject to an investigative procedure, or
- as a suspect not under arrest for the purposes of obtaining a forensic sample

When a detained person is placed into custody, the police officer will be required to manage all aspects of that custody and complete records. As the detaining of a person in most cases will occur in the field, ICOPS was designed to assist the police officer in that task. ICOPS would create a numbered custody record for each detained person, each of which would have a unique custody reference number (CRN). The custody would be created independently of charge information and could be inquired about by all officers.

Once a record is created, the officer entering the information will be deemed the custody manager and be able to add actions to that person's record. The results are improvements like reducing the time officers spend filling out forms and enabling investigative time to be monitored accurately. Custody management in ICOPS will allow the custody managers:

- Automatic calculation of investigative time remaining, taking into account timeouts and alerting the officer to requesting an extension of time if required (Fig. 6).
- Alerts to the officer, prompting him or her to request an extension of time prior to the investigative time finishing.
- All actions displayed on the same screen.
- A custody Management record output by the system listing all actions that took place during the person's time in custody.
- A list of all people currently in custody.

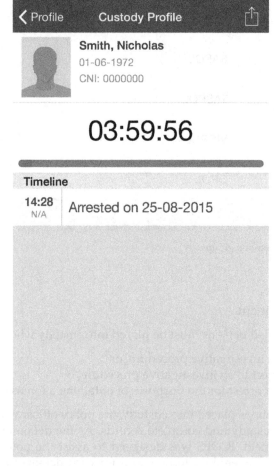

FIG. 6 Example of managing the custody of an arrested person.

3.5 Situational Awareness

Situational awareness typically refers to a person being aware of what is going on around him or her.

Law enforcement is an inherently dangerous occupation. At no time are officers more vulnerable than when they approach an unknown individual or a possibly mentally disturbed or impaired person, whether during a traffic stop, criminal investigation, or domestic violence call. Often, the best protection officers have is access to information about the person with whom they are dealing, the address to which they are dispatched, the vehicle and the driver they have stopped, and other information regarding activities in their jurisdictions. This information provides officers with situational awareness that could significantly increase officer and public safety.

When initiating a traffic stop, standard operating procedure is for an officer to run the vehicle license plate through a national database to acquire as much knowledge as possible about the vehicle owner (usually the driver) before approaching. A query to determine if there are any outstanding warrants on the registered owner of the vehicle, for example, could prompt the officer to request backup before approaching the vehicle. Once contact with the individual is initiated, the availability of additional information (i.e., identification of any other person in the vehicle) will further increase situational awareness.

Law enforcement officers need tools to provide accurate, timely, and complete information in the field. In addition, law enforcement agencies need access to a broad variety of technologies, such as geographic information systems (GIS) in order to build comprehensive situational awareness. Building enterprise-wide information sharing capabilities will enable agencies to improve situational awareness (Fig. 7).

Officers can also increase situational awareness through the use of social media or available online services. First responders to a disturbance at a large public event, for example, may acquire critical location and tactical information from public tweets via the Twitter platform or posted photos or video from cell phones. Images from Google Earth and other sources could inform officers responding to a crime in progress of potential escape routes or exposure to possible threats from suspects in or around a building. Real-time access to surveillance systems or traffic cameras via a handheld device could help officers target their response. However, the accuracy and reliability of information must be considered when utilizing public sources, especially in quickly developing situations. Policies governing the use of unsecure public information must be developed, and officers must be trained in the effective use of such tools.

3.6 Biometrics

As biometric technology expands, so do the methods by which a person can be identified and the accuracy with which an identification can be made.

Fingerprints are the only biometric that leaves something behind. The biometric traces left behind on a piece of physical evidence are called latent prints. They may also be referred to as tracing or markings. Latents are extremely important. And that is why, for the foreseeable future, fingerprints are going to remain law enforcement's most important biometric.

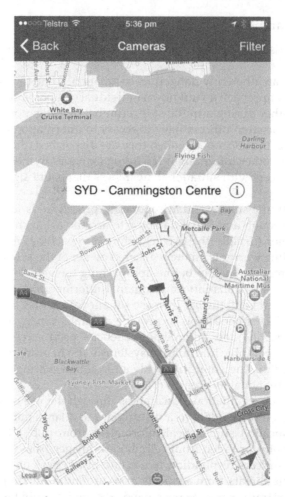

FIG. 7   Example of how situational awareness information might be pushed to the frontline officer.

Research is currently being conducted examining complete and fully automated approaches for the identification of low-resolution finger surface/texture images. This research and the obtained results are significant as they point towards the utility of touchless images acquired from the webcam for personal identification and its extension for other utilities like mobile phones.

3.6.1 Facial Recognition

Effective person identification is becoming increasingly central to law enforcement. The police are interested in whether they have already met a suspect before and what they know about them, such as whether they have a criminal record, whether they are armed and violent, etc.

Facial recognition is a relatively new biometric that is getting attention. Facial recognition has many advantages, a major one being that it is the only biometric that can routinely be obtained stealthily. Therefore it has value for use in surveillances. Facial recognition is not as accurate as fingerprints—at least, not yet—but it is becoming increasingly more accurate as new advances in the technology are made.

There are a number of different algorithms that scientists use to measure facial characteristics. New approaches continue to be developed by scientists at universities and in research labs of biometric companies. Each approach works differently, looking at different parts of the face or looking at the face in different ways. Ear shape, for example, is the focus of some facial recognition systems. Ear shape changes very little as we age. None of these facial recognition systems are 100 percent accurate, but some of them are approaching that level (Fig. 8).

As various facial recognition algorithms merge, the accuracy of facial recognition will increase. For instance, Imagus, a company based in Queensland, Australia, has a good facial recognition algorithm. They have developed a mobile app allowing police to run facial

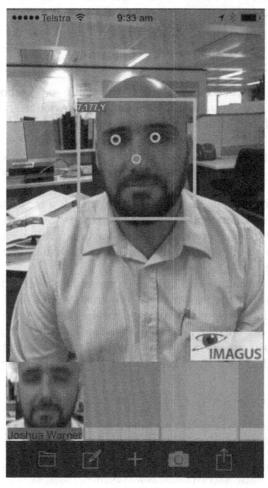

FIG. 8   Imagus facial recognition mobile app.

recognition in the field in a practical way without hindering normal police operation. As different methodologies merge, the result will be increased accuracy. Reliable applications in this field are not far off.

3.6.2 Iris Recognition

Iris recognition is another biometric of recent interest. The iris is the colored ring around the eye. Like fingerprints, the irises are formed in the womb after conception so that no two people, even twins, have the same iris.

Everyone has probably seen a very elderly person, such as a 100-year-old woman, photographed or interviewed on television. Sometimes in a close-up of her face you see her eyes sparkling, and they still look very youthful. The reason is she has the same irises as she did when she was a 19-year-old woman. Her skin may have wrinkled with age, but the iris has not changed at all. The iris can be used for both verification and identification. It is not useful in surveillance because no method yet exists to get close enough to the subject's iris without the subject's consent or cooperation.

4 CONCLUSION

Organizations need to better manage the working life expectations of a police officer. Technology needs to become an enabler to augment the knowledge and experience of new officers graduating from the police academy and working in the field. However, nothing can replace experience, which took earlier generations of police officers a decade to acquire enough. What is needed is change through innovation, implementing clear and practical strategies to deliver technology into the organization that makes police officers more effective and efficient, driving both time and costs down.

What policing organizations in Australia currently lack is a technology infrastructure that can collaborate with internal and external data sources, extracting, transforming, and loading data into a resource that each function within the organization can interrogate and then surface into a knowledge hub that will easily cause the collaboration process to occur both internally and externally.

However, achieving that alone will still not successfully contribute to police officers effectiveness and efficiency, if the information contained cannot reach the police officers to provide them the situational awareness required for them at the frontline. An organization's information can only be beneficial when it is directed and used by the appropriate responder.

Over the next 5 years, a change in the way policing is done needs to occur if a police officer's effectiveness and efficiency are to keep pace in this rapidly changing environment.

References

Choo, K.-K.R., 2011. Harnessing information and communications technologies in community policing. In: Putt, J. (Ed.), Community Policing in Australia. Research and Public Policy, vol. 111. Australian Institute of Criminology, Canberra, pp. 67–75.

Dervin, B., 1983. An overview of sense-making research: Concepts, methods and results. Paper presented at the annual meeting of the International Communication Association, Dallas, TX.

Dervin, B., 1992. From the mind's eye of the user: The sense-making qualitative-quantitative methodology. In: Glazier, J., Powell, R. R. (Eds.), Qualitative research in information management. Libraries Unlimited, Englewood, CA, pp. 61–84.

Dervin, B., 1996. Given a context by any other name: Methodological tools for taming the unruly beast. Keynote paper, ISIC 96: Information Seeking in Context. 1–23.

Hale, E., 2008. A critical analysis of Richard Paul's substantive trans-disciplinary conception of critical thinking. Unpublished dissertation, Union Institute and University.

Koper, C.S., Lum, C., Hibdon, J., 2015. The uses and impacts of mobile computing technology in hot spots policing. Eval. Rev. 39 (6), 587–624.

Ready, J.T., Young, J.T.N., 2015. The impact of on-officer video cameras on police–citizen contacts: findings from a controlled experiment in Mesa, AZ. J. Exp. Criminol. 11 (3), 445–458.

Tanner, S., Meyer, M., 2015. Police work and new 'security devices': a tale from the beat. Secur. Dialogue 46 (4), 384–400.

Victoria Police, 2014. Victoria Police Blue Paper: A Vision For Victoria Police In 2025. Blue Paper. Victoria Police, Melbourne.

Weick, K., 1995. Sensemaking in Organisations. Sage, London.

Additional reading materials

Bansler, J., Havn, E., 2006. Sensemaking in technology-use mediation: adapting groupware technology in organizations. Comput. Supported Coop. Work 15 (1), 55–91.

Borglund, E.A.M., Oberg, L.-M., Persson Slumpi, T., 2011. Success factors for police investigations in a hybrid environment: the Jamtland Police Authority case. Int. J. Police Sci. Manag. 14, 83–93.

Cosgrove, R., 2011. Critical thinking in the Oxford tutorial: a call for an explicit and systematic approach. High. Educ. Res. Dev. 30 (3), 343–356.

Cowan, P., 2016. Learning from the leaders in the region. http://www.itnews.com.au/news/top-tips-from-nz-polices-mobility-journey-417484.

Elliot, J., 2005. Biometrics roadmap for police applications. BT Technol. J. 23 (4), 37–44.

Knowledge workers, n.d. http://www.referenceforbusiness.com/management/Int-Loc/Knowledge-Workers.html.

Nunn, S., Quinet, K., 2002. Evaluating the effects of information technology on problem-oriented-policing: if it doesn't fit, must we quit? Eval. Rev. 26, 81–108.

Supervised Learning Based Detection of Malware on Android

F. Tchakounté, F. Hayata

University of Ngaoundéré, Ngaoundéré, Cameroon

Android has become the most popular open-source operating system for smartphones and tablets with an estimated market share of 70–80% (Canalys, 2013). A shipment of one billion Android devices has been forecast in 2017; over 50 billion applications have been downloaded since the first Android phone was released in 2008 (Llamas et al., 2013). The system is based on a Linux kernel and designed for Advanced RISC Machine (ARM) architectures. It includes various layers running on top of each other, with the lower ones providing services to the upper level layers. We give an overview of the architecture of Android presented in Fig. 1; existing studies (Brähler, 2015; Ehringer, 2010) give more details.

Linux Kernel: Android has taken the Linux kernel code and modified it to run in an embedded environment. Thus it does not have all the features of a traditional Linux distribution. The Linux Kernel is responsible for hardware abstraction and drivers, security, file management, process management, and memory management.

Libraries: A set of native C/C++ libraries is exposed to the application framework and to the Android runtime via the libraries component. It includes the Surface Manager, responsible for graphics on the device screen; 2D and 3D graphics libraries; WebKit, the web rendering engine that powers the default browser; and SQLite, the basic data store technology for the Android platform.

Android Runtime: Each application runs in its own instance of the Android runtime, and the core of each instance is a Dalvik virtual machine (DVM). The DVM is a mobile-optimized virtual machine, specifically designed to run fast on the devices that Android targets. Present in this layer and in each application runtime are also the Android core libraries, such as the Android class libraries (I/O).

Application Framework: The Application Framework provides high-level building blocks for applications in the form of various Android* packages. Most components in this layer are implemented as applications and run as background processes on the device.

Applications: This includes applications that developers write as well as applications from Google and other Android developers.

---

* API packages such as android.bluetooth, which provides classes that manage Bluetooth functionality.

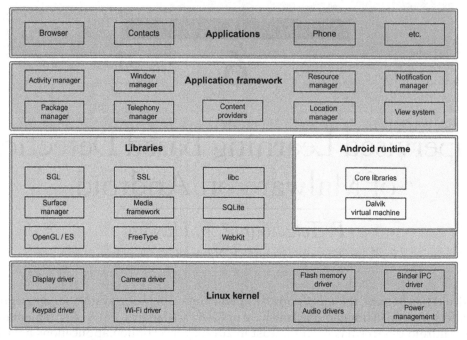

FIG. 1　Android architecture.

1 PERMISSION BACKGROUND

The model of security in Android is mainly based on permissions. A permission is a restriction limiting the access to a part of the code or data on a device. The limitation is imposed to protect critical data and code that could be misused to distort or damage the user's experience. Permissions are used to allow or restrict an application access to restricted APIs and resources. The INTERNET permission, for example, is required by applications to perform network communication, so, opening a network connection is restricted by the INTERNET permission. An application must have the READ_CONTACTS permission in order to read entries in a user's phonebook as well. The developer declares a <uses-permission> attribute to require a permission and specifies the name of the permission in the android:name field. They are both included in a file called the Android manifest or AndroidManifest.xml. This file describes the application capabilities of an application and includes the different components of the application. Fig. 2 presents two permissions: WRITE_EXTERNAL_STORAGE and INTERNET. The first one allows an application to write to external storage and the second one allows to open network sockets.

Android follows the Principle of Least Privilege (PLP) that stipulates entities having just enough privileges to do their job and no more as a prerequisite for security. For instance, if an application does not need Internet access, it should not request the Internet permission.

Table 1 describes some permissions.

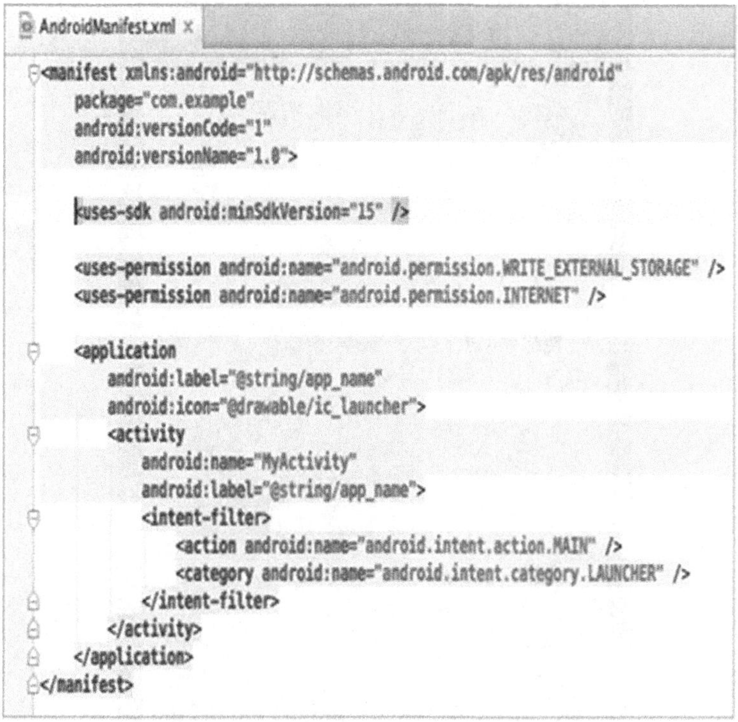

```
AndroidManifest.xml ×

<manifest xmlns:android="http://schemas.android.com/apk/res/android"
    package="com.example"
    android:versionCode="1"
    android:versionName="1.0">

    <uses-sdk android:minSdkVersion="15" />

    <uses-permission android:name="android.permission.WRITE_EXTERNAL_STORAGE" />
    <uses-permission android:name="android.permission.INTERNET" />

    <application
        android:label="@string/app_name"
        android:icon="@drawable/ic_launcher">
        <activity
            android:name="MyActivity"
            android:label="@string/app_name">
            <intent-filter>
                <action android:name="android.intent.action.MAIN" />
                <category android:name="android.intent.category.LAUNCHER" />
            </intent-filter>
        </activity>
    </application>
</manifest>
```

FIG. 2   Manifest file.

TABLE 1   Permission Examples

Permissions	Descriptions
CALL_PHONE	Allows an application to initiate a phone call without going through the dialer user interface to confirm the call being placed
MODIFY_PHONE_STATE	Allows modifications of the telephony state such as power on
WRITE_SMS	Allows an application to write SMS messages
READ_CONTACTS	Allows an application to read the user's contact data

A permission can be associated with one of the following Google Protection Levels (GPL) (Han et al., 2014):

- GPL0—Normal: A low-risk permission, which allows applications to access API calls (eg, SET_WALLPAPER) causing no harm to users.
- GPL1—Dangerous: A high-risk permission, which allows applications to access potential harmful API calls (eg, READ_CONTACTS) such as leaking private user data or control over the smartphone device. Dangerous permissions are explicitly shown to the user before an application is installed. The user must choose whether to grant a permission and to authorize whether the installation should continue.

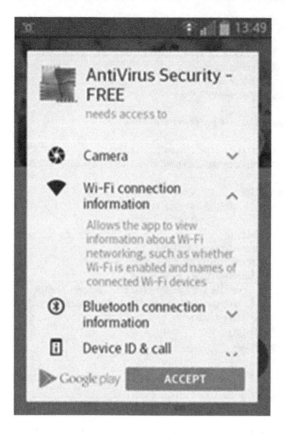

FIG. 3   Pre-installation.

- GPL2—Signature: A permission, which is granted if the requesting application is signed with the same certificate as the application, which defines the permission.
- GPL3—Signature-Or-System: Permissions of this type are used for certain special situations where multiple vendors have applications built into a system image and need to share specific features explicitly because they are being built together.

An Android application requires several permissions to work. Each application has to explicitly request permission from the user during the installation to perform certain tasks on the device, such as sending a messages. Before an application is being installed, the system prompts a list of permissions requested by the application and asks the user to confirm the installation. The user can either grant them all to install the application or refuse to install the application (as shown in Fig. 3).

1.1 Limitations of Permission Model

Android disposes several limitations and flaws, which can expose users to malicious actions, although it is the most used mobile OS. This section presents only those related to the permission system, which is the principal concern of this chapter. According to Fang et al. (2014), there are four general issues in the permission model.

1. **Coarse-granularity of permissions**: Most of Android permissions are coarse-grained. For instance, INTERNET permission (Barrera et al., 2010), READ_PHONE_STATE permission, and WRITE_SETTINGS permission give arbitrary accesses to certain resources (Jeon et al., 2015): INTERNET permission allows an application to send HTTP(S) requests to all domains and connect to arbitrary destinations and ports (Felt et al., 2010). The INTERNET permission therefore provides insufficient expressiveness to enforce control over the Internet accesses of the application (Barrera et al., 2010).

2. **Overclaim of permissions**: Overclaim of permissions is probably the most severe threat to Android security. It directly breaks the Principle of Least Privilege (PLP) (Saltzer, 1974). This violation of PLP exposes users to potential privacy leakage and financial losses. For example, if a stand-alone game application requests the SEND_SMS permission, which is unnecessary, the permission can be exploited to send premium rate messages without user's knowledge. Developers may make wrong decisions because of several reasons, concluded by Felt et al. (2010): At first, developers tend to request permissions with names that look relevant to the functionalities they design, even if the permissions are not actually required. Second, developers may request for permissions, which should be requested by deputy applications instead of their own application. Finally, developers may make mistakes due to using copy and paste, deprecated permissions, and testing artifacts. Other issues, including coarse-granularity of permissions, incompetent permission administrators, and insufficient permission documentation, are drivers of overclaim of permissions.

3. **Incompetent permission administrators**: Both developers and users lack professional knowledge in the process of permission. They have sometimes conflicting interests (Han et al., 2014). A developer may not precisely know user risks, once permissions declared in the Manifest are granted. Developers might choose to simply overclaim permissions to make sure that their applications work anyway (Barrera et al., 2010), while others might take time to learn individual permissions to request them appropriately. A survey done by Felt et al. (2012) shows that only 3% of respondents (users) answered correctly having understood permissions and 24% of the laboratory study participants demonstrated competence but imperfect comprehension.

4. **Insufficient permission documentation**: Google provides a great deal of documentation for Android application developers, but the content on how to use permissions on the Android platform is limited (Vidas et al., 2011). The insufficient and imprecise permission information confuses Android application developers, who may write applications with guesses, assumptions, and repeated trials. This leads to defective applications, which become threats with respect to security and privacy of users (Felt et al., 2011). The content of permissions is usually too technical for users to understand. Google describes the INTERNET permission as follows: "allows an application to create network sockets" (Android, 2015). This description seems to be too complex and abstruse for the user. The user might not know exactly risks related to this permission once granted.

Google made a change to the way application permissions work that has left a potential door opened to attackers in two points Google Play Help:

Permission's effect hidden to the user: Google defines permission groups according to resources to access and to certain objectives. The MESSAGES group contains, for instance, permissions that allow an application to send messages on behalf of the user or to intercept messages being received by the user. The application manager displays the group of resources which will be accessed after the user's approval. The user can scroll to see details on capabilities. The problem resides in the evaluation of risks to approve, because permissions requested are hidden behind a group of resources. Let's take for instance two categories C1 and C2 including respectively (P1: GPL normal, P2: GPL dangerous) and (P3: GPL dangerous, P4: GPL dangerous). Let's consider also an application, A, declaring P1, P2, P3, and P4. While installing A, C1 and C2 are displayed to the user because they contain permissions of GPL dangerous. Since P1 is of GPL normal, by definition, it is not displayed. The combination of P1 with P2 can be malicious on related resources. Permissions in C1 associated with those in C2 could have negative actions on resources.

Coarse-grained approval: A user will not need to review or accept permission groups already accepted for an application in the case that he has automatic updates turned on. Once a user approves an app's permissions, he actually approves all of the permission groups. For example, if an app want to read your incoming SMS, then it requires the "Read SMS messages" permission. But now installing an app, you are actually giving it access to all SMS-related permissions. The application developer can then include additional permissions from "SMS-related permissions Group," in a future update, which will not trigger any warning before installation. Then malicious developers can gain access to new dangerous permissions without user's knowledge by abusing this mechanism.

2 MALWARE LANDSCAPE

A malicious application or malware refers to an application that can be used to compromise the operation of a device, steal data, bypass access controls, or otherwise cause damage on the host terminal. Normal or benign applications or good software are, in contrast, those that do not perform any dangerous action on the system. Android malware is malicious software on the Android platform.

2.1 Malware Techniques

Zhou and Jiang (2012) categorize existing ways used by Android malware to install on user phones and generalize them into three main social engineering-based techniques: repackaging, update attack, and drive-by download.

2.1.1 Repackaging

It is one of the most common techniques that malware authors use to piggyback malicious payloads into popular applications. In essence, malware authors may locate and download popular applications, disassemble them, enclose malicious payloads, and then reassemble and submit the new applications to Google Play and alternative markets. Users are vulnerable by being enticed to download and install these infected applications.

2.1.2 Update Attack

Malware developers insert a special upgrade component into a legitimate application allowing it to be updated to a new malicious version, which is unlike the first technique that typically piggybacks the entire malicious payloads into applications.

2.1.3 Drive-by Downloads

The ability to install and download applications outside the official marketplaces allows malware developers to mislead users into downloading and installing malicious applications. It is a class of techniques where a web page automatically starts downloading an application when a user visits it. Drive-by downloads can be combined with social engineering tactics to appear as if they are legitimate. Because the browser does not automatically install downloaded applications on Android, a malicious Website needs to encourage users to open the downloaded file for actually infecting the device with malware.

2.1.4 Remote Control

Malware authors aim to access the device during the infection phase remotely. Zhou and Jiang noted that 1.172 samples (93.0%) turn the infected phones into bots for remote control during their analysis.

2.2 Tools for Malware Detection

There exist several tools to prohibit malware to infiltrate targeted devices. To help users in the task, free and paid tools are available to them. Three tools are commonly used for this purpose in discovery, assimilation, and destruction stages: firewalls, intrusion detection systems (IDS), and antivirus software. Their common mission is to track down and to eliminate potential malicious applications.

2.2.1 Firewall

A firewall is a barrier that protects information from a device or network when establishing communication with other networks such as the Internet. Its purpose is to protect the purity of the devices on which they are installed by blocking intrusions orchestrated from the Internet. Several benefits are associated with their use. First, they are well-known solutions. Then, they are also extensively used on other platforms (PC and server). Finally, they are very effective because they take advantage of the maturity gained by firewalls on PCs. A disadvantage is, that they are ineffective against attacks on the browser, Bluetooth, e-mail, SMS, and MMS; they are used as modules in antiviruses on Android.

2.2.2 Intrusion Detection Systems

An IDS represents a set of software and hardware components whose main function is to detect abnormal or suspicious activities on the analyzed target, a network or a host. This is a family of tools of many types: IDS, host intrusion detection system (H-IDS), network intrusion detection system (NIDS), IDS hybrid, intrusion prevention system (IPS), and kernel IDS/IPS kernel (K-IDS/IPS-K). IDS has two major advantages. First, it is able to detect new attacks, even those that seem isolated. Second, it can be easily adapted to any task. Unfortunately it generates a high consumption of resources and a high false alarm rate. Andromaly (Burguera et al., 2011) and Crowdroid (Burguera et al., 2011) are examples of an IDS dedicated to detecting malware on the Android platform. Crowdroid is specifically designed to recognize Trojans.

2.2.3 *Antiviruses*

Antiviruses are security software relying on application traits to recognize malicious behavior. Avast, AVG, and F-Secure are examples of renowned antiviruses. They are facing new constraints brought by the growing sophisticated techniques of malicious applications. Their efficiency is closely related to their detection methods, which are classified in three families by Filiol (Filiol, 2005).

1. Form analysis is detecting the presence of a threat in an application by static characters. It can be based on research of signatures, heuristics, or spectral analysis.
   (a) Research of signatures: Searches for patterns or bits, which are characteristics of a known threat. Its main disadvantage is that it is not able to detect unknown threats and known threats that are modified. It requires a permanent update of the signature database. It is simple to implement and is most often used by antivirus companies (Zhou and Jiang, 2012).
   (b) Spectral analysis: Scrutinizes statements commonly used by malware samples but rare in normal applications. It analyzes the frequency of such statements statistically to detect unknown threats. This approach is subject to false positive, ie, normal applications, which are incorrectly classified as malware.
   (c) Heuristic analysis: Its approach is to establish and maintain rules, which are used as a pattern to recognize malicious applications. It is also subject to false alerts, as the previous approach.
2. Integrity checking is based on the evidence that abnormal modifications of a file can reveal contamination by dangerous code. Dynamic behavior analysis is used to scrutinize the actions of an application when it is running.
3. The third method detects suspicious actions such as attempting to modify data of another application or to modify libraries and memory space reserved for the system.

The system built in this chapter uses the form analysis method.

3 MACHINE LEARNING

The rapid growth of the Android platform involves a pressing need to develop effective solutions. However, our defense capability is largely constrained by the limited understanding of the emerging malware and the lack of timely access to related samples. Moreover, Zhou and Jiang (2012) showed that malware is rapidly evolving and existing antimalware solutions are seriously becoming ineffective. For instance, it is not uncommon for Android malware to have encrypted root exploits or obfuscated C&C servers. The adoption of various sophisticated techniques greatly raises the bar for their detection. Conventional security measures relying on the analysis of security incidents and attack development inherently fail to provide a timely protection. As a consequence, users often remain unprotected over longer periods of time. The field of machine learning has been considered an ideal match for these problems, as learning methods are able to automatically analyze data, provide timely decisions, and support early detection of threats. Much work on mobile security based on this approach has produced interesting results.

3.1 Concepts

The concept of learning can be described in many ways including acquisition of new knowledge, enhancement of existing knowledge, representation of knowledge, organization of knowledge, and discovery of facts through experiments (Michalski et al., 1983). This approach can be used to acquire knowledge from malware and good software, in our case. A learning task may be considered the estimation of a function with sets of inputs and outputs. When such learning is performed with the help of computer programs, it is referred to as machine learning. A more fundamental way to distinguish machine learning is on the basis of the input type and the way in which the knowledge is used.

This division consists of learning for classification and regression, learning for acting and planning, and learning for interpretation and understanding. This work is based on the first; it is the most widely used method of learning. In this case, classification consists of assigning a new instance into one of the fixed classes from a finite set of classes. The learning scheme is presented with a set of classified examples from which it is expected to learn a way of classifying unknown instances. Regression involves the prediction of the new value on the basis of some continuous variable or attribute.

3.1.1 Dataset

A set of data items, the dataset, is a very basic concept of machine learning. A dataset is roughly equivalent to a two-dimensional spreadsheet or database table. A dataset is a collection of examples, with each instance consisting of a number of attributes.

- Training dataset: This is the sample of items or records (training items) used to determine rules to acquire knowledge for its items after the learning process.
- Testing dataset: This is a set of items or records (testing items) disjointed from the learning dataset. It is used to evaluate the capacity of the knowledge to classify unknown instances.

3.1.2 Attributes and Classes

Each instance that provides the input to machine learning is characterized by its values on a fixed, predefined set of features or attributes. The instances are the rows of the table and the attributes are the columns. They are generally in numeric (both discrete and real-value) or nominal form. Numeric attributes may have continuous numeric values, whereas nominal values may have values from a pre-defined set. The input data for a classification task are formally a collection of records. Each record, also known as an instance or example, is characterized by a tuple (x, y), where x is the attribute set and y is a special attribute, designated as the class label (also known as category, target attribute, or output). Table 2 shows a sample dataset used for classifying vertebrates into one of the following categories: mammal, bird, fish, reptile, or amphibian. The attribute set includes properties of a vertebrate such as its body temperature, skin cover, method of reproduction, ability to fly, and ability to live in water.

TABLE 2   Data for Classifying Vertebrates Into One of the Categories

Name	Body Temperature	Skin Cover	Gives Birth	Aquatic Creature	Aerial Creature	Has Legs	Hibernates	Class Label
Human	Cold-blooded	None	No	Semi	No	Yes	Yes	Amphibian
Python	Cold-blooded	Scales	No	No	No	No	Yes	Reptile
Whale	Warm-blooded	Hair	Yes	Yes	No	No	No	Mammal
Salmon	Cold-blooded	Scales	No	Yes	No	No	No	Fish

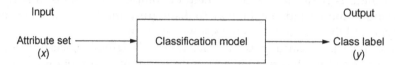

FIG. 4   Classification as the task of mapping.

The class label, on the other hand, must be a discrete attribute. This is a key characteristic that distinguishes classification from regression, a predictive modeling task in which y is a continuous attribute.

3.1.3 The Classification Model

Classification is the task of learning a target function f that maps each attribute set x to one of the predefined class labels y (Fig. 4). The target function is also informally known as a classification model.

The way in which knowledge is obtained is another important issue for machine learning. The learning element may be trained in different ways (Dietterich and Langley, 2003). For classification and regression, knowledge may be learned in a supervised, unsupervised, or semisupervised manner. Concerning supervised learning, the learner is provided with training examples with associated classes or values for the attribute to be predicted. Decision-tree and rule induction methods, neural network methods, the nearest neighbor approaches, and probabilistic methods are types of supervised learning. These methods differ in the way they represent the obtained knowledge and also in the algorithms that are used for learning. Unsupervised learning is concerned with the provision of training examples without any class association or any value for an attribute used for prediction. A third approach, which is essentially between the two described above, is that of semisupervised learning. In this type of learning, the set of training samples is mixed; that is, for some instances the associated classes are present, whereas they are absent for others. The goal in this case is to model a classifier or regression coefficient that accurately predicts and improves its behavior by using the unlabeled instances.

Fig. 5 illustrates the general lifecycle of the machine learning. It includes the learning phase to acquire the knowledge and the testing phase to test the capacity of the learning knowledge to predict the class of unknown samples. After the characterization of application samples into feature vectors, several learning algorithms such as Bayes, KNN, IBk, DT can be applied to generate a form of knowledge that can be used to identify the class of

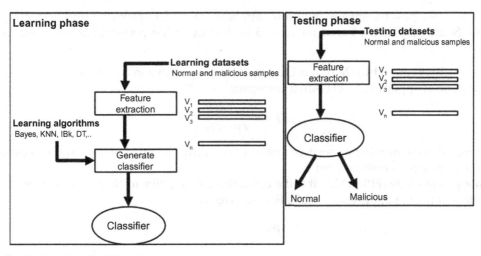

FIG. 5 Machine learning Lifecycle.

applications. Two major kinds of knowledge representation are used in learning: the decision tree and the classification rule. A classification rule is represented under the following form (Grzymala-Busse, 2010):

if (attribute1, value1) and (attribute2, value2) and ... and (attributen, valuen) then (decision, value).
or (attribute1, value1) δ (attribute2, value2) δ..δ(attributen, valuen)→ (decision, value).

Example. if (INTERNET='yes') and (WRITE_SMS='no') then application='normal'

The knowledge obtained during the learning phase can be applied to the test dataset to predict the class labels of unknown applications. It is often useful measuring the performance of the knowledge on the test dataset because such a measure provides an unbiased estimate of its generalization error.

3.1.4 Performance of Classification Models

The evaluation of the performance of a classification model is based on the counts of testing records correctly and incorrectly predicted by the model. These counts are represented in a table known as a confusion matrix (Witten et al., 2011). Table 3 depicts the confusion matrix for a binary classification problem.

TABLE 3 Confusion Matrix

Actual Class	Predicted Class	
	Yes	No
Yes	True positive	False negative
No	False positive	True negative

In our case, positive means malicious applications and negative means normal applications. Some metrics are based on Table 3 to determine the performance of classification models:

- True positive rate (TPR) (M1). It is the proportion of positive instances (ie, feature vectors of malicious applications) classified correctly:

$$TPR = \frac{TP}{TP + FN} \tag{1}$$

where TP is the number of positive instances correctly classified and FN is the number of positive instances misclassified.

- False positive rate (FPR) (M2). It is the proportion of negative instances (ie, feature vectors of benign applications) classified incorrectly:

$$FPR = \frac{FP}{FP + TN} \tag{2}$$

where FP is the number of negative instances incorrectly classified and TN is the number of negative instances correctly classified.

- Precision (M3). It is the number of true positives divided by the total number of elements labeled as belonging to the positive class.

$$Precision = \frac{TP}{TP + FP} \tag{3}$$

- The accuracy (M4) provides general information about how many samples are misclassified:

$$Accuracy = \frac{TP + TN}{TP + TN + FP + FN} \tag{4}$$

- Area under curve (AUC) (M5): This metric is the summary reflecting the classification ability. It represents the probability that a randomly chosen malicious sample will be correctly classified. The following guidelines are used to assess the classification quality (CQ) by the AUC value (Hanley and McNeil, 1982; Hosmer et al., 2013):

$$CQ = \begin{cases} Acceptable & if\ AUC \in [0.7, 0.8[\\ Excellent & if\ AUC \in [0.8, 0.9[\\ Outstanding & if\ AUC \geq 0.9 \end{cases} \tag{5}$$

3.1.5 Performance Evaluation of a Classifier

Cross validation is a method commonly used to evaluate the performance of a classifier on unknown samples (Tan et al., 2005). In this method, each record is used the same number of times for training and exactly once for testing in this approach. We partition the data into two equal-sized subsets as an example. We first choose one of the subsets for training and the other for testing. We then swap the roles of the subsets so that the previous training set becomes the testing set and vice versa. This approach is called a twofold cross validation. The total error is obtained by summing up the errors for both runs. Each record is used exactly once for training and once for testing in this example. The k-fold cross validation method generalizes this approach by segmenting the data into k equal-sized partitions. One of the partitions is chosen for testing, while the rest of them are used for training during each run. This procedure is repeated k times so that each partition is used for testing exactly once. Again, the total error is found by summing up the errors for all k runs. A special case of the k-fold cross validation method sets $k = N$, the size of the dataset.

3.2 Related Works: Machine Learning and Permissions

We investigate and discuss related works that focuses on requested permissions and those using classification learning for the detection of malware. The strategy starts by describing works that analyze the permissions requested to make decisions on behalf of the user. We then present works that use permissions individually and associatively to characterize applications. The last point proposes enhancements on these mechanisms.

3.2.1 Permission Analysis

This section presents works that analyze the requested permissions to make decisions on behalf of the user. Holavanalli et al. (2013) propose flow permissions, an extension to the permission mechanism. It is used to examine and grant explicit information flows within an application as well as implicit information flows across multiple applications. VetDroid (Zhang et al., 2013) is a dynamic analysis platform for reconstructing sensitive behavior in applications from the permission point of view. Felt et al. (2010) evaluate whether permissions of an application are effective in protecting users. Their results indicate a positive impact of permissions on the security. They also stipulate that this mechanism should be improved. This study reveals that users are frequently granting dangerous permissions during installation. Installation security warnings at installation therefore may not be an effective prevention tool for alerting users. Felt et al. (2012) provides guidelines to determine the most appropriate granting mechanism. Rosen et al. (2013) provide an approach to inform the user about the nature of applications by mapping API calls and privacy behaviors. Barrera et al. (2010) perform an empirical analysis on the expressiveness of some permission sets and propose some potential improvements. Their work is based on the verification of signature, the assignment of the UID, and their interrelation. Grace et al. (2012) describe mechanisms by which granted permissions to one application can be leaked to another. They built Woodpecker to examine capability leaks among pre-loaded apps in the phone firmware. Dini et al. (2012a) propose a multicriteria evaluation of applications to improve the understanding the trustworthiness degree of an application, from security and functional aspects. They assign a permission threat score according to the operations controlled by this permission. They compute then a global threat score for each application, which is a function of the threat score of all the required permissions, combined to information regarding the developer, the rating, and the number of downloads of the application.

3.2.2 Individual Permissions

Zhou and Jiang (2012) characterize existing malware from various aspects, including the permissions requested. They identified the permissions that are widely requested in both malicious and benign applications. Malicious applications clearly tend to request more frequently on the SMS-related permissions, such as READ_SMS, WRITE_SMS, RECEIVE_ SMS, and SEND_SMS. The result is the same with RECEIVE_BOOT_COMPLETED and CHANGE _ WIFI_STATE. Barrera et al. (2010) found no strong correlation between application categories and requested permissions and introduce a self-organizing method to visualize permission usage in different categories. Sanz et al. (2012) propose a method for categorizing Android applications through machine learning techniques. Their method extracts different feature sets including permissions. This classifies applications into several categories such as entertainment, society, tools, productivity, multimedia and video, communication, and puzzle and brain games. Orthacker et al. (2012) develop a method to circumvent the permission system by spreading permissions over two or more applications. Sato et al. (2013) is a method that analyzes the manifest by extracting four types of keyword lists: the permission, the intent filter, the process name, and the number of custom permissions. This approach determines the malignancy score by classifying individually permissions as malicious or benign.

3.2.3 Combinations of Permissions

DroidRanger (Zhou et al., 2012) is a system that characterizes and detects malware samples relying on two schemes: the first one provides footprinting based on the combination of permissions requested by known malware families; the second one is a heuristics-based filtering scheme. PermissionWatcher (Struse et al., 2012) is tool that analyzes permissions of other applications installed on the phone. They determined rules including association of permissions to classify application as suspicious. PermissionWatcher increases user awareness of potentially harmful applications through a home screen widget. Sarma et al. (2012) investigate the feasibility of using the permissions by an application, its category (such as games, education, social) and requested permissions in the same category to inform users about the risks. Rassameeroj and Tanahashi (2011) applies network virtualization and clustering algorithms to permissions. They determine irregular permission combinations requested by abnormal applications. Gomez and Neamtiu (2015) classify malicious applications into four classes of malware: DroidDream, DroidDreamLight, Zsone SMS, and Geinimi. This categorization is based on resources accessed by these four families, the infiltration technique and the payload used. Wei et al. (2012) present the nature, sources, and implications of sensitive data in an enterprise environment. They characterize malicious applications and the risks engendered. They finally propose several approaches for dealing with security risks for enterprises. Tang et al. (2011) introduce an extension of the security enforcement with a security distance model to mitigate malware. A security distance pair is the quantitative representation of the security threat that this pair of permissions may cause. A permission pair's security distance consists of a threat point, which represents the danger level and related characteristics. Canfora et al. (2013) propose a method for detecting malware based on three metrics: the occurrences of a specific subset of system calls, a weighted sum of a subset of permissions, and a set of combinations of permissions. Kirin (Enck et al., 2009) is a system to detect malware at install time based on an undesirable combination of permissions. Su and Chang (2014) determine whether an application is malware depending on a set of permissions. They compute a score depending on the number of occurrences of each permission like in other works (Huang et al., 2013; Sanz et al., 2013a,b; Liu and Liu, 2014). Liu and Liu (2014) considers the occurrence of two permissions to reflect malicious activities. Ping et al. (2014) propose a malware detection method based on the contrasting permission patterns. They specify three subsets used for the classification: the unique permission patterns in the malware dataset, the unique permission patterns in the normal dataset, and the commonly required permission patterns.

3.2.4 Machine Learning Techniques

Machine learning has been applied in some works for malware detection. Sanz et al. (2013b) introduced a method to detect malicious applications through machine learning techniques by analyzing the extracted permissions from the application itself. Classification features include the permissions required by the application (specified by the uses-permission tag) and the elements under the uses-features group. They employed supervised learning methods to classify Android applications into malware and benign software. MAMA is a method that extracts several features from the manifest to be trained with the ML classifiers to detect malware. These features are the requested permissions, and the uses-feature tag. They used four algorithms: K-nearest neighbors, decision trees, bayesian networks, and SVM for the classification. Huang et al. (2013) explore the performance for detecting malicious applications using the classification learning with four ML algorithms: adaBoost, naïve bayes, decision tree (C4.5), and Support Vector Machine. They extracted 20 features including required and requested permissions. The values of selected features are stored as a feature vector, which is represented as a sequence of comma-separated values. Aung and Zaw (2013) propose a framework to detect malware applications and to enhance security. This system monitors various permission-based features and events obtained from the applications; it analyses these features by using ML classifiers. The features are some requested permissions, such as INTERNET, CHANGE_CONFIGURATION, WRITE_SMS, SEND_SMS, CALL_PHONE and others not described in the paper. Shabtai et al. (2010) suppose that a successful differentiation between games and tools could provide a positive indication to differentiate malware. They extracted APK features, XML features, and DEX features to be trained with Machine Learning algorithms. Arp et al. (2014) combine required permissions and requested combined to six other features. Support Vector Machine algorithms are then applied to determine profiles for malicious and benign applications. Liu and Liu (2014) extract requested permissions, pairs of requested permissions and pairs of required permissions. The machine learning techniques and permissions are used to classify an application as benign or malicious. MADAM (Dini et al., 2012b) is a system to monitor the system at the Kernel level and at the user level. It combines permission features with kernel features such as system calls, and then train the samples. Crowdroid (Burguera et al., 2011) is a framework, which collects the traces of behaviour of applications from users based on crowdsourcing. Authors applied then the partitional clustering algorithm on these traces in order to differentiate between benign applications and malicious trojan applications. Andromaly (Shabtai et al., 2012) is a type of IDS that relies on the processor, the memory and the battery states to detect suspicious activities. Su and Chang (2014) detect whether an application is malware according to the permission combinations of the application. They used two different weighted methods to adjust the weights of the permissions. These methods are essentially based on permission occurrences in both samples and the frequency gap between samples. Protsenko and Müller (2014) use randomly metrics related to software code combined to features specific application structure, to detect malware with ML algorithms. Rovelli and Vigfusson (2014) design the system PMDS (Permission-based Malware Detection System). It is a cloud-based architecture based on the requested permissions with the main feature of detecting abnormal behavior. They build a

Machine Learning classifier on those features to automatically identify malicious combination of permissions. Wang et al. (2014) analyze only risks associated to individual permissions. They employ three feature ranking methods, namely, mutual information, correlation coefficient, and T-test to rank Android individual permissions with respect to their risk. They additionally use sequential forward selection as well as principal component analysis to identify risky permission subsets. Finally, they evaluate the usefulness of risky permissions for malware detection with support vector machine, decision trees, as well as random forest.

3.2.5 Limitations

The authors restrict their study to the most requested permissions or a set of permissions. The other permissions are ignored, although they could hide important information for the detection. The research works require ML techniques for the classification between benign and malicious applications. ML require a representative basis of data for training to provide a powerful tool for automatically inferring models. The quality of the detection model of such systems critically depends on the availability of representative malicious and benign applications (Arp et al., 2014). While the collection of benign applications is straightforward, gathering recent malware samples requires some technical effort. The number of features to extract from the Manifest (such as in Canfora et al. (2013) and Huang et al. (2013)) increases the computing overhead and the inefficiency of the solution. The choice of the feature to associate is relevant because its modification can give false results. Zhu et al. give acceptable results if the description is really filled by the developer; otherwise, the output could be false. This is also the case for the technique proposed by Gomez and Neamtiu (2015). It is inadequate to detect unknown malware because applications are classified using characteristics of known families of malware. Most of these works extract a feature set to represent the applications. There is no evidence to show which features give the best detection result, even if studies considers permissions as feature. The problem of usability of solutions remains urgent for the security. Many security solutions such as Flowdroid (Fritz et al., 2014; Chin et al., 2011) are harder to install even for expert users. The deployment is often not applicable in real devices, requiring installing components by command line. This fact discourages users and entices them to install risky solutions (Tchakounté and Dayang, 2013). Most of the approaches using ML classifiers are just theoretical: there is no inline system built to validate the results found. This shows eventually the difficulty of practicability of such mechanisms. Some works build the classifier inside a remote server, which receives some information necessary for the classification from the smartphone (Rovelli and Vigfusson, 2014). The server replies with the classification results to the client. Different users have different types of privacy and security concerns (Zhou and Jiang, 2012); one may need to protect their SMS while another may need to protect their contacts. Researches on permissions try to identify implicit concerns related to the user while categorizing permissions either in privacy threat, system threat, money threat (Dini et al., 2012a) or in privacy threat, monetary threat, and damage threat (Sarma et al., 2012). These views are too coarse and not resources oriented, and the user is not involved in the definition of the resources important in the smartphone.

3.2.6 Enhancements

Some efforts should be made to improve the effectiveness of permission-based solutions. For the sake of completeness, researchers should consider not only the 130 official permissions in Android, but also additional ones published in the GitHub (Android source, 2015) and third parties. The reason is to consider that a permission becomes risky when combining with others. The research should study all these permissions rather than focus on some. For sake of flexibility and performance, a detection mechanism should learn from samples historically close to the testing dataset. Older training datasets indeed cannot account for all malware lineages, and newer datasets do not contain enough representatives of most malware from the past (Allix et al., 2014). Building a reliable training dataset is essential to obtain the best performance. Authors should avoid using independent several features to construct the vector that represents an application. This could increase significant overhead, and there should be a relationship between them. None of the previous works that determine occurrences of permissions examine duplicated permissions in the Manifest. The extraction of permissions from applications should consider this possibility for the sake of precision. The percentage of permission occurrence in malware and benign software is one of the features often used by works aiming to characterize a malware sample. If a permission is required 10 times in normal applications more than in malware, this permission is not important to discriminate. The best approach should be to find a correlation between the permission frequency in malware and good software in such a way that even one presence is significant. We recommend implementing a lightweight system related to experiments. This could help to perform the testing phase. A survey on the usage could be performed to evaluate the usability in order to improve the design. There is no research work related to the permission analysis, which involve the user to give its view on what resources to be protected. This information represents the concern of the user on the security of the smartphone. A module could evaluate the risk according to this input and warn the user accordingly.

4 CHARACTERIZATION AND DETECTION WITH THE CONSIDERATION OF USER SECURITY SPECIFICATIONS

We propose a system to detect Android malware based on 222 permissions and structured in four layers, while considering limitations of related works elucidated in Section 3.2. The first layer is supported by a new model, based on the frequency of permissions and the proportion of requests by malicious applications within the whole sample. The second layer uses a model that relies on security risks related to granting permissions. The third layer uses a model that characterizes an application based on an association of vectors derived from the two first layers. The last layer involves the user to specify resources to be secured. Risk signals are generated to inform the user, depending on its specifications and the requested permissions.

We characterize applications in the first three layers using some models to translate them into vectors. For that, we collected a huge amount of normal and malicious samples.

4.1 Sampling

4.1.1 Applications for Learning Detection

We collected a dataset of 1993 normal applications from 2012 to 2015 in Google Play (2015) and VirusTotal (2015). In Google Play, we selected free ones from categories based on their descriptions, the number of downloads and the ratings given by users: only the top ones are picked. Each application taken from Google Play has been scanned by 57 engines from renowned antiviruses on VirusTotal, and only the ones that succeed all virus tests are considered "benign" and kept inside the dataset of normal applications.

The malware sample includes the dataset released by Drebin authors (Arp et al., 2014) to help the scientific community that often lacks this kind of data to carry out research. It is composed of 5560 malicious applications collected from 2010 to 2012, and includes 1260 malware samples grouped into 49 families (between August 2010 and October 2011) and released by Zhou and Jiang (2012). We additionally gather 1223 malicious applications from Contagio (2015) and VirusTotal from 2012 to 2014.

4.1.2 Applications for System Validation

Some applications constitute the dataset for evaluating and validating our security system. Normal applications have been collected from Google Play between 2013 and 2014, and the malicious ones from Contagio during the same period. According to Allix et al. (2014) learning and testing datasets must be historically coherent for good performance of the malware detection scheme; this justifies the period for the collection of the datasets.

4.1.3 Reengineering

Applications are dissembled to gather requested permissions from the manifest in a feature set. For this, it has used reengineering to investigate files included in the package of an application independently of its execution such as Android-apktool and JD-GUI. Some scripts have been developed to automate the tasks of extraction of information from applications. These scripts allow constituting the set of permissions to be scrutinize.

4.2 Layer 1

We will introduce some definitions required to define the model in this layer.

4.2.1 Definitions

Definition 1. We denote by $A^L = \left\{a_1^L, a_2^L, ..., a_{|A|}^L\right\}$, the training dataset of malicious applications and $B^L = \left\{b_1^L, b_2^L, ..., b_{|A|}^L\right\}$, the training dataset of normal applications with $|A^L|$ and $|B^L|$ the sizes of A^L and B^L.

Definition 2. We denote by $Perm = \left\{p_1, p_2, ..., p_{|Perm|}\right\}$ the set of permissions used in the model with $|Perm|$ the size of $Perm$, which constitutes permissions declared in Android GitHub (Saltzer, 1974). There are 206 permissions with complete descriptions provided. We consider 16 permissions not listed in previous sources, but only found in third party applications. Therefore $|Perm| = 222$. We denote $P(a)$ the set of all different permissions found in application a. P(a) does not contain repeated elements.

Definition 3. The function $presence(p, a)$ of the permission p in the application a is given by:

$$\forall p \in Perm, presence(p,a) = \begin{cases} 1 & if \ p \in P(a) \\ 0 & otherwise \end{cases} \quad (6)$$

Definition 4. The function $occurrence(p, E)$ of the permission p in the set of applications E is defined by:

$$occurrence(p, E) = \sum_{\forall p \in Perm, \forall a \in E} presence(p, a) \tag{7}$$

Definition 5. The function, gap_i between the occurrences of permission i in A^L and B^L is given by:

$$diff(i) = occurrence(i, A^L) \leq occurrence(i, B^L) \tag{8}$$

$$\forall i \in \{1, \ldots, | Perm |\}, gap_i = \begin{cases} 0 & if\ diff(i) \leq 0 \\ diff(i) & otherwise \end{cases} \tag{9}$$

Definition 6. The function $proportion(i)$ of requests of permission i by malicious applications is defined by:

$$proportion(i) = \frac{occurrence(i, A^L)}{occurrence(i, A^L) + occurrence(i, B^L)} \tag{10}$$

Readjustment of the normal sample. We adopted a probabilistic approach to estimate probable occurrences of permissions in a sample with 6783 normal applications, since the size of the malicious sample around five times the size of the normal applications. This solution is motivated by two reasons: the 1993 normal applications are diverse (of different categories), the most downloaded and the most recommended by Google. These selection criteria guarantee that the way permissions are requested in the same proportion follows the same tendency of permission requests by other normal applications in Google Play (Vennon and Stroop, 2010).

$$\forall i \in \{1, \ldots, | Perm |\}, p_i = \frac{occurrence(i, B^L)}{|B^L|} \tag{11}$$

p_i represents the probability of the request of the permission i. Probable occurrences of permissions in a sample of 6783 malicious applications will be estimated as follows:

$$\forall i \in \{1, \ldots, | Perm |\}, N_i = \lfloor |A^L| \times p_i \rfloor \tag{12}$$

N_i is the number of occurrences predicted for the permission p_i in Eq. (12).

4.2.2 Determination of Discriminating Metrics

This section describes the model which takes the requested permissions for applications and calculates their DM. The DM model is a novel approach to evaluate the popularity of a permission, and its definition includes two objectives: the first one concerns a measure that indicates the capacity for the permission to characterize malicious applications compared to normal ones. The second one is to evaluate the danger level, which may appear once the user grants this permission. The higher is the DM; more the permission is considered to be preferred by malicious applications and so it represents a high risk for devices. A question arises consequently: "From which value ε, is considered to be significant?" Two elements simultaneously guide to answer this question: $|A^L|$ and the DM's scale. We intuitively expect a scale of 10 (from zero to nine), that is 10 measures for permissions looking for more fine grained evaluation to be effectively used to discriminate applications. We finally determine ε as follows:

$$\varepsilon = \left\lfloor max\left(\frac{gap_i}{n-2}\right)\right\rfloor \tag{13}$$

where n is the number of levels.

We dedicate the scale nine (09) to permissions in the set *MalwarePermission*, specifically for malware pieces, since the scale goes until nine. This is the reason why we end at eight which is the size of scale minus two. We then model the DM by combining two strategies: the first one considers the occurrences of permissions in normal and malicious and the second one considers the proportion of requests of permission in malware.

First strategy: Discriminating Metric, DM1.

$$\forall i \in \{1,\ldots,| Perm |\}, DM1_i = \begin{cases} 0 & if\ gap_i \leq 0 \\ \dfrac{gap_i}{\varepsilon} & otherwise \end{cases} \tag{14}$$

Second strategy: Discriminating Metric, DM2.

$$\forall i \in \{1,\ldots,| Perm |\}, DM2_i = \begin{cases} (proportion(i)-0.5)\times 10 & if\ proportion(i) \geq 0 \\ 0 & otherwise \end{cases} \tag{15}$$

Determination of DM.

$$\forall i \in \{1,\ldots,| Perm |\}, DM_i = \begin{cases} 9 & if\ p_i \in MalwarePermission \\ max(DM1_i, DM2_i) & otherwise \end{cases} \tag{16}$$

MalwarePermission is the set of permissions that are requested only by malicious applications; that is those with no presence in normal applications.

4.2.3 Translation Into Vector Space

We associate with an application A a vector V of 10 elements. The element $V(i)$ of application A contains $n(A, i)$, the number of permissions requested by the application A with DM equals to i. Table 4 illustrates the vector representation.

4.3 Layer 2

This model aims to identify risks induced by application actions from a point of view of accessing resources through requested permissions.

TABLE 4   Vector Representation

$n(a, 0)$	$n(a, 1)$	$n(a, 2)$	$n(a, 3)$	$(a, 4)$	$n(a, 5)$	$n(a, 6)$	$n(a, 7)$	$n(a, 8)$	$n(a, 9)$	$n(a, 10)$

4.3.1 Risk and Category Definitions

We consider 10 categories of resources, which could intuitively be targeted by malware and risky permissions. The categories of resources are:

Messages: Users manipulate SMS and MMS messaging to communicate with each other. They could be sensitive for users if contents inside should be kept secret or should not be modified. Permissions in this category allow an application to send these resources on behalf of the user (SEND_SMS) to intercept (RECEIVE_SMS), and to read or modify messages (READ_SMS, WRITE_SMS). The permission is related to MMS: RECEIVE_MMS, which allows monitoring, recording, and processing on incoming MMS messages. If an application accesses SMS resources, there is no direct incidence on MMS resources. This is why RECEIVE_MMS is not combined with SMS permissions (Struse et al., 2012).
Contacts: Contacts could be launched without the user's knowledge when someone has the capacity to access (private) user contacts, calls, or even messages. It is therefore fundamental to consider these resources. Permissions considered in this group are READ_CONTACTS, WRITE_CONTACTS, and MANAGE_ACCOUNTS, which respectively allow an application to read the user's contact data, to write (but not read) them, and to manage the list of accounts in the AccountManager. We associate group accounts and contacts defined by Google separately. All combinations of the three permissions for this resource are considered.
Calls: Making calls represents one of the services mostly used on smartphones. They are associated with accessing contacts because calling requires having a phone number. Performing actions on calls without user consent could represent a privacy risk for him. Permissions investigated here are PROCESS_OUTGOING_CALLS (allowing an application to monitor, modify, or abort outgoing calls), READ_CALL_LOG (allowing an application to read the user's call log), WRITE_CALL_LOG (allowing an application to write, but not read, the user's contact data), CALL_PHONE (allowing an application to initiate a phone call without going through the dialer user interface, confirming the call being placed) and CALL_PRIVILEGED (allowing an application to call any phone number, including emergency numbers, without going through the dialer user interface, confirming the call being placed). Google defines a group called "telephony state," which is not limited to call-related permissions but also to permissions associated with accessing and modifying the telephony state. Calls can be launched without manipulating telephony state. We therefore create two groups: calls and telephony state.
Telephony state: It includes MODIFY_PHONE_STATE and READ_PHONE_STATE permissions, which respectively allow the modification of the phone state (such as power on, reboot) and allow read-only access to the phone state. All combinations are considered in this case such as MODIFY_PHONE_STATE and READ_PHONE_STATE.
Calendar: Users save events on a calendar to be reminded later. It could be harmful for the user if one can modify user events without any consent. In this case, meetings could easily be missed or canceled. Associated permissions are READ_CALENDAR and WRITE_CALENDAR, which respectively allow an application to read the user's calendar data and allow an application to write, but not read it. The only association is {READ_CALENDAR, WRITE_CALENDAR}. Location: This is a resource that is used to know the current location of the device owner. The access of this resource is often granted by default; in this case, the user can be tracked physically. ACCESS_FINE_LOCATION (that

allow an application to access the precise location from location sources such as GPS, cell towers, and Wi-Fi), ACCESS_COARSE_LOCATION (that allow an application to access an approximate location derived from a network location such as Wi-Fi), INSTALL_ LOCATION_PRO VIDER (that allows an application to install a location provider into the Location Manager), LOCATION_HARDWARE (that allows an application to use location features in hardware). This group includes sixteen combinations.

Wi-Fi: Google defines a group network used for permissions that provide access to networking services. We decide to create a group for Wi-Fi and Bluetooth network resources independently to detect effectively which network is frequently used by applications. This resource is mainly used for mobile data communication; if one can take the control of it, sensitive data can be transferred (from/to) the device without the user's knowledge. Permissions are: ACCESS_WIFI_STATE (that allows applications to access information about Wi-Fi networks), and CHANGE_WIFI_STATE (that allows applications to change the Wi-Fi connectivity state). We add moreover CHANGE_WIFI_ MULTICAST_STATE permission taken from the group AFFECTS _BATTERY defined by Google to complete the present group because it allows changing a property of the Wi-Fi resource. It allows specifically applications to enter the Wi-Fi Multicast mode connectivity state; the battery consumption is big in this case.

Bluetooth: This is a technology that lets your phone communicate without wire over short distances; it is similar to Wi-Fi in many ways. While it is not a danger to your phone, it does enable an application to send and receive data from other devices. Permissions are BLUETOOTH (that allows applications to connect to paired Bluetooth devices), and BLUETOOTH_ADMIN (that allows applications to discover and pair of Bluetooth devices). The only combination is {BLUETOOTH, BLUETOOTH_ADMIN}.

Network: This information concerns network socket states (open or closed) and the connectivity state (on or off). It is crucial for accessing a remote server via Internet sending retrieved sensitive data from a smartphone. Permissions included are: CHANGE_ NETWORK_STATE (that allows applications to change the network connectivity state), ACCESS_NETWORK_STATE (that allows applications to access information about network connectivity), and INTERNET (that allows applications to open network sockets).

Web Traces: Users usually save sensitive information (password, login, and banking codes) consciously when browsing across the Internet. Malicious applications try to gather this resource. Permissions included are WRITE_ HISTORY_BOOKMARKS (that allows an application to write, but not read, the user's sensitive data) and READ_ HISTORY_BOOKMARKS (that allow an application to read (but not write) the user's browsing history and bookmarks).

A category of permissions includes several permissions and the possible distinct combinations made from these permissions, as depicted in Appendix A. For instance, the category contacts has permissions READ_CONTACTS, WRITE_CONTACTS, MANAGE_ACCOUNTS, READ_CONTACTS & WRITE_CONTACTS, READ_ CONTACTS & MANAGE_ACCOUNTS, MANAGE_ACCOUNTS & WRITE_CONTACTS, READ_CONTACTS & WRITE_ CONTACTS & MANAGE_ACCOUNTS.

We define permission risks as follows:

$Risk_1 (R_1)$: The capability given by a permission to an application to directly read confidential information in the device. It is equal to one for the positive case and zero otherwise.

$Risk_2(R_2)$: The capability given by a permission to an application to directly modify user resources in the device. It is equal to one for the positive case and zero otherwise.

$Risk_3(R_3)$: The capability given by a permission to an application to perform some actions without knowledge of the user. It is equal to one for the positive case and zero otherwise.

$Risk_4(R_4)$: The capability given by a permission to an application to charge the user without any consent. It is equal to one for the positive case and zero otherwise.

The risk generated by a combination Cij of permissions j, in the category i is defined by:

$$\forall i \le 10, \forall j \le n_c(i), W(C_{ij}) = \sum_{k=1}^{4} R_k(C_{ij}) \tag{17}$$

$$if\ n \ge 2\ and\ C_{ij} = \{P_1 \cdots P_n\}, R_k(C_{ij}) = OR\left(R_k(P_1), R_k(P_2), \ldots, R_k(P_n)\right) \tag{18}$$

$$if\ n = 1\ and\ C_{ij} = \{P_1\} R_k(C_{ij}) = R_k(P_1) \tag{19}$$

$n_c(i)$ represents the number of combinations for the resource i and OR is the logical function $OR(x, y) = max(x, y)$.

In other words, the overall risk incurred in a category is the sum of individual risks generated by each combination of permission, in other words. Appendix A presents the whole different risks in categories of resources.

4.3.2 Translation Into Vector Space

The process to construct the vector profile is described by Algorithm 1:

ALGORITHM 1   CONSTRUCTION OF THE VECTOR

Input:
• An application a
• C_{ij}: set of combinations i belonging to resource j
Output: The Vector V associated to a
Variables: $S = / \emptyset$, the set of weight values
Begin
For resource j do
For C_{ij} of resource j do
if $presence(C_{ij}, a)$ then
$S = S \cup W(C_{ij})$
else $S = S \cup \{0\}$
end if
End For
$V(j) = Maximum(S)$
$S = / \emptyset$
End For
End

Let's consider an application with the following permissions:

- ACCESS_WIFI_STATE;
- READ_PHONE_STATE;
- RECEIVE_BOOT_COMPLETED;
- WRITE_EXTERNAL_STORAGE;
- ACCESS_NETWORK_STATE;
- INTERNET.

We obtain the following results after applying the process in Table 5:

Resource 1: Cij has no SMS/MMS permissions. $S = 0_1 \ldots 0_{16}$, $V(1) = MAX(S) = 0$
Resource 2: $S = 0_1 \ldots 0_7$, $V(2) = MAX(S) = 0$
Resource 3: $S = 0_1 \ldots 0_{32}$, $V(3) = MAX(S) = 0$
Resource 4: $S = 0_1 \ldots 0_4$, $V(4) = MAX(S) = 0$
Resource 5: $S = 0_1 \ldots 0_{15}$, $V(5) = MAX(S) = 0$
Resource 6: $C_{ij} = C_{16}$, $S = 1_1, 0_2 \ldots 0_{15}$, $V(6) = MAX(S) = 1$
Resource 7: $S = 0_1 \ldots 0_3$, $V(7) = MAX(S) = 0$
Resource 8: $C_{ij} = C_{18}, C_{28}, C_{48}$, $S = 2_1, 1_2, 0_3, 3_4, 0_5, 0_6, 0_7, 0_8, 0_9, 0_{10}$ $V(8) = MAX(S) = 3$
Resource 9: $C_{ij} = C_{29}$, $S = 0_1, 1_2, 0_3$ $V(9) = MAX(S) = 1$
Resource 10: $S = 0_1, 0_2, 0_3$ $V(10) = MAX(S) = 0$

The vector resultant is consigned in Table 5.

4.4 Layer 3

An application A is represented in this model as the association of the two vectors from the first two layers. That means that the vector is represented as in Table 6 where the first layer determines the first 10 features and the second layer the last 10. We then associate the two to obtain the vector characteristics for an application in this model.

4.5 Preliminary Learning

We perform a preliminary learning to identify algorithms that best fit for the samples. According to Fig. 5, the next step is the selection of learning algorithms, since we already have the samples and we already know the how to characterize applications. There are two reasons for that:

- The only possibility to compare algorithms is to apply several ones to samples and to retrieve best classification results.

TABLE 5 The Vector for the Example

0	0	0	0	0	1	0	3	1	0

TABLE 6 Representation of the Application Vector in Layer 3

$n(A, 0)$	$n(A, 1)$	$n(A, 2)$	$n(A, 3)$	$n(A, 4)$	$n(A, 5)$	$n(A, 6)$	$n(A, 7)$	$n(A, 8)$	$n(A, 9)$
Bluetooth	Calendar	Calls	Contact	Location	Message	Network	Telephony	Wi-Fi	Webtrace

- We would like to represent each of the learning approaches: divide and conquer (Suh, 2011), separate and conquer (Suh, 2011), Bayesian networks (Pearl, 1982), support vector machines (Vapnik, 2000), ensemble methods (Freund and Schapire, 1996), and K-nearest neighbors (Fix and Hodges, 1952).

We select seven algorithms: NaiveBayes (Kohavi, 1996), LibSVM (Vapnik, 2000), IBk (Fix and Hodges, 1952), AdaBoost M1 (Freund and Schapire, 1996), PART (Frank and Witten, 1998), J48 (Quinlan, 1993), and RandomForest (Breiman, 2001). They are available in Weka 3, a collection of machine learning algorithms for data mining tasks, to classify benign and malicious applications due to its simplicity and user-friendly interface.

Table 7 summarizes statistics concerning the preliminary evaluation of the models during the learning phase. For that, every model learns the whole dataset with seven classifiers to gather the capability of recognizing the class of a known application.

TABLE 7 Results of Classification

	Classifier	TP Rate	FP Rate	Precision	Recall	F-Measure	AUC
Layer 1	NaiveBayes	0.828	0.139	0.871	0.828	0.839	0.904
	LibSVm	0.9	0.231	0.897	0.9	0.897	0.834
	IBk	0.926	0.122	0.927	0.926	0.926	0.979
	AdaBoostM 1	0.875	0.28	0.871	0.875	0.872	0.928
	PART	0.911	0.164	0.911	0.911	0.911	0.963
	J48	0.911	0.15	0.912	0.911	0.912	0.946
	RandomForest	0.924	0.119	0.926	0.924	0.925	0.977
Layer 2	NaiveBayes	0.842	0.347	0.835	0.842	0.837	0.858
	LibSVm	0.884	0.309	0.886	0.884	0.877	0.787
	IBk	0.895	0.275	0.892	0.895	0.89	0.941
	AdaBoostM1	0.86	0.366	0.853	0.86	0.851	0.885
	PART	0.888	0.285	0.884	0.888	0.883	0.927
	J48	0.885	0.296	0.882	0.885	0.88	0.899
	RandomForest	0.894	0.275	0.891	0.894	0.889	0.94
Layer 3	NaiveBayes	0.806	0.14	0.864	0.806	0.819	0.892
	LibSVm	0.912	0.209	0.91	0.912	0.911	0.852
	IBk	0.95	0.116	0.949	0.95	0.949	0.991
	AdaBoostM1	0.879	0.272	0.875	0.879	0.876	0.932
	PART	0.935	0.153	0.934	0.935	0.934	0.979
	J48	0.926	0.168	0.925	0.926	0.925	0.957
	RandomForest	0.948	0.104	0.948	0.948	0.948	0.989

It is clearly shown that the best classifiers are IBk, RandomForest, and PART for the three layers. The first layer assimilates with a precision of around 92% and with an AUC, which tends to 98% with these classifiers. Layer 2 is less precise with around 89%; the AUC decreased to 94%. Layer 3 is more accurate with around 95% and with an AUC nearer to 1. All models are excellently able to assimilate profiles for normal and malicious applications according to these results, because they have an AUC greater than 90% (Hosmer et al., 2013). The third layer is almost perfect while assimilating application patterns. A testing and validation phase should, however, be done using cross validation; an implemented system is needed to confirm the performance in each layer. It is developed in the next chapter.

All models are complementary and can be combined to classify an application. The question now is which classification algorithm should be applied when an unknown application is assigned as normal or malicious.

4.6 Extracted Rules

The detection of malware with different characteristics is a big challenge. We are motivated to detect malware with varied characteristics with a set of detection rules extracted from the permission sets. The determination of characteristics is already effective (Sections 4.2, 4.3, and 4.4). We apply learning algorithms to extract rules based on these characteristics. RandomForest provides the best performance according to results shown in Table 7. However, this learning algorithm combines a set of independently learned decision trees and cannot construct explicit rules. It is the same for IBk. On the contrary, PART provides explicit rules that can be used for detection.

The first layer includes 71 decision rules constructed with the 222 permissions using all the learning dataset composed of the whole benign and malicious samples. Each rule has a condition as a conjunction of attribute values and a consequence as a class label. The class label is either *normal* or *malicious* in our case. Note that in a rule the conjunction of attribute values forms a sufficient condition for detecting malware, but not a necessary condition. In this layer, attributes correspond to DM values. As an example, detection Rules 1 and 5 are depicted as

---

Rule 1:
eight > 0 AND zero <= 5 AND six > 0 AND zero <= 3 AND four <= 1 AND one <= 4 AND nine <= 0 AND zero <= 2: malware

...

Rule 5:
eight <= 0 AND four <= 1 AND six <= 0 AND zero > 2 AND five <= 0 AND zero <= 4 AND one <= 2 AND three <= 0: normal

---

In the previous excerpt, Rule 1 indicates a normal application and Rule 5 describes a malicious characteristic. The Rule 1 can be interpreted as follows. An application is considered as malware if it has the corresponding profile: It requests at least one permission belonging to a DM equals to 8 and with at most five permissions with a DM equals to zero and at least one permission with DM equals to six and with at most one permission with a DM equals to four and at most four permissions with DM equals to one.

The second layer consists of 53 decision rules. Note that in a rule the conjunction of attribute values forms a sufficient condition for detecting malware, but not a necessary condition. In this layer, the attributes correspond to risk values associated to resource accessed. As an example, detection Rules 28 and 49 are depicted as

---

Rule 28:

calls > 1 AND telephony > 0 AND Wi-Fi <= 1 AND message <= 3 AND location > 0 AND webtrace <= 0 AND message <= 1: malware

...

Rule 49:

location > 0 AND telephony <= 1: normal

In the previous excerpt, Rule 49 indicates a normal application and Rule 28 profiles a malicious application. The Rule 28 can be interpreted as follows. An application with the following profile is to be considered as a malware: application requests permissions inducing a risk concerning calls greater than one, a risk concerning telephony greater than zero, a risk concerning Wi-Fi resource at most equals to one, risk concerning message resources at most equals to three, a risk concerning location resources at least equals to zero, and no risk concerning web trace resources.

The third layer consists of 128 decision rules. As an example, detection Rule 1 is depicted as:

Rule 1:

eight > 1 AND zero <= 3 AND message > 0 AND telephony > 0 AND network > 1 AND four> 0: malware

...

Rule 1 combines attributes from Layers 1 and 2. This rule can be interpreted as follows. An application is considered as a malware sample in Layer 3 if it requests at least two permissions with DM equals to three, at most three permissions with DM equals to zero, at least one permission with DM equals to four; and it requests permissions inducing risks concerning message and telephony at least equal to zero, and risk concerning network greater than one.

4.7 Classifier

An experiment has been conducted to study different possibilities to associate the models of the different layers. As presented in Fig. 6, the procedure includes two steps.

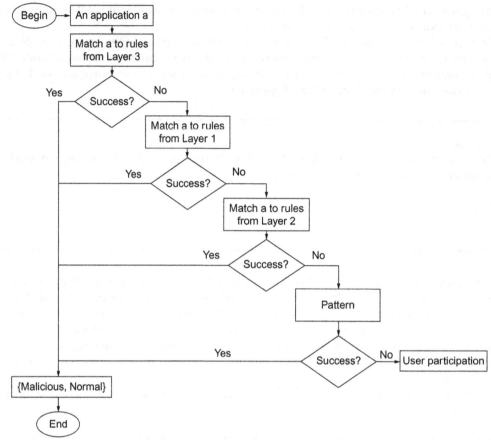

FIG. 6   Classifier.

Step 1. Selection of the association that minimizes FPR and FNR. In case the number of FP and FN remains the same, complete Step 2. The objective here is to investigate whether a misclassified application in a model can be truly classified in a different one. As we have three models, there are six associations possible to check:

- Model 1–Model 2–Model 3: Taken misclassified applications in Model 1; transfer them to Model 2 to determine if they get well classified; if not then they are transferred to Model 3 for the same purpose.
- Model 1–Model 3–Model 2: Taken misclassified applications in Model 1; transfer them to Model 3 to determine if they get well classified; if not then they are transferred to Model 2 for the same purpose.
- Model 2–Model 1–Model 3: Taken misclassified applications in Model 2; transfer them to Model 1 to determine if they get well classified; if not then they are transferred to Model 3 for the same purpose.

- Model 2–Model 3–Model 1: Taken misclassified applications in Model 2; transfer them to Model 3 to determine if they get well classified; if not then they are transferred to Model 1 for the same purpose.
- Model 3–Model 1–Model 2: Taken misclassified applications in Model 3; transfer them to Model 1 to determine if they get well classified; if not then they are transferred to Model 2 for the same purpose.
- Model 3–Model 2–Model 1: Taken misclassified applications in Model 3; transfer them to Model 2 to determine if they get well classified; if not then they are transferred to Model 1 for the same purpose.

Six possible association sets are obtained, and they provide the same outputs *GoodClassifiedPositive* and *GoodClassifiedNegative* after applying Algorithm 1. The second step is therefore performed.

ALGORITHM 2   SELECTION OF THE ASSOCIATION

<u>Input</u>: $M = model1, model2, model3$

<u>Output</u>:

- *GoodClassifiedPositive*: applications misclassified as malware at the beginning but finally classified as normal
- *GoodClassifiedNegative*: applications misclassified as normal at the beginning but finally classified as malware

<u>Variables</u>:

- $f_p' = f_n' = \varnothing$
- fp_i: Set of applications belonging to FP for the model i
- fn_i: Set of applications belonging to FN for the model i

<u>Begin</u>

<u>For</u> m in M do

  $M = M \setminus \{m\}$

  FalsePositive $= fp_m$

  FalseNegative $= fn_m$

  <u>For</u> n in M do

    $fp' = fp_n \cap FalsePositive$

    GoodClassifiedPositive $= GoodClassifiedPositive \cup \{FalsePositive \setminus fp'\}$

    FalsePositive $= fp'$

    $fn' = fn_n \cap FalseNegative$

    GoodClassifiedNegative $= GoodClassifiedNegative \cup \{FalseNegative \setminus fn'\}$

    FalseNegative $= fn'$

  <u>End For</u>

    GoodClassifiedPositive, GoodClassifiedNegative $= \varnothing$

<u>End For</u>

<u>End</u>

TABLE 8   Detection Results Obtained With the Known Dataset

	TP	FN	FP	TN	TPR (%)	FPR (%)	Precision (%)	Accuracy (%)	AUC (%)
IBk	6628	155	286	1707	97.7	14.4	95.86	94.97	99.1
PART	6589	194	378	1615	97.1	19,00	94.6	93.48	97.9
RandomForest	6580	203	251	1742	97.00	12.6	96.32	94.82	98.9

Step 2. Selection of the model with the best precision. Model 3 has the best precision (around 0.94 of AUC), as shown in Table 8; Model 1 follows with around 0.92 of AUC.

The selected association is therefore Model 3—Model 1—Model 2. The whole classifier for the classification of an unknown application, *app*, requires sequentially three phases:

- Phase 1: Apply Model 3 to *app*. Classify the application within this model. If *app* is found as malware, we believe it is malware. If app is classified as normal, we believe it is normal. In these cases, the classifier sends the results to the displaying module. If app has a profile that is not found within the rules defined in the model, then the classifier checks it in Model 1.
- Phase 2: Apply Model 1 to *app*. Classify the application within this model. If *app* is found as malware, we believe it is malware. If app is classified as normal, we believe it is normal. In these cases, the classifier sends the results to the displaying module. If app has a profile that is not found within rules defined in the model, then the classifier checks it in Model 2.
- Phase 3: Apply *Model 2* to *app*. Classify the application within this model. If *app* is found as malware, we believe it is malware. If *app* is classified as normal in the first two steps, we believe it is normal. In these cases, then the classifier sends the results to the displaying module. If *app* has a profile that is not found within the rules defined in the model, the classifier checks if *app* matches the rule *if the Manifest file declared only one system permission and if it is READ_LOGS, INSTALL_PACKAGES, or READ_USER_DICTIONARY, then the application is malicious.* The classifier will transfer it to the user participation module defined in the next section if *app* does not match with any permission pattern until this step.

4.8 User Participation

This module receives applications, which do not succeed in the classification process (Fig. 7). The only possibility is to require user to express their security points of view and define which resources have to be considered as sensitive and then to be protected. The module retrieves the permission requested by the application according to this information and computes the features of Model 2. Depending on the result, the modules define the types of alerts to display to the user and sends them to the displaying module.

The type of alerts depends on the resources selected by the user and the answer to the question determined with the help of Model 2: Does the application fit the user's security requirements?

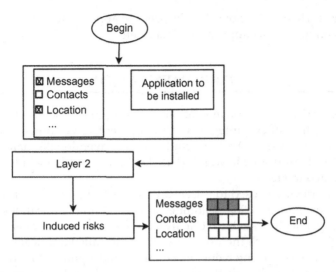

FIG. 7 User participation.

The following resources are displayed to the user with descriptions:

- SMS/MMS: User messages.
- Contact: User contacts.
- Agenda: User events and meetings.
- Call: Information related to user calls: caller contact, callee contact, etc.
- Location: The user's geographic position at any time.
- Telephony state: It includes resources used to track the user with his current location, his unique device ID, and his phone number. They are accessed to modify the phone state in order to shut down the device or to intercept outgoing calls.
- Network: It includes resources accessed to use the Internet. They are also requested by an application to take user information to the Internet or to transfer sensitive information from the Internet to the user device. Therefore, user information can be leaked without his/her knowledge.
- Bluetooth: It includes resources manipulated in a user's open Bluetooth network to take information to a nearby mobile device or to transfer sensitive information from a nearer mobile device to the device. Therefore, user information can be leaked without his/her knowledge.
- Wi-Fi: It includes resources, which open the communication to the Internet or to a remote device via Wi-Fi. Therefore, user information can be leaked without his/her knowledge.
- Information for browsing: It is information saved by the user like passwords, logins, banking codes, online payment codes, etc. when browsing in the Internet.

By default, all the resources are selected. Additionally, clear descriptions of possible activities with requested permissions are presented; after that the user selects the resources to protect. For that, it is scaled results within the interval (Canalys, 2013; Ehringer, 2010) to emphasize security risks linked to the intention of the application compared to the requirement specified by the user. There are actions that the user can apply on the application: To uninstall, remove the application, display application details, etc.

5 IMPLEMENTATION

We have proceeded to the implementation after designing the whole system. We used the Android Studio, the official Integrated Development Environment (IDE) for Android developers, to build the system Android studio. It is conventionally named "Look at your Resources and Detect Android Malware" (LaReDAMoid) and it includes five interrelated modules, as presented in Fig. 8.

The module of retrieving is used to extract and list user applications. The module of analysis is responsible for characterizing, scanning, and classifying applications coming from the module of retrieving. It includes selective analysis, in which the user scans some applications, and complete analysis, in which the user scans all the installed applications. The module of automatic analysis listens and intercepts installations and updates to renew the characterizations of applications; then it calls the module of analysis and notifies the user about the results. The module of preferences is used to define settings such as specifying resources to protect and activate automatic analysis. The module of interpretation and presentation of results is responsible to interpret results from the modules of analysis and preferences and to present them in comprehensible manner to the user.

LaReDAMoid deals with update vulnerability. It reclassifies the application while considering new permissions included in the modified version to inform the user.

5.1 Interfaces

This section presents some interfaces LaReDAMoid. Fig. 9 represents a screenshot, which depicts a list of user applications. This interface appears after clicking on the *List Apps* button on the home screen in Fig. 10.

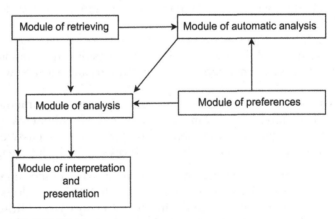

FIG. 8   Architecture of LaReDAMoid.

FIG. 9   List of user applications.

Fig. 11 represents an interface to perform the complete analysis. This interface is obtained after clicking on the button *Scan Apps* from the home screen. The item *Analyse all* is then selected to launch the complete analysis. The button *Scan All Now* is used to launch the complete scanning; the user can rather select the item *Select Apps* used to select specific applications for scanning as shown in Fig. 12.

Fig. 13A depicts views for the analysis results. The first one displays applications with their status and corresponding icons to highlight statuses. The user clicks on the application icon to obtain Fig. 13A, to go deeper into the results. This figure shows actions that the user can take according to results and settings made on resources. A risk value under scale of 4 is displayed to indicate to the user whether his security requirements have been considered for each selected resource. The user can then decide to run the application or to remove it.

The user is invited to specify how he will be informed of the results of the automatic analysis: with a notification or with an alert dialog. Additionally, the user selects resources to protect in order to evaluate security risks. These two previous functionalities are shown in Fig. 14A. He is then notified after a new installation or a new update, as shown in Fig. 14B.

FIG. 10   Home screen.

6 EVALUATION AND DISCUSSION

This section aims to evaluate LaReDAMoid in several objectives:

- Performance detection and performance prediction: is LaReDAMoid able to detect known samples and unknown samples?
- Comparison of LaReDAMoid detection of malware families against related works.
- Comparison of LaReDAMoid with renowned antiviruses.
- Comparison of LaReDAMoid with related works.

6.1 Detection Performance

The first step in this section consists of evaluating the detection performance of LaReDAMoid on known samples provided during the training. We consider the three best classifiers, IBk, PART, and RandomForest. Table 8 presents the detailed results.

The system is able to detect 97% of the malware samples used in the training with 99% of AUC. This proves that the model is outstanding with a precision of 95% at least. But, what is the situation when it has to predict the class of unknown samples? We build the experiments to

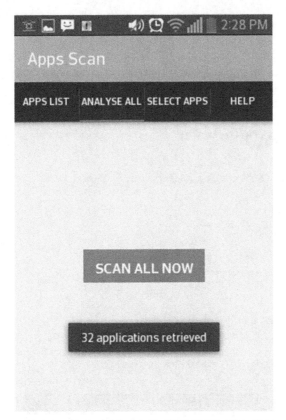

FIG. 11   Complete analysis.

evaluate the prediction performance of LaReDAMoid. We determine first of all the performance with the 10-fold cross validation, a case of the k-fold cross validation method, described as applying the classifier to the data 10 times, and each time with a 90-10 configuration; that is, 90% of data for training and 10% for testing; Table 9 summarizes the average of these 10 iterations. We keep the same metrics and the same classifier used to determine detection performance.

The model remains outstanding; it is able to detect 95 % of the malware samples with 93% precision. We randomly split the partitions into known and unknown ones. We apply three cases:

- known partition (60%) and unknown one (40%);
- known partition (66%) and unknown one (34%);
- known partition (70%) and unknown one (30%).

We repeat them 10 times and take the average results. The partitioning cases ensure that the reported results refer to the capacity of the system to predict unknown malware during the learning phase.

The results of these experiments are consigned in Table 10, where only the AUC metric with classifiers IBk, PART and RandomForest is considered.

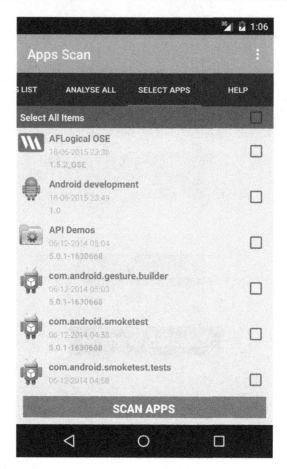

FIG. 12   Selective analysis.

The system is able to efficiently detect unknown malware with 95–97% of AUC, corresponding to 95–97 samples of unknown malware when installing 100 applications. It is an excellent model according to Hosmer et al. (2013).

6.1.1 Model Validation

We collected a testing dataset including 51 malicious applications published at the end of 2014 by antivirus companies and research groups and 34 normal applications from Google Play to achieve the validation of the model. Normal applications have been tested in VirusTotal to confirm their normality. After eliminating duplicates and removing corrupted packages, we are left with 30 malicious applications and 33 normal applications. The results obtained are the following:

- LaReDAMoid detects correctly 30 pieces of malware out of 30.
- LaReDAMoid detects correctly 25 normal applications among 30; eight are misclassified, among which are the antivirus software AVAST, AVG, McAfee, F-SECURE Mobile Security, which require accessing the user's whole sensitive information of the user: personal information (accounts, phone calls, messages, personal information, location,

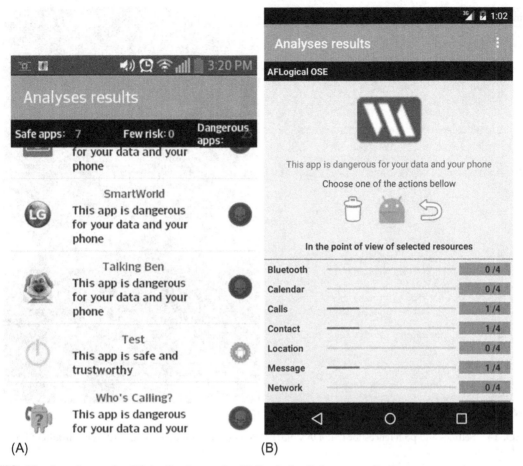

FIG. 13   Scanning results. (A) Application results. (B) Result details for one application.

services that cost money), hardware information (network communication, storage, hardware controls, and system tools). They request respectively 42, 57, 70, and 59 permissions, too much for an application. This result indicates that the false positives could be considerable due to the fact that an application that requires many permissions tends almost all resources considered in the model. Therefore it will be considered as risky according to the second layer.

6.2 Comparison Between Layer Models

The objective of this section is to determine, which layer models offers independently better results. Fig. 15 (A–C) illustrates respectively AUC, precision, and true positive rate results on these models for the best classifier RandomForest.

The third model outperforms the two others, according to AUC, precision, and TPR results. We discover however an exception with classifier PART about the precision criteria. It indicates that Model 1 is more precise than the others (Fig. 16).

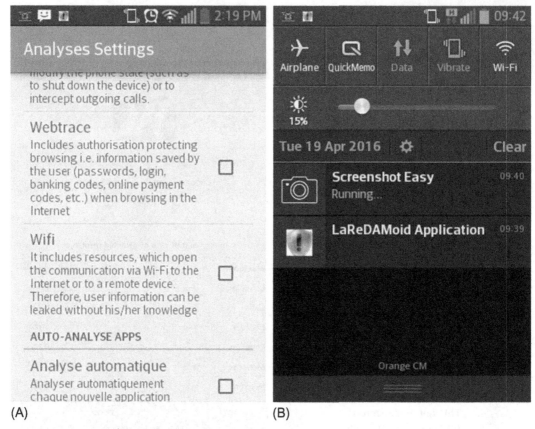

FIG. 14   Settings and preferences for LaReDAMoid. (A) Settings concerning resources. (B) A notification for new application

TABLE 9   Prediction Results Simulating the Unknown Dataset

	TP	FN	FP	TN	TPR (%)	FPR (%)	Precision (%)	ACC (%)	AUC (%)
IBK	6468	315	497	1496	95.4	24.9	92.9	90.74	95.7
PART	6427	356	418	1575	94.8	21,00	93.9	91.18	94.7
RandomForest	6475	308	432	1561	95.5	21.7	93.7	91.56	96.6

6.3 Detection of Malware Families

A malware family is a group of applications with similar attack techniques. Zhou and Jiang (2012) released 49 malware families in 2012 that reflect always the behavior of nowadays malware (Wang et al., 2014). An important experiment consists therefore to evaluating specifically the performance detection of every sample for the forty-nine families. The family names and the number of samples for each family are listed in Table 11. The detection

TABLE 10   Values of AUC for Every Partition

Partitions	Classifier	AUC
Splitting 60-40	IBk	0.952
	PART	0.952
	RandomForest	0.964
Splitting 66-34	IBk	0.957
	PART	0.95
	RandomForest	0.965
Splitting 70-30	IBk	0.955
	PART	0.95
	RandomForest	0.966

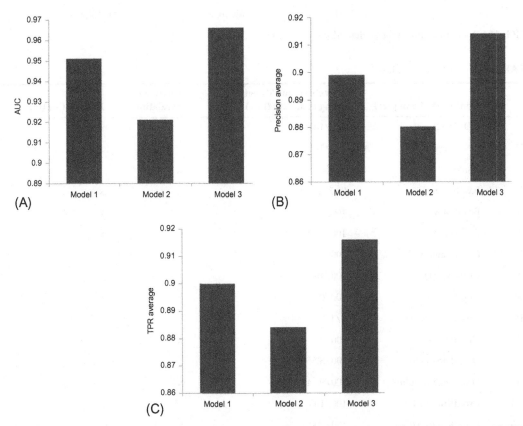

FIG. 15   Model 3 outperforms Models 1 and 2 with RandomForest. (A) AUC criteria. (B) Precision criteria. (C) TPR criteria.

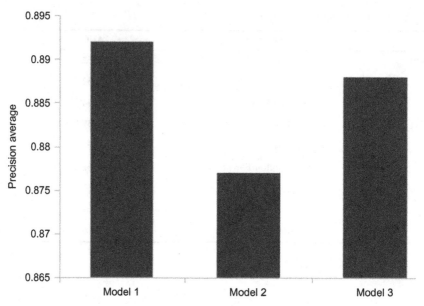

FIG. 16 Model 1 is more precise than Models 2 and 3 in PART.

TABLE 11 Malware Families

	Families(# of Samples)	Detection Our Model/Model Wang et al. (2014) (%)	Privilege Escalation	Remote Control
F1	ADRD(22)	100/100		x
F2	AnserverBot(187)	100/100		x
F3	Asroot(8)	75/50	x	
F4	BaseBridge(122)	95.72/83.60	x	x
F5	BeanBot(8)	100/87.5		x
F6	BgServ(9)	100/100		x
F7	CoinPirate(1)	100/0		x
F8	Crusewin(1)	100/100		x
F9	DogWars(1)	100/0	x	x
F10	DroidCoupon(1)	0/100	x	
F11	DroidDeluxe(1)	100/0	x	x
F12	DroidDream(16)	100/87.5		x
F13	DroidDreamLight(46)	100/93.47	x	x
F14	DroidKungFu1(34)	100/100	x	x
F15	DroidKungFu2(30)	100/100	x	x
F16	DroidKungFu3(309)	100/97.41		x
F17	DroidKungFu4(96)	100/97.91	x	x

TABLE 11   Malware Families—cont'd

	Families(# of Samples)	Detection Our Model/Model Wang et al. (2014) (%)	Privilege Escalation	Remote Control
F18	DroidKungFuSapp(3)	100/100		
F19	DroidKungFuUpdate(1)	100/100		x
F20	Endofday(1)	100/100		
F21	FakeNetflix(1)	100/100		
F22	FakePlayer(6)	100/100		
F23	GamblerSMS(1)	100/100		x
F24	Geinimi(69)	100/100		
F25	GGTracker(1)	100/100	x	x
F26	GingerMaster(4)	100/100		x
F27	GoldDream(47)	100/100		
F28	Gone60(9)	100/100		
F29	GPSSMSSpy(6)	100/100		
F30	HippoSMS(4)	100/100		
F31	Jifake(1)	100/0		x
F32	jSMSHider(16)	100/37.5		x
F33	KMin(52)	100/100		
F34	LoveTrap(1)	100/100		
F35	NickyBot(1)	100/100		x
F36	NickySpy(2)	100/100		x
F37	Pjapps(58)	100/100		x
F38	Plankton(11)	100/63.63		x
F39	RogueLemon(2)	100/100		
F40	RogueSPPush(2)	100/100		
F41	SMSReplicator(1)	100/0		
F42	SndApps(10)	100/80		x
F43	Spitmo(1)	100/100		
F44	TapSnake(2)	100/50		
F45	Walkinwat(1)	100/0		x
F46	YZHC(22)	100/100	x	
F47	Zhash(11)	100/100	x	
F48	Zitmo(1)	100/100		
F49	Zsone(12)	100/91.66		

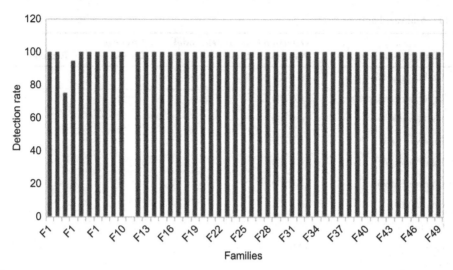

FIG. 17　Detection per malware family.

performance of the whole system for each family is illustrated in Fig. 17. Our classifier is able to reliably detect all families with an average accuracy of 99.20% (1250/1260) at a false positive of 0.79% (10/1260). All families can be perfectly identified at 100%, except three of them: Asroot, Basebridge, and Droiddeluxe. Basebridge shows a detection rate of more than 95.72% (112 correctly detected out of 119), Asroot shows a detection rate of 75% (6 correctly detected out of 8) and Droiddeluxe (with just one sample) cannot be detected. These families commonly rely on the root privilege to function well. They leverage known root exploits (rageagainstthecage, Asroot) without asking the user to grant the root privilege to these samples to escape from the built-in security sandbox. Our system is based on static analysis of requested permissions. Therefore we cannot identify applications exploiting root exploits with no permission requested. Dynamic analysis for mitigation should be associated, to scrutinize the runtime behavior of the installed application. The system rather detects perfectly other families with samples performing privilege escalation and remote control presented in Table 11.

Fig. 17 summarizes the detection performance of malware families.

Drebin authors (Arp et al., 2014; Wang et al., 2014) investigated similarly the detection of malware families. The first work focuses only on 20 families whereas the second focuses on all the families. The following point has been drawn in a conjoint comparison:

- Our system perfectly detects the Kmin family like Drebin.
- Our system outperforms Drebin in the detection of other families with 100% of the detection rate. Drebin stands with average 90% detection of those families.
- Wang et al. (2014) detect 94.92% (119) of malware family samples whereas ours detects about 99.20%. The second column of Table 12 presents details of both detection by our model and Wang et al. (2014). Most of the case, we outperforms their detection. The exception appears only with the family Droidcoupon with one sample.

TABLE 12 Detection Results on Unknown Malware

No		AVG	Avast	F-Secure				LaReDAMoid
				MP	SP	FPr	NP	
1	ING Bank N.V.	×	✓		●			✓
2	AlfSafe	×	✓			●		✓
3	Android System	×	✓	●				✓
4	Awesome Jokes	✓	✓				●	✓
5	BaDoink	×	✓				●	✓
6	BaseApp	×	✓			●		✓
7	Battery Doctor	×	✓			●		✓
8	Battery Improve	×	✓				●	✓
9	Black Market Alpha	×	✓			●		✓
10	Business Calendar Pro	✓	✓				●	✓
11	Chibi Fighter	×	×				●	✓
12	com.android.tools.system	×	✓			●		✓
13	Dendroid	×	✓	●				✓
14	Détecteur de Carrier IQ	×	✓				●	✓
15	FlvPlayer	×	✓	●				✓
16	Install	×	✓				●	✓
17	Jelly Matching	×	✓		●			✓
18	Mobile Security	×	✓		●			✓
19	o5android	×	✓			●		✓
20	PronEnabler	✓	✓			●		✓
21	Radardroid Pro	×	✓			●		✓
22	SberSafe	×	✓			●		✓
23	Se-Cure Mobile AV	×	✓				●	✓
24	SoundHound	×	✓		●			✓
25	SPL Meter FREE	×	✓	●				✓
26	System Service	×	✓			●		✓
27	VkSafe	×	✓			●		✓
28	41CA3EFD	×	✓		●			✓
29	sb.apk	×	✓				●	✓
30	ThreatJapan_D09	×	✓			●		✓

×, misclassified; ✓, correctly classified.

6.4 Antivirus Scanners

We have compared our model to three renown antiviruses: AVG, Avast, and F-Secure. The reason is that thay scan applications based on permissions. This experiment uses the testing dataset (Section 6.1.1) with 30 unknown samples of malware and 30 unknown normal applications collected for validation. Table 12 presents the detection results for LaReDAMoid and antiviruses.

Table 13 reveals that the system correctly detects 30 samples of malware whereas AVG only alerts to three samples: Awesome Jokes, Business Calendar Pro, and PronEnabler. AVG provides therefore a TP of three, a TN of 33, a FN of 27 and a FP of null. Avast detects 29 malware samples and fails to detect the Chibi Fighter malware. Avast gets therefore a TP of 29, a TN of 33, a FN of one and FP of null. The applications are classified in four categories: many privacy issues (MP), some privacy issues (SP), few privacy issues (FPr), and no privacy issues (NP) concerning F-Secure. Only four malware samples are correctly classified. Five samples are detected as applications with some privacy issues and 12 are classified as applications with few issues. F-Secure incorrectly classifies nine samples as applications with NP. F-Secure Mobile Security has TP of nine (we consider MP and SP as malicious classes), a TN of 24 (NP), FP of nine (normal applications belonging to MP, SP, and FPr), and a FN of nine (malware belonging to NP).

Our scheme is the best in determining malware with 100% of TPR, followed by Avast, which fails to determine just one malware sample. The accuracy indicates that LaReDAMoid records the best performance after Avast. LaReDAMoid is therefore considered as reliable compared to existing antiviruses.

Zhou and Jiang experienced that the best antivirus (Lookout) detects 79.6% of 1260 samples from the 49 malware families. We have also taken from this work on other antiviruses (Norton, Trend Micro and Avg). Table 14 shows that LaReDAMoid outperforms Lookout and the others on this dataset.

6.5 Related Works

We compare the performance of the detection system with three well-known approaches in the literature, based on requested permissions as features Kirin (Enck et al., 2009),

TABLE 13   Detection Results

	TP	FN	FP	TN	TPR	FPR	Accuracy
AVG	3	27	0	33	10.00%	0.00%	57.14 %
Avast	29	1	0	33	96.66%	0.00%	98.41%
F-Secure	9	21	9	24	30.00%	27.00%	52.38 %
LaReDAMoid	30	0	8	25	100.00%	24.24 %	88.00%

TABLE 14   Detection AV on Malware Families

LaReDAMoid	Avg	Lookout	Norton	Trend Micro
99.20%	54.7%	79.6%	20.2%	76.7%

RCP+RPCP (Rare Critical Permissions and Rare Pair Critical Permission) (Sarma et al., 2012) and PermissionWatcher (Struse et al., 2012). Kirin identifies nine permission rules for applications to be considered potential malicious. RCP+RPCP measures the permission risks by evaluating the popularity of permissions within applications of the same category. The performance of RCP+RPCP is generated with the rule #RCP(2)+#RPCP(1) $\geq \theta$, the best performing one. PermissionWatcher classifies an application based on 16 rules of combination of permissions.

Table 15 presents the performance results in terms of TPR, FPR, Precision, Accuracy, and AUC, after applying these methods to the learning dataset defined in Section 5.1.

We can observe from Table 16 that our method has better performance than the other methods. Kirin only has nine manually defined security rules, not enough to distinguish malicious applications from benign applications. #RCP(2)+#RPCP(1) uses arbitrary 26 critical permissions to generate the risk signal for an application. This approach does not consider other permissions, which could generate maliciousness. The consequence is the low positive rate. PermissionWatcher includes permission combinations of Kirin and those not sufficient to profile applications. Our method uses ML and captures the permissions patterns of both benign and malicious applications. We consider security risks related to sensitive resources besides the requested permissions. We have better performance with this combination. #RCP(2)+#RPCP(1) however detects 74 normal applications more than the detection system. These two methods are similarly precise, although LaReDAMoid outperforms the three other methods concerning the accuracy and the AUC, given the capacity to predict unknown samples. We notice that the important prerequisite for a good detection is the precise determination of features. The semantics of features must reflect the sample profiles, and features contribute significantly to classification.

6.6 Limitations

The previous evaluation demonstrates the efficiency of the system in the detection of recent malware. The system uses machine learning techniques to learn malware profiles.

The system, however, lacks the capabilities of a run-time analysis. Some strains of malware make use of obfuscation or load code dynamically, which hinders any static inspection.

The system is less accurate in the detection of normal applications. This is justified by the fact that we focus only on permissions. Applications such as Avg, which require more than 30 permissions, will be considered as malware by our system because they access several resources; therefore the calculated risk in the second layer is higher.

TABLE 15 Detection Performance

	TP	FN	FP	TN	TPR	FPR	Precision	Accuracy	AUC
Kirin	4076	2707	271	1722	60.09 %	13.5 %	93.76 %	57.52 %	66.9 %
#RCP(2)+#RPCP(1) $\geq \theta$	5657	1126	177	1816	83.39 %	8.88 %	96.96 %	85.15 %	58.5 %
PermissionWatcher	5342	1141	502	1491	76.39	25.18	91.40	77.86	85.4%
Our scheme	6580	203	251	1742	97.00%	12.6 %	96.32 %	94.82 %	99.00%

TABLE 16 Risk Determination

No	Resources	C_{ij}	Permissions and Combinations	R_1	R_2	R_3	R_4	W_{ij}
1	Messages	$C_{1,1}$	SEND_SMS	1	0	1	1	3
		$C_{2,1}$	RECEIVE_SMS	1	0	0	0	1
		$C_{3,1}$	RECEIVE_MMS	1	0	0	0	1
		$C_{4,1}$	READ_SMS	1	0	0	0	1
		$C_{5,1}$	WRITE_SMS	0	1	0	0	1
		$C_{6,1}$	SEND_SMS, RECEIVE_SMS	1	0	1	1	3
		$C_{7,1}$	SEND_SMS, READ_SMS	1	0	1	1	3
		$C_{8,1}$	SEND_SMS, WRITE_SMS	0	1	1	1	3
		$C_{9,1}$	RECEIVE_SMS, READ_SMS	1	0	0	0	1
		$C_{10,1}$	RECEIVE_SMS, WRITE_SMS	1	1	0	0	2
		$C_{11,1}$	READ_SMS, WRITE_SMS	1	1	0	1	3
		$C_{12,1}$	SEND_SMS, RECEIVE_SMS, READ_SMS	1	0	1	1	3
		$C_{13,1}$	SEND_SMS, RECEIVE_SMS, WRITE_SMS	1	1	1	1	4
		$C_{14,1}$	SEND_SMS, READ_SMS, WRITE_SMS	1	1	1	1	4
		$C_{15,1}$	WRITE_SMS, READ_SMS, RECEIVE_SMS	1	1	0	0	2
		$C_{16,1}$	READ_SMS, SEND_SMS, RECEIVE_SMS, WRITE_SMS	1	1	1	1	4
2	Contacts	$C_{1,2}$	READ_CONTACTS	1	0	0	0	1
		$C_{2,2}$	WRITE_CONTACTS	0	1	0	0	1
		$C_{3,2}$	MANAGE_ACCOUNTS	1	1	0	0	2
		$C_{4,2}$	READ_CONTACTS, WRITE_CONTACTS	1	1	0	0	2
		$C_{5,2}$	READ_CONTACTS, MANAGE_ACCOUNTS	1	1	0	0	2
		$C_{6,2}$	MANAGE_ACCOUNTS, WRITE_CONTACTS	1	1	0	0	2
		$C_{7,2}$	READ_CONTACTS, WRITE_CONTACTS, MANAGE_ACCOUNTS	1	1	1	0	3
		$C_{2,3}$	READ_CALL_LOG	1	0	0	0	1
		$C_{3,3}$	WRITE_CALL_LOG	0	1	1	0	2
		$C_{4,3}$	CALL_PHONE	1	0	1	1	3
		$C_{5,3}$	CALL_PRIVILEGED	1	0	1	1	3
		$C_{6,3}$	PROCESS_OUTGOING_CALLS, READ_CALL_LOG	1	0	1	1	3
		$C_{7,3}$	PROCESS_OUTGOING_CALLS, WRITE_CALL_LOG	1	1	1	1	4
		$C_{8,3}$	PROCESS_OUTGOING_CALLS, CALL_PHONE	1	0	1	1	3

TABLE 16 Risk Determination—cont'd

No	Resources	C_{ij}	Permissions and Combinations	Risks				Weight
				R_1	R_2	R_3	R_4	W_{ij}
		$C_{9,3}$	PROCESS_OUTGOING_CALLS, CALL_PRIVILEGED	1	0	1	1	3
		$C_{10,3}$	READ_CALL_LOG, WRITE_CALL_LOG	1	1	0	0	2
		$C_{11,3}$	READ_CALL_LOG, CALL_PHONE	1	0	1	1	3
		$C_{12,3}$	READ_CALL_LOG, CALL_PRIVILEGED	1	0	1	1	3
		$C_{13,3}$	WRITE_CALL_LOG, CALL_PHONE	1	1	1	1	4
		$C_{14,3}$	WRITE_CALL_LOG, CALL_PRIVILEGED	1	1	1	1	4
		$C_{15,3}$	CALL_PHONE, CALL_PRIVILEGED	1	0	1	1	3
		$C_{16,3}$	PROCESS_OUTGOING_CALLS, READ_CALL_LOG, WRITE_CALL_LOG	1	1	1	1	4
		$C_{17,3}$	PROCESS_OUTGOING_CALLS, READ_CALL_LOG, CALL_PHONE	1	0	1	1	3
		$C_{18,3}$	PROCESS_OUTGOING_CALLS, READ_CALL_LOG, CALL_PRIVILEGED	1	0	1	1	3
		$C_{19,3}$	PROCESS_OUTGOING_CALLS, WRITE_CALL_LOG, CALL_PHONE	1	1	1	1	4
		$C_{20,3}$	PROCESS_OUTGOING_CALLS, WRITE_CALL_LOG, CALL_PRIVILEGED	1	1	1	1	4
		$C_{21,3}$	PROCESS_OUTGOING_CALLS, CALL_PHONE, CALL_PRIVILEGED	1	1	1	1	4
		$C_{22,3}$	READ_CALL_LOG, WRITE_CALL_LOG, CALL_PRIVILEGED	1	1	1	1	4
		$C_{23,3}$	READ_CALL_LOG, CALL_PHONE, CALL_PRIVILEGED	1	0	1	1	3
		$C_{24,3}$	WRITE_CALL_LOG, CALL_PHONE, CALL_PRIVILEGED	1	1	1	1	4
		$C_{27,3}$	PROCESS_OUTGOING_CALLS, READ_CALL_LOG, WRITE_CALL_LOG, CALL_PHONE	1	1	1	1	4
		$C_{28,3}$	PROCESS_OUTGOING_CALLS, READ_CALL_LOG, WRITE_CALL_LOG, CALL_PRIVILEGED	1	1	1	1	4
		$C_{29,3}$	PROCESS_OUTGOING_CALLS, READ_CALL_LOG, CALL_PHONE, CALL_PRIVILEGED	1	0	1	1	3
		$C_{30,3}$	PROCESS_OUTGOING_CALLS, WRITE_CALL_LOG, CALL_PHONE, CALL_PRIVILEGED	0	1	1	1	3
		$C_{31,3}$	READ_CALL_LOG, WRITE_CALL_LOG, CALL_PHONE, CALL_PRIVILEGED	1	1	1	1	4

Continued

TABLE 16 Risk Determination—cont'd

				Risks				Weight
No	Resources	C_{ij}	Permissions and Combinations	R_1	R_2	R_3	R_4	W_{ij}
		$C_{32,3}$	PROCESS_OUTGOING_CALLS, READ_CALL_LOG, WRITE_CALL_LOG, CALL_PHONE, CALL_PRIVILEGED	1	1	1	1	4
4	Calendar	$C_{1,4}$	READ_CALENDAR	1	0	0	0	1
		$C_{2,4}$	WRITE_CALENDAR	0	1	1	0	2
		$C_{3,4}$	READ_CALENDAR, WRITE_CALENDAR	1	1	1	0	3
		$C_{2,5}$	ACCESS_COARSE_LOCATION	1	0	1	0	2
		$C_{3,5}$	INSTALL_LOCATION_PROVIDER	1	0	1	0	2
		$C_{4,5}$	LOCATION_HARDWARE	1	0	1	0	2
		$C_{5,5}$	ACCESS_FINE_LOCATION, ACCESS_COARSE_LOCATION	1	0	0	0	1
		$C_{6,5}$	ACCESS_FINE_LOCATION, INSTALL_LOCATION_PROVIDER	1	0	0	0	1
		$C_{7,5}$	ACCESS_FINE_LOCATION, LOCATION_HARDWARE	1	0	0	0	1
		$C_{8,5}$	ACCESS_COARSE_LOCATION, INSTALL_LOCATION_PROVIDER	1	0	0	0	1
		$C_{9,5}$	ACCESS_COARSE_LOCATION, LOCATION_HARDWARE	1	0	0	0	1
		$C_{10,5}$	INSTALL_LOCATION_PROVIDER, LOCATION_HARDWARE	1	0	0	0	1
		$C_{11,5}$	ACCESS_FINE_LOCATION, ACCESS_COARSE_LOCATION, INSTALL_LOCATION_PROVIDER	1	0	0	0	1
		$C_{12,5}$	ACCESS_FINE_LOCATION, ACCESS_COARSE_LOCATION, LOCATION_HARDWARE	1	0	0	0	1
		$C_{13,5}$	ACCESS_FINE_LOCATION, INSTALL_LOCATION_PROVIDER, LOCATION_HARDWARE	1	0	0	0	1
		$C_{14,5}$	ACCESS_COARSE_LOCATION, INSTALL_LOCATION_PROVIDER, LOCATION_HARDWARE	1	0	0	0	1
		$C_{15,5}$	ACCESS_FINE_LOCATION, ACCESS_COARSE_LOCATION, INSTALL_LOCATION_PROVIDER, LOCATION_HARDWARE	1	0	0	0	1
6	Wifi	$C_{1,6}$	ACCESS_WIFI_STATE	1	0	0	0	1
		$C_{2,6}$	CHANGE_WIFI_STATE	0	1	0	0	1
		$C_{3,6}$	CHANGE_WIFI_MULTICAST_STATE	0	1	0	0	1
		$C_{4,6}$	ACCESS_WIFI_STATE, CHANGE_WIFI_STATE	1	1	0	0	2

TABLE 16 Risk Determination—cont'd

No	Resources	C_{ij}	Permissions and Combinations	Risks				Weight
				R_1	R_2	R_3	R_4	W_{ij}
		$C_{5,6}$	ACCESS_WIFI_STATE, CHANGE_WIFI_MULTICAST_STATE	1	1	0	0	2
		$C_{6,6}$	CHANGE_WIFI_STATE, CHANGE_WIFI_MULTICAST_STATE	0	1	0	0	1
		$C_{7,6}$	ACCESS_WIFI_STATE, CHANGE_WIFI_STATE, CHANGE_WIFI_MULTICAST_STATE	1	1	0	0	2
7	Bluetooth	$C_{1,7}$	BLUETOOTH	1	1	1	0	3
		$C_{2,7}$	BLUETOOTH_ADMIN	1	1	1	0	3
		$C_{3,7}$	BLUETOOTH, BLUETOOTH_ADMIN	1	1	1	0	3
8	Network	$C_{1,8}$	INTERNET	1	0	1	0	2
		$C_{2,8}$	ACCESS_NETWORK_STATE	1	0	0	0	1
		$C_{3,8}$	CHANGE_NETWORK_STATE	0	1	0	0	1
		$C_{4,8}$	INTERNET, ACCESS_NETWORK_STATE	1	1	1	0	3
		$C_{5,8}$	INTERNET, CHANGE_NETWORK_STATE	1	1	1	0	3
		$C_{6,8}$	ACCESS_NETWORK_STATE, CHANGE_NETWORK_STATE	1	1	0	0	2
		$C_{7,8}$	INTERNET, ACCESS_NETWORK_STATE, CHANGE_NETWORK_STATE	1	1	1	0	3
9	Telephony	$C_{1,9}$	MODIFY_PHONE_STATE	0	1	0	0	1
		$C_{2,9}$	READ_PHONE_STATE	1	0	0	0	1
		$C_{3,9}$	READ_PHONE_STATE, MODIFY_PHONE_STATE	1	1	0	0	2
10	Web traces	$C_{1,10}$	WRITE_HISTORY_BOOKMARKS	0	1	0	0	1
		$C_{2,10}$	READ_HISTORY_BOOKMARKS	1	0	0	0	1
		$C_{3,10}$	READ_HISTORY_BOOKMARKS, WRITE_HISTORY_BOOKMARKS	1	1	0	0	2

A number of malware samples exactly the same permissions that are requested by normal applications. This gives negative impact on the detection accuracy by the first layer (Wang et al., 2014).

Some malware does not need to request any permissions (Lineberry et al., 2015). In this case, relying on only permissions is not feasible for the detection of malware pieces. The developers may request overprivileged permission requests that are never actually used in the application. This leads to false positives if only the permission information is used for the detection.

Another limitation is that detection performance critically depends on the availability of representative malicious and benign applications.

7 CONCLUSION AND PERSPECTIVES

In this work, we provide a flexible machine learning-based mechanism to effectively detect Android malware based only on requested permissions. For that, we first described the Android ecosystem for a better understanding of the Android security limitations. Then we presented important aspects of the malware landscape. Next, we explored machine learning techniques used to learn and train application profiles, to detect and to predict application status: malicious or normal. Then we explored how to determine detection performance. Next we presented our model and its implementation. Finally, we evaluated and discussed the system with renowned antiviruses and related works.

Our system is built of three layers. The first layer is supported by a model, which aims to characterize applications based on proportion of permission requests. The second layer uses a model, which relies on security risks related to granting permissions. For that, we defined 10 resource categories including related permissions and distinct combination of these permissions. The last layer uses a model, which characterizes an application based on an association of vectors derived from the two first layers. We apply supervised learning with several learning algorithms, namely, NaiveBayes, LibSVM, IBk, AdaBoostM1, PART, J48, and RandomForest, on a collection of 6783 cases of malware and 1993 normal applications, which have been tested and validated. Then we determined detection rules to profile applications. Additionally, our system requires the user to specify sensitive resources to protect and takes it in account during the process of characterization of applications.

Our framework is good in detecting around 98% accuracy and in predicting with around 96% of the true positive rate. This means that it is capable to discriminate almost all cases of malware in detection and prediction. The AUC is between 97% and 99%, which confers the property of the outstanding model according to Hosmer and Lemeshow (2000).

Some limitations exist because the system only considers the permissions as features. The first one is that normal applications with several permissions are likely considered as malware since they seem to be accessing several resources. The second one is that they are normal applications, which requests the same permission as a normal application. In this case, the detection will fail. The last case is that the system is not able to scrutinize an application with no permission.

For future work, we plan to associate runtime analysis and other static features to strengthen the system.

APPENDIX A DIFFERENT COMBINATIONS OF PERMISSIONS AND DETERMINATION OF RISKS

Table 16 shows data for different combinations of permissions and determination of risks.

APPENDIX B NORMAL APPLICATIONS FOR TESTING

AVG, McAfee Security, Safety Care, Who's Calling, Fsecure Mobile Security, Avast Mobile Security, CSipSimple, German, Talking Ben, 100% Anglais, Alphabets & Numbers Writing, Apk Extractor, AppPermissionWatcher, AppPermissions, Baby Ninja Dance, Candy Crush

Saga, LaReDAMoid, File Manager, Important Dates, Kids Songs, Learn Numbers in French Lang, Malware Tracker, My Permissions, Noms Abc, Permission Friendly Apps, Permission Monitor Free, Polaris Viewer 4, Pregnancy Tracker, Screenshot Easy, Smartworld, Test, Malware Tracker.

Acknowledgments

The authors would like to thank the Computer Security Group of the University of Göttingen for sharing the Drebin dataset, and Zhou Y., Jiang X., for sharing the dataset of Genome Project. We acknowledge founders of VirusTotal and Contagio, who provide us samples.

References

Allix, K., Bissyande, T.F.D.A., Klein, J., Le Traon, Y., 2014. Machine Learning-Based Malware Detection for Android Applications: History Matters! University of Luxembourg, Walferdange.

Android, 2015. Manifest permissions. http://developer.android.com/reference/android/Manifest.permission.html.

Android-apktool, A tool for reverse engineering Android apk files. http://code.google.com/p/android-apktool/.

Android source. 2015. https://github.com/android/platform_frameworks_base.

Android studio, http://developer.android.com/tools/studio/index.html.

Arp, D., Spreitzenbarth, M., M. Hübner, H.G., Rieck, K., 2014. DREBIN: effective and explainable detection of android malware in your pocket. Proceedings of 17th Network and Distributed System Security Symposium (NDSS). The Internet Society, San Diego, CA.

Aung, Z., Zaw, W., 2013. Permission-based android malware detection. Int. J. Sci. Technol. Res. 2 (3), 228–234.

Barrera, D., Kayacik, H.G., van Oorschot, P.C., Somayaji, A., 2010. A methodology for empirical analysis of permission-based security models and its application to Android. In: Proceedings of the 17th ACM Conference on Computer and Communications Security (CCS'10). ACM, New York, pp. 73–84.

Brähler, S., 2015. Analysis of the android architecture. https://os.itec.kit.edu/downloads/sa:2010_braehler-stefan_android-architecture.pdf.

Breiman, L., 2001. Random forests. J. Mach. Learn. 45 (1), 5–32.

Burguera, I., Zurutuza, U., Nadjm-tehrani, S., 2011. Crowdroid: behavior-based malware detection system for android. In: Proceedings of the 1st ACM Workshop on Security and Privacy in Smartphones and Mobile devices (SPSM'11). ACM, New York, pp. 15–26.

Canalys, 2013. Over 1 billion android-based smart phones to ship in 2017. http://www.canalys.com/newsroom/over-1-billion-android-based-smart-phones-ship-2017.

Canfora, G., Mercaldo, F., Visaggio, C.A., 2013. A classifier of malicious android applications. In: Proceedings of Eighth International Conference on Availability, Reliability and Security (ARES). IEEE, pp. 607–614.

Chin, E., Felt, A.P., Greenwood, K., Wagner, D., 2011. Analyzing inter-application communication in Android. In: Proceedings of the 9th Annual International Conference on Mobile Systems, Applications and Services (MobiSys'11). ACM, New York, pp. 239–252.

Contagio. 2015. http://contagiodump.blogspot.com/.

Dietterich, T., Langley, P., 2003. Machine learning for cognitive networks: technology assessments and research challenges. http://core.ac.uk/download/pdf/10195444.pdf.

Dini, G., Martinelli, F., Matteucci, I., Petrocchi, M., Saracino, A., Sgandurra, D., 2012. A multi-criteria-based evaluation of android applications. In: Proceedings of Trusted Systems. Springer, Berlin, pp. 67–82.

Dini, G., Martinelli, F., Saracino, A., Sgandurra, D., 2012. Madam: a multi-level anomaly detector for android malware. In: Proceedings of the 6th International Conference on Mathematical Methods, Models, and Architectures for Computer Network Security. MMM-ACNS-12. Springer, Berlin, pp. 240–253.

Ehringer, D., 2010. The dalvik virtual machine architecture. Technical Report.

Enck, W., Ongtang, D., McDaniel, P., 2009. On lightweight mobile phone application certification. In: Proceedings of the 16th ACM Conference on Computer and Communications Security. ACM, New York, pp. 235–245.

Fang, Z., Weili, H., Yingjiu, L., 2014. Permission based android security: issues and countermeasures. Comput. Sec. 43, 205–218.

Felt, A.P., Greenwood, K., Wagner, D., 2010. The effectiveness of install-time permission systems for third-party applications. University of California at Berkeley, Berkeley, CA. Technical report UCB/EECS-2010-143.

Felt, A.P., Chin, E., Hanna, S., Song, D., Wagner, D., 2011. Android permissions demystified. In: Proceedings of the ACM Conference on Computer and Communications Security (CCS). ACM, New York, pp. 627–638.

Felt, A.P., Ha, E., Egelman, S., Haney, A., Chin, E., Wagner, D., 2012. Android permissions: user attention, comprehension, and behavior. In: Proceedings of the Eighth Symposium on Usable Privacy and Security (SOUPS'12). ACM, New York, pp. 1–14.

Filiol, E., 2005. Évaluation des logiciels antiviraux: quand le marketing s'oppose à la technique. Journal de la sécurité informatique MISC 21.

Fix, E., Hodges, J.L., 1952. Discriminatory analysis-nonparametric discrimination: consistency properties. 11. USAF School of Aviation Medicine, pp. 280–322.

Frank, E., Witten, I.H., 1998. Generating accurate rule sets without global optimisation. In: Proceedings of the Fifteenth International Conference on Machine Learning (ICML' 98). Morgan Kaufmann, San Francisco, CA, pp. 144–151.

Freund, Y., Schapire, R.E., 1996. Experiments with a new boosting algorithm. In: Proceedings of the 13th International Conference on Machine Learning (ICML'96). Morgan Kaufmann, San Francisco, CA, pp. 148–156.

Fritz, C., Arzt, S., Rasthofer, S., Bodden, E., Bartel, A., Klein, J., le Traon, Y., Octeau, D., McDaniel, P., 2014. FlowDroid: precise context, flow, field, object-sensitive and lifecycle-aware taint analysis for Android apps. In: Proceedings of the 35th ACM SIGPLAN Conference on Programming Language Design and Implementation (PLDI'14). ACM, New York, pp. 259–269.

Gomez, L., Neamtiu, I., 2015. A characterization of malicious android applications. http://www.lorenzobgomez.com/publications/MaliciousAppsTR.pdf.

Google Play, 2015. https://www.play.google.com.

Google Play Help, About app permissions. https://support.google.com/googleplay/answer/6014972?p=app_permissions&rd=1.

Grace, M., Zhou, Y., Wang, Z., Jiang, X., 2012. Systematic detection of capability leaks in stock android smartphones. In: Proceedings of the 19th Annual Symposium on Network and Distributed System Security (NDSS'12). The Internet Society, San Diego, CA.

Grzymala-Busse, J.W., 2010. Rule Induction. Data Mining and Knowledge Discovery Handbook. Springer, New York, pp. 249–265.

Han, W., Fang, Z., Yang, L.T., Pan, G., Wu, Z., 2014. Collaborative policy administration. IEEE Trans. Parallel Distrib. Syst. 25 (2), 498–507.

Hanley, J.A., McNeil, B.J., 1982. The meaning and use of the area under a receiver operating characteristic (ROC) curve. Radiology 143 (1), 29–36.

Holavanalli, S., Manuel, D., Nanjundaswamy, V., Rosenberg, B., Shen, F., Ko, S.Y., Ziarek, L., 2013. Flow permissions for android. In: Proceedings of the 28th IEEE/ACM International Conference on Automated Software Engineering (ASE2013). Palo Alto, CA, pp. 652–657.

Hosmer, D.W., Lemeshow, S., 2000. Applied logistic regression. Wiley, New York.

Hosmer, D., Lemeshow, S., Sturdivant, R., 2013. Applied Logistic Regression. Wiley Series in Probability and Statistics Wiley.

Huang, C.Y., Tsai, Y.T., Hsu, C.H., 2013. Performance evaluation on permission-based detection for Android malware. In: Proceedings of Advances in Intelligent Systems and Applications. Springer, Berlin, pp. 111–120.

JD-GUI, http://java.decompiler.free.fr/?q=jdgui.

Jeon, J., Micinski, K.-K., Vaughan, J.-A., Reddy, N., Zhu, Y., Foster, J.-S., Millstein, T., 2013. Dr. Android and Mr. Hide: Fine-grained security policies on unmodified android. http://drum.lib.umd.edu/bitstream/1903/12852/1/CS-TR-5006.pdf.

Kohavi, R., 1996. Scaling up the accuracy of naive-bayes classiers: a decision-tree hybrid. In: Proceedings of the Second International Conference on Knowledge Discovery and Data Mining. AAAI Press, Portland, OR, pp. 202–207.

Lineberry, A., Richarson, D.L., Wyatt, T., 2015. These aren't the permissions you're looking for. https://www.defcon.org/images/defcon-18/dc-18-presentations/Lineberry/DEFCON-18-Lineberry-Not-The-Permissions-You-Are-Looking-For.pdf.

Liu, X., Liu, J., 2014. A two-layered permission-based android malware. Detection scheme. In: Proceedings of the 2nd IEEE International Conference on Mobile Cloud Computing, Services, and Engineering (MOBILECLOUD'14). IEEE, Washington, DC, pp. 142–148.

Llamas, R., Reith, R., Shirer, M., 2013. Apple cedes market share in smartphone operating system market as android surges and windows phone gains, according to IDC. http://www.idc.com/getdoc. jsp?containerId=prUS24257413.

Michalski, R.S., Carbonell, J.G., Mitchell, T.M. (Eds.), 1983. Machine Learning: An Artificial Intelligence Approach. Springer, Berlin.

Orthacker, C., Teufl, P., Kraxberger, S., Lackner, G., Gissing, M., Marsalek, A., Leibetseder, J., Prevenhueber, O., 2012. Android security permissions—can we trust them? In: Proceedings of Security and Privacy in Mobile Information and Communication Systems. Springer, Berlin, pp. 40–51.

Pearl, J., 1982. Reverend bayes on inference engines: a distributed hierarchical approach. In: Proceedings of the American Association of Artificial Intelligence (AAAI'82). AAAI Press, Portland, OR, pp. 133–136.

Ping, X., Xiaofeng, W., Wenjia, N., Tianqing, Z., Gang, L., 2014. Android malware detection with contrasting permission patterns. Commun. China 11 (8), 1–14.

Protsenko, M., Müller, T., 2014. Android malware detection based on software complexity metrics. In: Proceedings of the 11th International Conference on Trust, Privacy and Security in Digital Business (TrustBus'14). Springer, Munich, pp. 24–35.

Quinlan, J.R., 1993. C4.5: Programs for Machine Learning. Morgan Kaufmann, San Francisco, CA.

Rassameeroj, I., Tanahashi, Y., 2011. Various approaches in analyzing Android applications with its permission-based security models. In: Proceedings of 2011 IEEE International Conference on Electro/Information Technology (EIT). IEEE, Mankato, MN, pp. 1–6.

Rosen, S., Qian, Z., Mao, Z.M., 2013. Appprofiler: a flexible method of exposing privacy-related behavior in android applications to end users. In: Proceedings of the third ACM Conference on Data and Application Security and Privacy. ACM, New York, pp. 221–232.

Rovelli, P., Vigfusson, Y., 2014. PMDS: permission-based malware detection system. In: Proceedings of the 10th International Conference on Information Systems Security (ICISS). Springer, Hyderabad, India, pp. 338–357.

Saltzer, J.H., 1974. Protection and the control of information sharing in Multics. Commun. ACM 17 (7), 388–402.

Sanz, B., Santos, I., Laorden, C., Ugarte-Pedrero, X., Bringas, P.G., 2012. On the automatic categorisation of android applications. In: Proceedings of IEEE Consumer Communications and Networking Conference (CCNC). IEEE, Las Vegas, NV, pp. 149–153.

Sanz, B., Santos, I., Laorden, C., Ugarte-Pedrero, X., Bringas, P.G., Álvarez, G., 2013. PUMA: permission usage to detect malware in Android. In: Proceedings of the International Joint Conference CISIS'12-ICEUTE'12-SOCO'12 Special Sessions. Springer, Berlin, pp. 289–298.

Sanz, B., Santos, I., Laorden, C., Ugarte-Pedrero, X., Nieves, J., Bringas, P.G., Álvarez Marañón, G., 2013. MAMA: manifest analysis for malware detection in Android. J. Cybern. Syst. 44 (6–7), 469–488.

Sarma, B.P., Li, N., Gates, C., Potharaju, R., Nita-Rotaru, C., Molloy, I., 2012. Android permissions: a perspective combining risks and benefits. In: Proceedings of the 17th ACM Symposium on Access Control Models and Technologies (SACMAT'12). ACM, New York, pp. 13–22.

Sato, R., Chiba, D., Goto, S., 2013. Detecting android malware by analyzing manifest files. In: Proceedings of the Asia-Pacific Advanced Network (Asia JCIS). IEEE, Tokyo, pp. 23–31.

Shabtai, A., Fledel, Y., Elovici, Y., 2010. Automated static code analysis for classifying android applications using machine learning. In: Proceedings of 2010 International Conference on Computational Intelligence and Security (CIS). IEEE, Nanning, pp. 329–333.

Shabtai, A., Kanonov, U., Elovici, Y., Glezer, C., Weiss, Y., 2012. Andromaly: a behavioral malware detection framework for android devices. J. Intell. Inf. Syst. 38 (1), 161–190.

Struse, E., Seifert, J., Uellenbeck, S., Rukzio, E., Wolf, C., 2012. Permissionwatcher: creating user awareness of application permissions in mobile systems. In: Proceedings of Ambient Intelligence. Springer, Berlin, pp. 65–80.

Su, M.-Y., Chang, W.-C., 2014. Permission-based malware detection mechanisms for smartphones. In: Proceedings of IEEE 2014 International Conference on Information Networking (ICOIN). Phuket, Thailand, pp. 449–452.

Suh, S.C., 2011. Practical Applications of Data Mining. Jones and Bartlett Publishers, USA.

Tan, P.-N., Steinbach, M., Kumar, V., 2005. Introduction to Data Mining. Addison-Wesley, Boston, MA.

Tang, W., Jin, G., He, J., Jiang, X., 2011. Extending Android security enforcement with a security distance model. In: Proceedings of 2011 International Conference on Internet Technology and Applications (iTAP). IEEE, pp. 1–4.

Tchakounté, F., Dayang, P., 2013. Qualitative evaluation of security tools for android. Int. J. Sci. Technol. 2 (11), 754–838.

Vapnik, V., 2000. The Nature of Statistical Learning Theory. Information Science and Statistics. Springer, Berlin.

Vennon, T., Stroop, D., 2010. Threat analysis of the android market. Technical report, SMobile Systems.

Vidas, T., Christin, N., Cranor, L., 2011. Curbing Android permission creep. In: Proceedings of the 2011 Web 2.0 Security and Privacy Workshop (W2SP2011). Oakland, CA.

VirusTotal, 2015. Virustotal—free online virus, malware and URL scanner. https://www.virustotal.com.

Wang, W., Wang, X., Feng, D., Liu, J., Han, Z., Zhang, X., 2014. Exploring permission-induced risk in android applications for malicious application detection. IEEE Trans. Inf. Forensics Secur. 9 (11), 1869–1882.

Wei, X., Gomez, L., Neamtiu, I., Faloutsos, M., 2012. Malicious Android applications in the enterprise: what do they do and how do we fix it? In: Proceedings of 2012 IEEE 28th International Conference on Data Engineering Workshops (ICDEW). IEEE, pp. 251–254.

Weka 3, Data Mining Software in Java. http://www.cs.waikato.ac.nz/ml/weka/.

Witten, I.H., Eibe, F., Hall, M.A., 2011. Data Mining Practical Machine Learning Tools and Techniques, third. Morgan Kaufmann, San Francisco, CA.

Zhang, Y., Yang, M., Xu, B., Yang, Z., Gu, G., Ning, P., Wang, X.S., Zang, B., 2013. Vetting undesirable behaviors in Android apps with permission use analysis. In: Proceedings of the ACM SIGSAC Conference on Computer & Communications Security (CCS'13). ACM, New York, pp. 611–622.

Zhou, Y., Jiang, X., 2012. Dissecting android malware: characterization and evolution. In: Proceedings of IEEE Symposium on Security and Privacy (SP12). IEEE, Washington, DC, pp. 95–109.

Zhou, Y., Wang, Z., Zhou, W., Jiang, X., 2012. Hey, you, get off of my market: detecting malicious apps in official and alternative android markets. In: Proceedings of the 19th Annual Network and Distributed System Security Symposium (NDSS'2012). The Internet Society, San Diego, CA, pp. 5–8.

On Discovering Vulnerabilities in Android Applications

X. Li[*], *L. Yu*[†], *X.P. Luo*[†]

[*]Chinese Academy of Sciences, Beijing, China [†]The Hong Kong Polytechnic University, Kowloon, Hong Kong

1 INTRODUCTION

The prosperity of the app economy boosts the number of mobile apps. More than two million Android apps[1] have been published in Google Play and around 2.5 million iOS apps[2] are listed in the Apple store. It is expected that the app economy could reach $101 billion in 2020.[3] At the same time, smartphones have become an indispensable part of our daily lives, and many apps have been downloaded and installed. A recent report shows that Android users will install on average 95 apps from June 2014 to January 2015 (Sawers, 2015).

Not all apps are well designed and developed. Recent studies illustrate that many apps are prone to various attacks because of their internal vulnerabilities. For example, HP research found that 90% apps are vulnerable after analyzing 2107 apps from companies on the Forbes Global 2000 (Seltzer, 2013). The latest application security report from Arxan shows that 90% of 126 mobile health and finance apps under investigation contain at least two critical security vulnerabilities (Arxan, Inc., 2016). Our study of 557 randomly collected apps with at least one million installations reveals that 375 apps (67.3%) had at least one vulnerability (Qian et al., 2015). There are many potential reasons for this embarrassing situation, such as short development cycles, lack of security awareness, insufficient security development guidelines.

In this chapter, we survey the vulnerabilities found in Android apps by collecting vulnerability reports from many sources, such as common vulnerabilities and exposures (CVE), because Android has occupied more than 80% of global market. Besides introducing major vulnerabilities in Android apps, we model how to discover them as graph traversals so that

---

[1] http://www.statista.com/statistics/266210/number-of-available-applications-in-the-google-play-store/

[2] http://www.pocketgamer.biz/metrics/app-store/

[3] http://venturebeat.com/2016/02/10/the-app-economy-could-double-to-101b-by-2020-research-firm-says/

Mobile Security and Privacy
http://dx.doi.org/10.1016/B978-0-12-804629-6.00007-9

VulHunter (described in Section 2.3) can use them to check whether an app has such vulnerabilities. Note that VulHunter uses Android property graphs (APGs) to represent apps and store them in the graph database. We also review the approaches for discovering various vulnerabilities in apps, which could leverage static analysis or dynamic analysis or the hybrid approach. Moreover, we discuss the limitations of existing approaches and suggest future directions of research (Heelan, 2011).

The chapter is organized as follows: Section 2 gives an introduction to the taxonomy of vulnerabilities in Android apps and the architecture of VulHunter. We introduce and model various common vulnerabilities in Section 3. Section 4 reviews existing approaches for discovering vulnerable apps and Section 5 discusses their limitations. We conclude the paper in Section 6.

2 BACKGROUND

2.1 Security Mechanisms of Android

We introduce three security mechanisms that are closely related to major vulnerabilities in apps: process sandbox, permission mechanism, and signature mechanism. There are other important security mechanisms in Android, such as interprocess secure communication mechanism, memory management mechanism, system partitions, and loading mechanism. Interested readers can refer to the relevant papers (Enck et al., 2009; Drake et al., 2014) for details.

Process sandbox. Android's process sandbox mechanism achieves a separation between apps. It creates a Dalvik virtual machine (DVM) instance for each app and grants a UID as the identification in the app installing process. In the Linux kernel, UID acts as the identification for different users. By default, different apps are separated. If they need to visit each other directly, they can set their SharedUserID to the same value.

Permission mechanism. Android's permission mechanism defines whether the app has the ability to access protected APIs and resources. The main functionalities of the permission mechanism include: permission confirmation during installation, permission check, permission use, and permission management during execution. A permission statement includes the permission name, the group it belongs to, and the protection level, which includes normal, dangerous, signature, signature or system. Developers can declare permissions required by the app through <uses-permission> tag in AndroidManifest.xml.

Signature mechanism. All apps must be signed with a private key before being released. The signature can be used to confirm the identity of developers, to test whether an app has any changes, and to establish a trusted relationship between two apps. Signature methods are divided into debug mode and release mode. The signature in debug mode is used for program testing during development, and the signature in release mode is used for publishing apps to markets.

2.2 Taxonomy of Android App Vulnerability

We have made a collection of 242 Android vulnerabilities, which have detailed information from many sources such as, vulnerability databases, security communities, and so on. After analyzing these vulnerabilities according to CERT Secure Coding Standards (CERT, 2015) and the OWASP's Mobile Security Project (OWASP, 2015), we classify the 242 vulnerabilities into 20 categories, as shown in Fig. 1, and number them M1-M20 (M20 can be negligible,

Name	Vulnerability Name	Name	Vulnerability Name
M1	Weak server side controls	M11	Linux kernel universal vulnerability
M2	Insecure data storage	M12	Program logic design flaw
M3	Insufficient transport layer protection	M13	Signatures vulnerability
M4	Unintended data leakage	M14	Code execution vulnerability
M5	Poor authorization and authentication	M15	Malicious application behavior vulnerability
M6	Broken cryptography	M16	Mobile terminal web vulnerability
M7	Client side injection	M17	Applications communications vulnerability
M8	Security decisions via untrusted inputs	M18	Configuration error vulnerability
M9	Webview vulnerability	M19	Denial of service vulnerability
M10	Linux kernel driver vulnerability	M20	others

FIG. 1   Taxonomy of Android vulnerability.

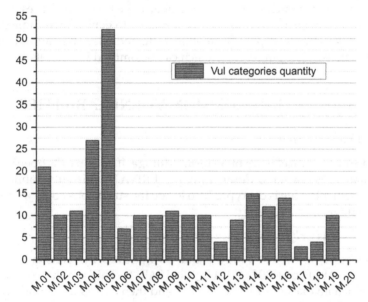

FIG. 2   Distribution of Android vulnerabilities.

because its number is very small). It is worth noting that M1-M8 are based on OWASP Mobile Risk Top10. Fig. 2 depicts the distribution of these vulnerabilities. It shows that most of the reported vulnerabilities result from poor authorization and authentication as well as unintended data leakage.

2.3 VulHunter

We proposed and developed Vulhunter to discover common vulnerabilities in Android apps (Qian et al., 2015). Given an app, Vulhunter will turn its dex file into an APG which integrates the abstract syntax tree (AST), interprocedure control-flow graph (ICFG), method call graph (MCG), and system dependency graph (SDG) of the app, and is stored in a graph database. Moreover, we model five common vulnerabilities as graph traversals and perform them over APGs to determine whether an app is vulnerable. We have demonstrated in Qian et al. (2015) how to discover syntax level, control flow level, and data flow level vulnerabilities. In this chapter, we will cover more vulnerabilities and model how to identify them as graph traversals following (Qian et al., 2015). For ease of explanation, we will use the following symbols in this chapter:

$$MATCH^p_{label};\tag{1}$$

$$ARG(N)_i;\tag{2}$$

$$N_1 - [R^p_{type}]^{len} \rightarrow N_2,\tag{3}$$

where,

- $MATCH^p_{label}$ represents matching nodes with label `label` and properties p.
- $ARG(N)_i$ indicates traversing from *Invoke-Stmt* node N to get its *i*th argument.
- $N_1 - [R^p_{type}]^{len} \rightarrow N_2$ denotes a path from node N1 to node N2. The path is connected by relationship `type` with length of `len`, which can be omitted if it equals 1.

3 MODELING COMMON VULNERABILITIES

3.1 Insecure Data Storage

Sensitive information disclosure on external storage. If an app calls openFileOutput() but the second parameter is not set to Context.MODE_PRIVATE, this vulnerability may happen depending on whether the file is encrypted. To locate the suspicious code, we can conduct the following graph traversals:

$$MATCH^{p3}_{ast} \circ ARG(N)_2 \circ MATCH^{p2}_{stmt},\tag{4}$$

where p2 refers to `openFileOutput` and p3 indicates the constant parameter node `MODE_WORLD_READABLE` or `MODE_WORLD_WRITEABLE`. This graph traversal first locates the **statement** which invokes `openFileOutput` and then checks its second parameter. If the parameter in the AST tree is p3, the app may have such vulnerability.

3.2 Insufficient Transport Layer Protection

SSL/TLS trusts all certificates. When using SSL, if the app invokes setHostnameVerifier() with the parameter ALLOW_ALL_HOSTNAME_VERIFIER, this vulnerability exists, which could make the app vulnerable to the MITM (man-in-the-middle) attack. To detect the problematic code, we can use the following graph traversals:

$$MATCH^{p2}_{ast} \circ ARG(N)_1 \circ MATCH^{p1}_{stmt}\tag{5}$$

where p1 represents `setHostnameVerifier` and p2 denotes `ALLOW_ALL_HOSTNAME_ VERIFIER`. This graph traversal first matches the statements which invoke method p1, and then checks whether its first parameter in the AST tree matches p2. If so, the vulnerability exists.

3.3 Unintended Data Leakage

Log sensitive information disclosure. If an app uses one of the following methods to save sensitive information: Log.d(), Log.e(), Log.i(), Log.v(), Log.w(), such a vulnerability may exist, because when the terminal is connected to the PC, Log information can be accessed. To detect such a vulnerability, we can use the following graph traversal:

$$MATCH_{stmt}^{p1} - [R_{SDG_{Data}}]^+ -> MATCH_{stmt}^{p2} \tag{6}$$

where p1 denotes sink functions, such as *Log.i()*, *Log.d()*, and p2 refers to source functions that collect sensitive information, such as *getDeviceID()*. If there exists a path from source functions to sink functions, the vulnerability may exist. The edges on this path have a data dependency relationship.

3.4 Poor Authorization and Authentication

Exposed components (e.g., `contentProvider`, `service`). In the <provider> or <activity> tag of AndroidManifest.xml, if there is not the android:exported="false" statement for apps that set either `android:minSdkVersion` or `android:targetSdkVersion` to a value less than 17 or if the value of the statement is true, such a vulnerability may exist.

Intent leakage or tampering caused by permission granting. If there is an implicit intent broadcasting method call and there is a permission statement with a property value of FLAG_GRANT_WRITE_URI_PERMISSION or FLAG_GRANT_READ_URI_PERMISSION, then such a vulnerability may exist. To locate the suspicious code, we can use the following graph traversal:

$$MATCH_{stmt}^{p1} - [R_{SDG_{Data}}]^+ -> MATCH_{stmt}^{p2} \tag{7}$$

$$MATCH_{ast}^{p3} \circ ARG(N)_1 \circ MATCH_{stmt}^{p2} \tag{8}$$

where p1 refers to *Context.sendBroadcast()*, p2 denotes *intent.addFlags()*, and p3 indicates FLAG_GRANT_WRITE_URI_PERMISSION. After finding the statements that call *Context. sendBroadcast()*, we check the intent initialization function *intent.addFlags()*. If any of them uses FLAG_GRANT_WRITE_URI_PERMISSION as a parameter, this vulnerability may exist.

3.5 Broken Cryptography

Weak AES encryption mode. AES encryption is initialized using javax.crypto.Cipher. If an app uses the ECB mode, the same plaintext will lead to the same ciphertext, which is vulnerable to dictionary attacks. We could use the following graph traversal to identify the corresponding problematic code:

$$MATCH_{stmt}^{p1} \tag{9}$$

$$MATCH_{ast}^{p2} \circ ARG(N)_1 \circ MATCH_{stmt}^{p1} \tag{10}$$

where p1 refers to *Ciper.getInstance* and p2 denotes *AES/ECB/PKCS5Padding*. We first identify the statements that call *Ciper.getInstance*, and then check whether their first parameter is *AES/ECB/PKCS5Padding*. If so, the vulnerability may exist.

3.6 Webview Vulnerability

WebView malicious code execution. Such vulnerability exists in the system with API level less than 17. If the method webView.addJavascriptInterface() is called, and the applicable versions of the app in AndroidManifest.xml are not limited to API level 17 or above, the vulnerability may exist. We can use the following graph traversal to identify the vulnerable code:

$$MATCH_{stmt}^{p1} \tag{11}$$

where p1 denotes *webView.addJavascriptInterface*. After finding a statement that invokes this method, we check whether the minSdkVersion in manifest file is less than 17. If so, the vulnerability may exist.

3.7 App Communication Vulnerability

Content disclosure of implicit Intent broadcast. Intent is used for exchanging information between components in the same app or between apps. Note that using implicit Intent broadcast may lead to the disclosure of Intent contents. More precisely, if there is an invocation of the implicit Intent broadcasting method Context.sendBroadcast(), it will cause this problem. Therefore we can easily identify this issue using the following graph traversal:

$$MATCH_{stmt}^{p1} \tag{12}$$

where p1 denotes Context.sendBroadcast().

3.8 Configuration Error Vulnerability

Information disclosure due to the incorrect setting. Before releasing an app, the developer should ensure that the app is not debuggable in AndroidManifest.xml (android:debuggable="false"). Otherwise, such a vulnerability may exist.

4 DISCOVERING VULNERABILITIES

In this section, we review mechanisms for discovering vulnerabilities. They can be classified into three categories: static analysis-based methods, dynamic analysis-based methods, and hybrid methods. The static analysis-based methods usually investigate the Dalvik bytecode in the dex file or the Java class files converted from the dex file without running the app. The dynamic analysis-based methods commonly execute the app and monitor its behaviors, based on which vulnerabilities could be identified. Since both static analysis and dynamic analysis have their pros and cons, researchers propose hybrid methods that leverage the advantages of static and dynamic analysis.

4.1 Static Analysis-Based Approaches

Grace et al. studied the vulnerability of capability leaks, which belongs to M5 in Fig. 1, and developed a static analysis-based detection tool named Woodpecker, which could discover both explicit and implicit capability leaks (Grace et al., 2012). Woodpecker builds CFGs of apps and then leverages the CFGs to determine whether there is privilege leakage. Specifically, for the explicit capability leakage, it inspects the preinstalled apps in the system by checking whether their components are exposed. If so, it conducts further path analysis to determine whether the leakage exists. For the implicit capability leakage, it checks each app's sharedUserId in Manifest. If it is used, this app's capability in terms of requested permissions is exposed to the apps with the shared UID.

Wei et al. proposed and developed Amandroid (Wei et al., 2014), a static analysis framework, for detecting intercomponent communication vulnerabilities, which include those in M4 and M17 in Fig. 1. More precisely, given an app, it first turns the Dalvik bytecode into intermediate representation (IR) and then constructs the IDFGs (intercomponent data flow graph) and DDGs (data dependence graph). After that, Amandroid looks for potential vulnerabilities from IDFGs and DDGs, including data leakage, data injection, and APIs misuse. Note that when building IDFGs, Amandroid computes the point-to information for all objects and fields in order to find the target of intent precisely.

Lu et al. developed CHEX (Lu et al., 2012) to identify component hijacking vulnerabilities, which cover those in M4, M5, and M7 in Fig. 1, such as permission disclosure, unauthorized data acquisition, intent deception, etc. CHEX employs data flow summaries to model the execution of entry points, and utilizes data flow analysis based on data dependency graphs to locate hijacking vulnerability. They further enhanced CHEX by proposing AAPL (Lu et al., 2015) to detect privacy leakage vulnerabilities. AAPL can reduce false positives. It combines a variety of static analysis methods, including opportunistic constant evaluation, object origin inference, and joint flow tracking, to detect more invisible data flows. Furthermore, AAPL employs a new approach called peer voting to filter out most of the legitimate privacy disclosures from the results, purifying the detection results for automatic and easy interpretation.

Gordon et al. proposed DroidSafe (Gordon et al., 2015) for statically detecting the apps' data stream related vulnerabilities, which include those in M4 in Fig. 1. DroidSafe creates models for 117 classes in the Java standard library as well as the Android library, Android runtime, and apps hidden state maintained by the Android runtime. It makes global resolution of Intent and Uri, and traces IntentFilter. By analyzing the sensitive data flows in apps, DroidSafe establishes the data flow graphs from sources to sinks. DroidSafe has covered all possible forms of communication to ensure a high coverage. Experimental results show that compared to other methods, DroidSafe increases the detection rate of sensitive data flow by about 10%.

Cao et al. designed and realized EDGEMINER (Cao et al., 2015) to address the issue of implicit control flow transitions through the Android framework. It analyzes the Android framework and constructs the call graphs to find potential callbacks. By using backward data flow analysis to identify registration-callback pairs, EDGEMINER outputs framework summary and then employs other static analysis tools for further analysis of apps.

Fahl et al. developed MalloDroid (Fahl et al., 2012) for studying the MITM vulnerability in Android apps. This tool can be integrated into the app market or installed in the user's mobile device. MalloDroid will inspect apps during installation. If it identifies potential SSL MITM vulnerability in an app, users will be alerted.

4.2 Dynamic Analysis-Based Approaches

Xing et al. discovered the severe vulnerability relevant to Android's upgrading mechanism. In particular, malware that lurks in the lower version system could get privilege rights after the system upgrades, then get access to users' data privacy. To spot such a vulnerability, the authors have developed the detection tool named SecUP. It constructs a database for saving exploit entry points and has a scanner for vulnerability identification. The detection module has constraint rules for determining the existence of vulnerabilities.

Wang et al. investigated the mobile-end same-origin policy (SOP) bypass vulnerability (Wang et al., 2013), and proposed a detection mechanism named Marbs. This system marks the source of information for each communication message and strengthen the SOP strength. The core of Marbs includes setOriginPolicy and checkOriginPolicy, which are implanted into DVM thread. SetOriginPolicy is open to all apps, and checkOriginPolicy is for the system kernel.

Wu et al. investigated the security impact of vendor customization on the Android system (Wu et al., 2013) and designed a system named SEFA to detect potential vulnerabilities. SEFA consists of three parts: including provenance analysis, permission usage analysis, and vulnerability analysis. First, it conducts provenance analysis, classifying the system apps into three categories, namely AOSP native applications, vendor-specific apps, and third-party apps. Then it performs the authorization analysis on the apps in order to check whether sensitive permissions are used. Finally, it checks whether there are redelegation vulnerabilities and privacy disclosure vulnerabilities.

Schrittwieser et al. studies the vulnerabilities in mobile messaging and VoIP apps (Schrittwieser et al., 2012). By conducting dynamic testing, it found vulnerabilities in VoIP and message apps' authentication mechanisms. The vulnerable apps make the user's phone number as the only certification basis, triggering a series of safety risks, such as account hijacking, spoof sender-IDs, and enumerating subscribers.

Hay et al. examined the IAC (Inter-Application Communication) vulnerability (Hay et al., 2015) and developed a new system named INTENT-DROID. It triggers sensitive APIs by constructing and sending probe intents. The externally observable indications are used to validate the test. The experimental result shows that INTENT-DROID can find a lot of IAC vulnerabilities in apps.

4.3 Hybrid Approaches

Sounthiraraj et al. investigated the SSL MITM vulnerability (Sounthiraraj et al., 2014). It first conducts static analysis to identify apps that may have such a vulnerability by examining the implementation of X509TrustManager and HostNameVerifier. More precisely, it identifies key entry points and builds the input function set for the next phase of dynamic trigger detection. Then, it applies UI automation to the key entry points of windows for triggering HTTPS communications, whose traffic will go through the MITM proxy. At the same time, the log of dynamic analysis will be recorded and used to determine whether the SSL MITM vulnerability exists.

Bhoraskar et al. developed Brahamstra (Bhoraskar et al., 2014) for detecting third-party component vulnerabilities in apps. It addresses the weakness of existing GUI testing tools and can efficiently locate the triggering points of third-party libraries. First, the Execution Planner constructs page transition graphs to find execution paths to third-party libraries through static analysis. Then, the Execution Engine triggers apps in the simulator following the executable paths. Finally, the Runtime Analyzer captures and records running apps' operating status to determine whether there are third-party library vulnerabilities. To improve the speed of execution engine, Brahmastr rewrites app binaries to insert code that automatically invokes the callbacks triggered by the user.

Zhou et al. examined two types of vulnerabilities related to content providers, including passive content leakage and content pollution (Zhou and Jiang, 2013). They developed a detection tool named ContentScope. It firstly filters out apps that do not have exported content providers. Then, ContentScope determines the vulnerable apps by traversing the path from public content provider interface to the low-level database-operating routines in control flow graph. It will conduct dynamic analysis to confirm the vulnerability in apps.

5 DISCUSSION

5.1 Limitations in Static Analysis-Based Methods

By analyzing the bytecode instead of executing the app, static analysis may quickly locate problematic codes and achieve high code coverage. However, it suffers from several limitations. First, since it does not run the app, it is difficult to investigate codes using dynamic language features. For example, Java reflection is widely used in many apps, but it is challenging to investigate it in a precise and scalable manner (Smaragdakis et al., 2014). Moreover, apps could use dynamic class loading to dynamically extend its functionality. Static analysis cannot examine the dynamically loaded class if it is on the remote server. Besides using dynamic language features, more and more apps will employ the hardening services (or packing services) to protect themselves (Zhang et al., 2015b). Note that the dex file in the packed app does not contain the app's major functionalities, thus impeding static analysis.

Second, UI components can be dynamically added, and they will usually react to certain events, such as user input. Without executing the app, static analysis may miss such dynamic UI components and/or the reactions to certain events (Rountev and Yan, 2014; Shao et al., 2014). Third, the callback mechanism provided and orchestrated by the Android framework introduces challenging issues to static analysis (Cao et al., 2015), such as how to trace the information flow through the Android framework, etc. Note that the majority of existing studies just focus on apps, and they will be affected by the issues introduced by the Android framework. Fourth, there are still many open problems in static program analysis, such as pointer analysis, implicit flow analysis, and concurrent program analysis, to name a few (Hind, 2001). Moreover, given more than two million apps, how to quickly spot vulnerable apps is non-trivial.

5.2 Limitations in Dynamic Analysis-Based Methods

Since dynamic analysis executes apps, it has a high accuracy rate and will not be affected by hardening services. However, it also has some limitations. First, the code coverage rate of dynamic analysis is low because it will take a very long time to execute all paths. Second, many existing dynamic analysis methods use emulator (e.g., QEMU) for analyzing apps. However, emulators may not support all features in a real smartphone, such as various sensors, USB, etc. Furthermore, a number of approaches for detecting emulator have been proposed (Jing et al., 2014), which may render many existing approaches useless. Third, the majority of existing approaches do not handle implicit flows. Note that tracking implicit flows could reveal more security vulnerabilities. However, it is challenging to track implicit flows (King et al., 2008).

5.3 Future Directions

Based on the above analysis, we list a few future directions to stir up research efforts into this important area. First, since static analysis and dynamic analysis have their own advantages and disadvantages, it is a promising approach to combine them together. For example, static analysis can quickly locate suspicious codes, guide the fuzzing test, generate GUI test cases, etc. Dynamic analysis can track the information flows, handle dynamic language features, etc. Second, since more and more apps employ various obfuscation and hardening techniques to protect themselves from being reverse engineered and analyzed, such techniques also make the detection of vulnerability more difficult. How to effectively and efficiently recover the original dex file is an interesting research problem. Third, although we summarize a number of vulnerabilities, there is a lack of formal approaches to represent them. Moreover, methods for discovering new vulnerability patterns are desirable. Leveraging machine learning techniques and incorporating more information in addition to code (Zhang et al., 2015a) would be a promising approach.

6 SUMMARY

In this chapter, we survey the vulnerabilities found in Android apps by collecting vulnerability reports from many sources, such as CVE. Besides introducing major vulnerabilities in Android apps, we model how to discover them as graph traversals following the definition in VulHunter Qian et al. (2015). We also review the approaches for discovering various vulnerabilities in apps, which could leverage static analysis, dynamic analysis, or the hybrid approach. Moreover, we discuss some limitations in existing approaches and suggest future directions of research.

References

Arxan, Inc, 2016. 5th annual state of application security report. https://goo.gl/mAqfx3.

Bhoraskar, R., Han, S., Jeon, J., Azim, T., Chen, S., Jung, J., Nath, S., Wang, R., Wetherall, D., 2014. Brahmastra: driving apps to test the security of third-party components. In: Proceedings of the 23rd USENIX Security Symposium (USENIX Security 14), USENIX Association. pp. 1021–1036.

Cao, Y., Fratantonio, Y., Bianchi, A., Egele, M., Kruegel, C., Vigna, G., Chen, Y., 2015. Edgeminer: automatically detecting implicit control flow transitions through the android framework. In: Proceedings of the ISOC Network and Distributed System Security Symposium (NDSS).

CERT, 2015. Secure coding standards. https://www.securecoding.cert.org/confluence/pages/viewpage.action?pageId=111509535 (accessed August 15, 2015).

Drake, J.J., Lanier, Z., Mulliner, C., Fora, P.O., Ridley, S.A., Wicherski, G., 2014. Android Hacker's Handbook. John Wiley & Sons, New York.

Enck, W., Ongtang, M., McDaniel, P., 2009. Understanding android security. IEEE Secur. Privacy 7 (1), 50–57.

Fahl, S., Harbach, M., Muders, T., Baumgartner, L., Freisleben, B., Smith, M., 2012. Why eve and mallory love android: an analysis of android SSL insecurity. In: Proceedings of ACM CCS.

Gordon, M.I., Kim, D., Perkins, J., Gilham, L., Nguyen, N., Rinard, M., 2015. Information-flow analysis of android applications in droidsafe. In: Proceedings of the Network and Distributed System Security Symposium (NDSS). The Internet Society.

Grace, M., Zhou, Y., Wang, Z., Jiang, X., 2012. Systematic detection of capability leaks in stock android smartphones. In: Proceedings of NDSS.

Hay, R., Tripp, O., Pistoia, M., 2015. Dynamic detection of inter-application communication vulnerabilities in android. In: Proceedings of the 2015 International Symposium on Software Testing and Analysis.

Heelan, S., 2011. Vulnerability detection systems: think cyborg, not robot. IEEE Secur. Privacy 9 (3), 74–77.

Hind, M., 2001. Pointer analysis: haven't we solved this problem yet? In: Proceedings of the 2001 ACM SIGPLAN-SIGSOFT Workshop on Program Analysis for Software Tools and Engineering. ACM, pp. 54–61.

Jing, Y., Zhao, Z., Ahn, G.J., Hu, H., 2014. Morpheus: automatically generating heuristics to detect android emulators. In: Proceedings of ACSAC.

King, D., Hicks, B., Hicks, M., Jaeger, T., 2008. Implicit flows: can't live with 'em, can't live without 'em. Information Systems Security, Springer, New York, pp. 56–70.

Lu, L., Li, Z., Wu, Z., Lee, W., Jiang, G., 2012. Chex: statically vetting android apps for component hijacking vulnerabilities. In: Proceedings of CCS.

Lu, K., Li, Z., Kemerlis, V., Wu, Z., Lu, L., Zheng, C., Qian, Z., Lee, W., Jiang, G., 2015. Checking more and alerting less: detecting privacy leakages via enhanced data-flow analysis and peer voting. In: Proceedings of NDSS.

OWASP, 2015. OWASP mobile security project. https://www.owasp.org/index.php/Projects/OWASP_Mobile_Security_Project_-_Top_Ten_Mobile_Risks (accessed August 15, 2015).

Qian, C., Luo, X., Le, Y., Gu, G., 2015. Vulhunter: toward discovering vulnerabilities in android applications. IEEE Micro 35 (1), 44–53.

Rountev, A., Yan, D., 2014. Static reference analysis for GUI objects in Android software. In: Proceedings of the International Symposium on Code Generation and Optimization, pp. 143–153.

Sawers, P., 2015. Android users have an average of 95 apps installed on their phones, according to yahoo aviate data. http://goo.gl/cfs1bf.

Schrittwieser, S., Frühwirt, P., Kieseberg, P., Leithner, M., Mulazzani, M., Huber, M., Weippl, E.R., 2012. Guess who's texting you? evaluating the security of smartphone messaging applications. In: Proceedings of NDSS.

Seltzer, L., 2013. HP research finds vulnerabilities in 9 of 10 mobile apps. http://goo.gl/esxBkb.

Shao, Y., Luo, X., Qian, C., Zhu, P., Zhang, L., 2014. Towards a scalable resource-driven approach for detecting repackaged android applications. In: Proceedings of the 30th Annual Computer Security Applications Conference (ACSAC).

Smaragdakis, Y., Kastrinis, G., Balatsouras, G., Bravenboer, M., 2014. More sound static handling of java reflection. Technical report.

Sounthiraraj, D., Sahs, J., Greenwood, G., Lin, Z., Khan, L., 2014. SMV-hunter: large scale, automated detection of SSL/TLS man-in-the-middle vulnerabilities in android apps. In: Proceedings of NDSS.

Wang, R., Xing, L., Wang, X., Chen, S., 2013. Unauthorized origin crossing on mobile platforms: threats and mitigation. In: Proceedings of the 2013 ACM SIGSAC of Conference on Computer & Communications Security. ACM, pp. 635–646.

Wei, F., Roy, S., Ou, X., et al., 2014. Amandroid: a precise and general inter-component data flow analysis framework for security vetting of android apps. In: Proceedings of the 2014 ACM SIGSAC Conference on Computer and Communications Security. ACM, pp. 1329–1341.

Wu, L., Grace, M., Zhou, Y., Wu, C., Jiang, X., 2013. The impact of vendor customizations on android security. In: Proceedings of ACM CCS.

Zhang, T., Jiang, H., Luo, X., Chan, A.T., 2015. A literature review of research in bug resolution: tasks, challenges and future directions. Comput. J. 59 (5), 741–773.

Zhang, Y., Luo, X., Yin, H., 2015. Dexhunter: toward extracting hidden code from packed android applications. In: Proceedings of ESORICS.

Zhou, Y., Jiang, X., 2013. Detecting passive content leaks and pollution in android applications. In: Proceedings of NDSS.

ABOUT THE AUTHORS

Xiaoqi Li received his B.S. from Central South University and is a graduate student at the Chinese Academy of Sciences. His research focuses on Android security and vulnerability.

Le Yu received his B.S. and M.S. from Nanjing University of Posts and Telecommunications. He is currently a research assistant at Hong Kong Polytechnic University. His research focuses on Android security and privacy.

Xiapu Luo is a research assistant professor in the Department of Computing at Hong Kong Polytechnic University. His research focuses on smartphone security, network security and privacy, and Internet measurement.

A Study of the Effectiveness Abs Reliability of Android Free Anti-Mobile Malware Apps

J. Walls*, K.-K.R. Choo*,†

*University of South Australia, Adelaide, SA, Australia

†University of Texas at San Antonio, San Antonio, TX, United States

1 INTRODUCTION

Smartphones are popular for both personal and corporate use, and they are becoming the new personal computer due to their portability, ease of use, and functionality (e.g., video conferencing, Internet browsing, email correspondence, persistent wireless and data connectivity, worldwide map location services, and countless mobile apps). It is, therefore, not surprising that the number of smartphone devices reached 336 million units worldwide, which was an increase of 19.3% in the first quarter of 2015. Continued growth is expected throughout 2015 and 2016, particularly for devices running Android operating system (OS). The latter's worldwide market share is 78.9% at the end of the first quarter 2015. With a majority of the smartphone market share worldwide, the Android OS also surpassed a billion shipments of devices in 2014 (Rivera and Goasduff, 2015; Rivera and van der Meulen, 2015).

Given the flexibility and ease of operation that mobile OS permits, hardware manufacturers are able to develop faster and more powerful devices that incorporate a wide range of functionalities for everyday use; for example, larger display screens, integrated browsing, media support for video, audio and images, a gyroscope and other real-world sensors, access to Global System for Mobile Communications (GSM), Enhanced Data for GSM Evolution (EDGE), 3G, 4G Long-Term Evolution (LTE) data, Bluetooth, Wi-Fi, a built-in digital camera, and Global Positioning System (GPS) components.

Vulnerabilities in hardware and software functionalities can, however, be exploited by criminals. Examples include "phishing" attacks facilitated by mobile apps, such as instant messaging apps (see Chu et al., 2013). Apps can be designed to provide access to sensitive user data (e.g., contact lists and geolocation information) should the permissions be granted by the user.

Unfortunately, with the openness and widespread adoption of the Android OS, the platform is the most targeted of the four popular mobile platforms by malware authors (Symantec Corporation, et al., 2014; APWG, 2013). Another recent study of mobile malware, for example, reported that "Android devices are currently the most targeted, accounting for 60% of the infections observed in the mobile network" (Alcatel-Lucent, 2013, p. 7), and examples of mobile malware targeting Android devices including Android.Ackposts, a malicious mobile app (also known as "Battery Long") designed to steal personal data from a compromised device and upload details to a remote server, were detected (Symantec Intelligence, 2012). Other malware includes short message service (SMS) Trojan viruses, false advertising modules that contain malware, and sophisticated web-based malware that use various exploits in order to gain root access.

In this chapter, we investigate the effectiveness and reliability of 15 popular free antimobile malware apps in detecting malware on three Android devices running three different Android flavors, namely KitKat (4.4.x), Jelly Bean (4.1.x), and Ice Cream Sandwich (4.0.x). Two newer Android flavors were also taken into consideration, specifically Lollipop (5.x), which was released in late 2014, and Marshmallow (6.0), which was released in late 2015. However, the relative number of devices running Lollipop (23.5% distribution) and Marshmallow (distribution not currently available) were considerably lower than that of earlier versions, such as KitKat, where distribution is 38.9% (Dashboards as of Oct. 11, 2015, Android Developers Dashboards, 2015). Along with higher distribution across multiple devices, KitKat, Jelly Bean, and Ice Cream Sandwich demonstrate enough history and stability for this study, whereas Lollipop and Marshmallow would have too much flux and unknown variables; thus they were not included within this study and are subject to further analysis. This is, to the best of our knowledge, the first academic systematic study that has been conducted through a manual experiment process of 15 popular free antimalware apps for Android devices. Our findings will contribute to a better understanding of the effectiveness and reliability of such apps for Android devices, and it potentially serves as a guide for future antimalware app developers.

The chapter is organized as follows: In Section 2, we present an overview of Android OS and app security and describe the malware threats and existing countermeasures. Our experiment setup and findings are presented in Sections 3 and 4, respectively. Section 3 outlines the experiment process in detail, in which 15 popular free antimalware apps are measured against a suit of 15 known malware samples. Each test will be performed manually to replicate a day-to-day user who unknowingly installs a malicious app. The results will hopefully demonstrate the effectiveness and reliability of how well the antimalware app performed. After the experiment process, Section 4 outlines the findings of all the test results against their respective metric values, which allow for possible analysis of particular performance issues and their improvements. The last section concludes this chapter and discusses future research topics.

2 AN OVERVIEW OF ANDROID

2.1 The Android OS

2.1.1 System Framework and Architecture

A major advantage of the Android OS is that it is part of the Open Handset Alliance (OHA) consortium, which provides flexibility for device manufacturers and software and app developers, as the environment has fewer restrictions and compatibility issues across multiple hardware devices. The core building blocks of the Android software platform, which is based on the open-source Linux OS and uses the Linux Kernel, have been modified specifically for smartphones (Nimodia and Deshmukh, 2012).

The Android OS system architecture comprises five main architecture layers, each with its own functionality and benefits for interoperability across different devices (Fig. 1). The Linux Kernel is the first layer, residing at the bottom of the architecture. It is considered to be the core layer, as it includes all physical-level operations, such as hardware device drivers. The remaining layers build on the Linux Kernel and perform their own functions. The second layer is Libraries, where native libraries are developed in C/C++ to ensure smooth OS functionality when accessing multiple apps at once. Additional features facilitate Internet-related functions and data storage, such as web browsing (Nimodia and Deshmukh, 2012).

The third layer is the Android Runtime (ART). This layer uses Java programming and operates its own virtual environment, Dalvik Virtual Machine (DVM), for developing Android apps. Application Framework is the fourth layer and comprises several individual components that manage various application frameworks, such as built-in default apps, including email and a web browser (e.g., open-source WebKit browser or Chrome in later versions). Due to the many components and its functionality, this is one of the main layers within the Android system framework (Nimodia and Deshmukh, 2012).

Finally, Applications is the fifth layer. This represents the top of the architecture, and it is where app downloads and installs are located (Nimodia and Deshmukh, 2012). These five layers make up the overall Kernel, and assist with the operation and functionality of the Android OS architecture as a whole.

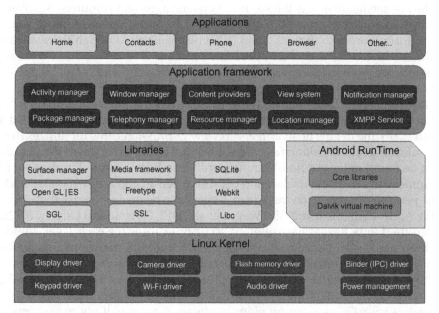

FIG. 1 Android OS system architecture. *Adapted from Android Platform Security Architecture, Android software stack, viewed 28 June 2014. https://source.android.com/devices/tech/security/index.html#android-platform-security-architecture.*

Although these five underlying layers give Android OS immense development capabilities and allow developers to produce a variety of features and variables in their apps, security measures must be considered in order to help protect hardware devices, network resources, and software design, such as ensuring the security and privacy of user data and avoiding the exploitation of app privileges.

2.1.2 Security Architecture

Within the Linux Kernel, there are a number of security features in place throughout each of the five layers that have their own functions but work together by layering on top of each other to provide a security model. This enables the Android OS to become more secure and restrict access to core file system activities and storage locations, such as root system files. Some of these features include the following:

Linux Kernel—The fundamental purpose of the Kernel is a user-based permission model. Key security features include device encryption to prevent unauthorized access, independently isolating processes, the ability to remove unsecured or unnecessary sections of the kernel, and allow integration between the additional system layers. The Linux Kernel also refers to file system permissions, which isolate resources from one another; for example, preventing User A from altering User B's files. The Linux Kernel also provides an application sandbox environment within the libraries and ART layer (Vargas et al., 2012).

Libraries and ART—A primary security feature of the Android OS is the application sandbox environment, where the Linux Kernel enforces security between apps and the system so they are unable to interact with each other. This effectively isolates resources and data files from other apps by assigning each installed app a unique user ID (UID) and a group ID (GID). As in the example above, User A will not have the level of permission to alter User B's files (Vargas et al., 2012).

Application communication—As the security between apps and resources is isolated by default, interapp communication is possible by way of the application communication feature that uses an Inter-Process Communication (IPC) mechanism. Although there are additional functionalities with how IPC interacts, the basic principle is to gather the two main sections of information, one from the receiving end and one from where data shall be passed, which allows purposeful interaction (Ongtang et al., 2012).

Application permissions: Any installed app must have a digital signature, or security certificate, that validates the legitimacy of an app and confirms the app developer's details. As the user can verify the details of an app and review permissions, this minimizes the security risk of downloading and installing fake apps. Essential information about the permissions of an app can be found in the AndroidManifest.xml file, which is located in the root directory. This is an important security consideration because when an app is downloaded and the user accepts the permissions shown on the screen, a check can be made to verify these permissions through the AndroidManifest.xml file (Vargas et al., 2012; Pieterse and Olivier, 2012).

Although the Linux Kernel has different security features for each layer, these features have not been used in all version releases of the Android OS. New versions are becoming more frequent as development continues, contributing to the software improvements outlined in Table 1. For example, earlier Android versions, such as 2.3 (Gingerbread), have a less advanced security model compared with that of newer versions, such as 4.3 (Jelly Bean). Unfortunately, earlier OS versions on older hardware devices will not receive any software updates, as a hardware upgrade is required. This is mainly due to improved hardware and

TABLE 1 Android Version History as of Oct. 11, 2015 (Amadeo, 2014; Android Developers Dashboards, 2015)

OS Name	Version	Release Dates	Application Programming Interface (API)	Distribution	Key Features and Improvements
n.a.	1.0	Sep. 2008	–	–	Initial release of Android with full handset functionality and features such as Android Market, Google Maps/Calendar/Contacts, Short Message Service (SMS)/Multimedia Messaging Service (MMS), telephony, web browser, email, video, camera, Wi-Fi, and Bluetooth capability
n.a.	1.1	Feb. 2009	–	–	Maintenance release to 1.0 and device hardware
Cupcake	1.5	Apr. 2009	–	–	Uses Linux Kernel 2.6.27; additions include screen rotation, various widget support, enhanced animation, predictive text and soft keyboard, browser update, Picasa introduction, and YouTube video uploads
Donut	1.6	Sep. 2009	–	–	Uses Kernel 2.6.29; faster searching, picture and video gallery, battery indicator, text-to-speech, and new API framework
Eclair	2.x	Oct. 2006–Jan. 2010	–	–	Uses Kernel 2.6.29; introduces the use of multiple accounts, Google Maps navigation, calendar and contacts sync with Gmail/Exchange, HTML5 support, live wallpaper, additional APIs introduced, and optimized hardware
Froyo	2.2.x	May 2010–Nov. 2011	8	0.7%	Uses Kernel 2.6.32; improved performance, Java process improvement in DVM, Chrome, tethering, wireless access point (WAP), Adobe Flash, cloud-to-device messaging (C2DM), data access control, and additional user interface frameworks
Gingerbread	2.3.x	Dec. 2010–Sep. 2011	10	13.5%	Uses Kernel 2.6.35; introduces near field communication (NFC), control battery usage for apps, front and rear camera, SIP telephony, native development environment, Google Talk video chat, overall enhanced performance for screen, video, and audio

Continued

TABLE 1 Android Version History as of Oct. 11, 2015 (Amadeo, 2014; Android Developers Dashboards, 2015)—cont'd

OS Name	Version	Release Dates	Application Programming Interface (API)	Distribution	Key Features and Improvements
Jelly Bean	4.3.x	Jul. 2012– Jul. 2013	18	9.0%	Based on Kernel 3.0.31; introduces Google Now, keymaps, multiple user and onscreen support, Google Cloud Messaging (GCM), OpenGL ES 3.0 support for game graphics, filesystem write performance, security and performance enhancements, developer logging, and analysis
	4.2.x		17	19.7%	
	4.1.x		16	27.8%	
KitKat	4.4.x	Oct. 2013– Jun. 2014	19	17.9%	Uses Kernel 3.4.0; various user interface changes, wireless printing, a new storage access framework, more synchronization between accounts and Google+, further security enhancements, bug fixes, and the new runtime virtual machine called ART which, although not enabled by default, will eventually replace DVM for increased performance and battery life
Lollipop	5.0	Oct. 2014	21	15.6%	The Dalvik DVM has been replaced with a newer ART virtual machine, with ahead-of-time (AOT) compilation and 64-bit processor support. Lock screen no longer support widgets but provides application and notification support, guest and multiple user accounts, Tap and Go quick data transfers and migration to new devices, device protection improved for lost or stolen—device stays locked until Google account sign in, even if device has been factory reset
	5.1	Feb. 2015	22	7.9%	
Marshmallow	6.0	Oct. 2016	23	n.a	Key features include fingerprint authentication, confirm credential (time out app protection and password authentication based on use), App Linking (associate an app with a web domain), Auto Backup for Apps (full backups and app restores), Direct Share (share data with other users through apps, such as social media, more intuitively), Voice Interactions with apps, Android for Work (silent app installs, enterprise owned devices, and further control over device such as security certificate control)

OS capabilities, where added software and security features have been introduced to support changes (Vargas et al., 2012). By not upgrading the hardware, users are unable to upgrade their Android OS and therefore become more susceptible to malicious attacks.

Android version history, distribution, and key features and improvements throughout the various release dates are represented in Table 1 (Android, Developers Guide, 2014; Android Dashboards, 2015).

In addition to the Linux Kernel security architecture, we need to consider environmental and physical factors when it comes to the security of an Android OS smartphone. These factors include the Memory Management Unit (MMU), which is a hardware prerequisite component that handles the memory and cache of a smartphone. This means the device needs sufficient internal memory to carry out processes. The MMU is important to the Linux Kernel, as it assists in the separation of processes and reduces access privileges. Type Safety is a second factor to consider. It is a programming language that prevents discrepancies between programming variables and enforces a standard code format, therefore preventing conspicuous code from being executed. A final factor to consider is the Mobile Carrier/Network Operator, where authentication of the Subscriber Identity Module (SIM) and associated protocols adhere to the mobile network's basic security principles. This helps to avoid intrusion, which can target user identification, voice and data charges, and monitoring (Shabtai et al., 2010). For example, in Sep. 2014, fake mobile phone towers were reportedly discovered in the United States that could give those who were in control of the towers "the ability to attack mobile phones through eavesdropping and installing spyware" (Sky News, 2014).

2.1.3 Vulnerabilities

Having an open-source OS encourages rapid development because multiple developers can identify vulnerabilities in the OS and prepare patches to fix the identified vulnerabilities to avoid widespread exploitation of such vulnerable devices.

The core layers for potential vulnerabilities were discussed above (Linux Kernel platform, the open-source OS, and third-party apps), thus emphasizing that understanding the Android OS security architecture will assist in mitigating vulnerabilities in core apps and services. However, hardware resources may also be affected and include a number of additional vulnerabilities. Hardware resources at risk may include battery power, memory and central processing unit (CPU) resources, removable storage media, and cameras. For example, the contents of a secure digital (SD) card have no security measure in place, thus allowing private content to be exploited (Shabtai et al., 2009).

Although the impact of vulnerabilities depends upon the type of threat, a standard (non-modified and nonrooted) Android OS is typically well protected because the core components of the Linux Kernel cannot be replaced. However, source code, such as framework, DVM, and the native libraries, can be modified, thus increasing the risks of vulnerabilities. For example, previous studies have highlighted a number of poorly designed and insecure mobile apps that request excessive and unnecessary permissions and, consequently, increase the security risk (Shabtai et al., 2009). In a more recent work, Choo and D'Orazio (2015) identified vulnerabilities and design weaknesses in the Australian Government Medicare Express Plus app for iOS devices, which allows an attacker to expose the device user's sensitive data and personally identifiable information (PII) stored on the device. Due to the time lag between the discovery of a vulnerability and the availability of an update or patch, users of affected devices are vulnerable to attacks (Husted et al., 2011).

2.1.4 Rooted Android Devices

Rooting an Android device is a process that allows a user to obtain root privileges, allowing them to easily interact with the OS and make changes to the device. Such changes include interface customizations, unlocking hidden features, installing the latest OS releases, and removing software preinstalled by hardware manufacturers. Rooted devices also allow third-party app installations that offer additional features not supported by nonrooted Android smartphones, such as apps that tweak the battery life, speed, and performance of a smartphone (Liebergeld and Lange, 2013).

While the rooting process removes existing restriction and allows more flexibility, it may result in additional security risks, as malicious apps may be able to bypass the device's built-in security measures. For example, third-party apps having root access to the device would be able to interact directly with the device and system files and therefore be able to access information on the device that includes private and sensitive data. Third-party apps that have root access may also modify files and/or disable the device, rendering it unusable (Liebergeld and Lange, 2013).

2.2 Android Application Security

2.2.1 App Permissions

Android is a popular app development platform and offers open-source flexibility in an unrestricted marketplace. This has contributed to the growing availability of Android OS and also allows for an extensive API, which defines how the app interacts with most areas of the hardware functionality, such as user data and phone settings, wireless connectivity, GPS system, and built-in digital camera.

The security of app permissions is managed through the Linux Kernel, specifically the Libraries and ART layers, and is based on isolating activities and permissions in terms of what the app is able to perform and access on the device. As each app has its own process and is managed in its own sandbox environment, apps are unable to "talk" to each other, which means less information can be shared. App permissions need to be declared in the AndroidManifest.xml file, as mentioned earlier in the Security Architecture. If such permissions are not listed within this file, then the Kernel will carry out its task of restricting, known as a "runtime exception," preventing any malicious activity from running (Vidas et al., 2011).

According to Vidas et al. (2011), there are close to 130 app-level permissions incorporated within the Android framework that are declared before an installation occurs. The user initiates installation and needs to accept such permissions before the installation can occur. This allows some control over what permissions are being executed by an app. However, the majority of users are not aware of how permissions work and what they are intended for. Thus, apps may comprise privileged permissions that are not required for the purpose of the app, such as location access and network access, which may have an impact on the privacy, security, and vulnerability of the device (Vidas et al., 2011).

The development of an Android app is based on four protection levels. The app developer can select the appropriate protection level in conjunction with Component Type permissions. The four protection levels are Normal, where minimal permissions are needed; Dangerous, where a substantial risk is present and therefore more permissions are requested, but only on a user's confirmation; Signature, which allows apps with the same signature permissions to talk to each other; and, finally, SignatureOrSystem, which is a signature permission that has access to the image file system. As app permission requests are granted, the protection layers declare the app's permissions to the user for approval and grant access to the smartphone. In the event of permissions being declined, the app will not install (Ongtang et al., 2012).

2.2.2 Component Permissions

To assist in the selection of app permissions and protection levels, predetermined component types need to be identified in relation to an app's purpose. There are four component types defined by Android to securely identify an app's purpose and what areas of the system it will access. The first component type is Activity, which relates to onscreen user functionality. For example, onscreen app activity generally displays only one or two options per screen due to the screen size of smartphone devices. Having too many app activities on one screen will be hard to read and thus affect option selection by users. The second component type is Service, where an app will continue to perform a particular process in the background, even if the app has been temporarily closed from onscreen display; for example, downloading a music file and returning to the home screen (Enck et al., 2009).

The third component type is Content Provider, which enables the sharing and storing of data through a relational database that can describe the content it contains. Finally, the fourth component type is Broadcast Receiver, which can be defined as a mailbox for receiving messages from other internal apps only and with no external interference so that the message can then be broadcasted to its intended destination (Enck et al., 2009).

2.2.3 Signing Apps

Before an app can be added to the Android marketplace, the app must be digitally signed with a certificate to identify the author. This ensures that both the app code and noncode resources are authenticated. If the app does not have a valid certificate, it will not be packaged as an Android application package (APK) file format for distribution. An app can also be self-signed by the developer and not necessarily through a Certificate Authority (CA), a commercial entity that issues digitally signed certificates. The APK is the driving force for app installation on an Android device. Therefore if the APK file is not digitally signed, it will be deemed as an invalid or unauthenticated file and will not be published. A digital signed app is verified as being from a legitimate/trusted source (developer) (Android, Developers Guide, 2013).

2.2.4 Privacy

Apps can be installed quickly and easily without having many options to configure, unlike traditional computer system software installations. Although app permissions are presented to the user, they are often simply accepted for immediate use without much consideration. In a survey of 250 university students and academic staff members, for example, it was found that device users would allow app permissions that appeared unnecessary on their mobile devices (Imgraben et al., 2014). Once the app has been installed, all included permissions will have been given access to parts of the smartphone, and the user will be unable to change, modify, or select certain permissions after the installation.

As a result, there may be leaking of personal and sensitive data to third parties (e.g., advertisement companies) and sending of SMS/MMS messages, and as well as calls made without the user's knowledge. It may be impossible for users to know what information is being captured and how data is gathered and used (Feth and Pretschner, 2012). A developer may have legitimate reasons for gathering data, such as user interaction feedback and usage statistics, although data transmitted to a third party without the user's knowledge can infringe on the user's privacy (Dietz et al., 2011). For example, mobile advertising is usually present in free apps, where app developers are financially compensated through a referral system when a user generates impressions (clicks) on specific advertisements (Leontiadis et al., 2012). Additionally, malicious apps can masquerade as legitimate apps that may inadvertently be installed by the user and read their personal data without the user even knowing (La et al., 2013).

As the number of mobile apps continue to increase, so will the need for privacy-enhancing and monitoring components. One example is the "permissions request" monitoring system that allows a user to actively manage and monitor what tasks/data the apps are conducting/collecting with their approved permissions. A "permissions request" monitoring system would also check permission requests at runtime and not at deployment time. For example, permitting an app to access the Internet every so often allows control over the runtime of the app, rather than accepting all permissions and allowing the app to access the Internet all the time without user consent (Feth and Pretschner, 2012).

"Permissions request" monitoring gives the user flexibility and a degree of control over app permissions, thus assisting with the protection of personal and sensitive data. If the user is uncomfortable with available options after finding out what the permissions are, apps can be easily uninstalled by the user's request without question in order to protect data privacy.

2.3 Android Malware Threats and Countermeasures

As smartphones are mostly always on and connected to the Internet through either mobile data or wireless home connections, possible attack vectors will make use of such available connectivity. Given that a user can allow elevated permissions unknowingly, this generates a number of avenues for an attack. By browsing untrusted websites on an Android smartphone, the user leaves the door open for drive-by exploitation, which is a common vector that spreads malware by identifying and exploiting mobile web browsers. Phishing is another common vector by which information is gathered under false pretences via emails or websites that masquerade as official or legitimate. Other than technical attacks, there are also human factors to consider such as social engineering, which is an attack vector that targets a user by manipulation, coercing them into making a particular decision that will actually help the attacker perform its relevant functions.

Threats of this nature make an everyday smartphone a potential target for attacks that can compromise private information, steal data, make use of hardware resources, and leave the device partially or fully unusable. Not only will this have a huge impact on an individual smartphone, potential threats, such as phishing, have the capability to spread and infect other smartphones through contacts stored on the device. For example, SMS/MMS messages may be distributed unknowingly to stored contacts, which may result in unwanted charges. This can also extend to email accounts, social media networks, and cloud-based services.

With the Android OS, there are several security measures in place in the underlying core framework and Linux Kernel. Although these areas are protected, it is possible to manipulate the hardware in order to uncover vulnerabilities in the framework, thus allowing root access. Therefore rooted devices will be more susceptible to security threats, such as SMS Trojan horses (Shabtai et al., 2009). The Android OS also uses various components, such as Java, which can also render a smartphone vulnerable to exploitation. As malicious code needs to be inserted into Android binaries.dex files, Java code is generally unable to infect class file formats to make this adjustment, and the Java code does not have write privileges to any APK files (Shabtai et al., 2009).

Malware is a "classic" threat to Android OS. It presents additional concerns as the Android OS platform becomes more versatile and the storage of personal data increases, making it an ideal target for malware apps. Malware can be designed to capture personal data and control a smartphone without the consent of the user by impersonating a useful or legitimate functionality, such as a Trojan or a botnet (La et al., 2013).

Since Android is an open-source platform and the system framework and architecture use a sandbox environment, there is an onus on users as they make the choice to download apps from the Google Play store or alternative sources, some of which can be untrustworthy.

However, even trusted sources, such as the Google Play store, have had malicious apps, as there is no initial review of an app's code before the app is posted. For example, a user may see an app they would like to download from a social media network but when they click on the link to download the app, they are redirected to an untrusted Android app download website and not the Google Play store. The user downloads, accepts, and installs the app, giving elevated permissions to the Android platform and allowing a potential malicious attack, such as phishing, to take place (Delac et al., 2011).

One example of a malware app was Trojan-SMS.AndroidOS.FakePlayer.b, which surfaced in 2010 and targeted Android phones by masquerading as a fake music player that users had to manually install. This example relates to the app permissions mentioned above. If users are not aware of the permissions being granted, they may render their smartphones vulnerable to security threats by unknowingly authorizing access. The purpose of this malware was to send SMS messages to premium-rate telephone numbers without the user's consent or knowledge. In this particular example, the malware app was able to take control of software resources, but it is also had further capability to access and manipulate hardware resources, such as by changing or deleting memory card data (La et al., 2013). Therefore, having antimalware protection in place will help mitigate a potential security threat in order to protect personal data and corporate data, particularly as bring your own device (BYOD) policies are becoming acceptable in the workplace environment (Wang et al., 2012).

To counteract malware within the Google Play store, Google introduced an automatic system named Bouncer in early 2012 that was designed to automatically sweep apps for malicious code. Although Bouncer was responsible for a 40% reduction in malware apps in the Google Play store, malware is evolving at such a speed that it will always find new vulnerabilities that make automatic systems, such as Bouncer, struggle to keep up to date. Therefore being personally aware of what apps are being downloaded and their permissions is a vital security measure to prevent any security threat (Hou, 2012).

There is a vast range of apps to download, and malicious apps may leverage this to their advantage by conducting an IPC between one another. Apps for the Android platform are comprised of four main components that share information and data from the receiving components that need to be passed through each one, as introduced in Section 2.2. As each component has its own purpose, the interaction between them may cause a possible threat to occur and initiate IPC between two apps that are of a malicious nature. Therefore if one component of an app is configured by a developer to attempt contact with a different or same component of another app, then personal data could be leaked and shared with external sources for later use.

Apps, mobile web browsers, email clients, hardware capability, and access to a wide network of social elements all present different avenues for security threats. Smartphones, with increasing connectivity options and data storage, are a consistent source of valuable information, making them ideal targets for strategic attack. There are a number of different strategic attack actors, which include attempts to capture information over a period of time to explore and gain resourcefulness in sensitive information for the purpose of exposing data. Possible reasons behind such attack actors may include financial gain, information gathering, or an exposure of truth. For example, a politically motivated threat may relate to wanting deception exposed for political gain.

Each attack vector has a method and logic to it. Thus the choice of malware, phishing, social engineering, or botnet attacks may depend on the intended outcome. For example, malware may exploit a smartphone to become a botnet (zombie) without the user even knowing. This causes the device to perform automated tasks across the Internet without the knowledge of the user and with the aim of targeting and compromising confidentiality, integrity, and availability of services (Pieterse and Olivier, 2012).

There are a number of countermeasures to such threats, which have been introduced by security providers. The countermeasures include virus, malware and spyware protection, and the ability to wipe the smartphone remotely if it is lost or stolen. However, antivirus/malware signature repositories need to be constantly updated with the latest definitions in order to remain effective as security threats continue to rise (Shabtai et al., 2009).

The various attack vector and actor methods are outlined in Table 2.

2.3.1 Antimalware

Malware apps have the ability to compromise the integrity of personal data to take advantage of software and hardware functionality. According to the Fortinet Threat Landscape Report (2014), for example, a record number of malware families specifically targeting the Android OS were detected in 2013, and the Android OS was the most targeted platform OS for the majority of attacks. Over 50,000 malware samples were collected per day in the first quarter of 2013, and by the end of the fourth quarter, a staggering 450,000 malware samples were collected on a daily basis. It was then that the first ransomware malware sample targeting the Android OS was discovered, called Locker/SLocker Ransomware (Spreitzenbarth, Forensic Blog, 2014), though ransomware is not a new threat to computer-based systems.

Android devices continue to be one of the most targeted mobile devices in the first quarter of 2014, with a notable focus on Trojans, which are repackaged apps designed to facilitate social engineering and the sending of messages to a premium-rate number without the user's knowledge (F-Secure Mobile Threat Report, 2014). It is, therefore, not surprising that Android Jelly Bean (v. 4.2) added an option for the user to allow or block suspicious SMS messages sent from apps. The report also highlighted the rise of Windows Trojan hops, Tor network threats, and Bootkit, targeting older versions of the Android OS, as well as Cryptominer and Dendroid toolkits, designed to repackage apps and take advantage of remote access facilities.

TABLE 2 Example of Android Attack Vectors/Actors and Possible Mitigation Strategies

Potential Attack Vector/Actors	Description	Examples	Mitigation Strategies
Mobile network services	SMS/MMS, voice calls, emails	Messages presented to the user that appear to be from a legitimate source, where the user may be sent to external untrusted website. Various unknown phone calls claiming to be authorized agencies with the intention to obtain information verbally, or a user is asked to call a number that charges a nominal fee, where the user is unaware.	Delete unknown messages, user awareness, do not reply or call back, mark unwanted emails as spam/block sender, hang up phone call, awareness of sharing personal information over phone, identification and verification of source, call-block features
Mobile Internet access	3G/4G services, Wi-Fi	Always on and connected, exposing mobile device to threats, easy connectivity to public Wi-Fi hotspots, as well as untrusted and open wireless networks	Turn off GPS and location options, do not access sensitive uniform resource locator (URL) links (e.g., banking websites) over public Wi-Fi, turn off other connectivity tools if not used (also saves battery), be aware of apps constantly using data/internet services, install antivirus/malware defenses
Social engineering	Deception, vulnerability aimed at the user and social surroundings	Includes fake webpages impersonating as trusted sources, fraud, scams, hoaxes, tricking the user into doing something they should not be doing	Password and change management, two-factor authentication, physical device security, classifying the sensitivity of information (what is important to keep safe and not share), educating users on identifying legitimacy and authenticity, Android apps, Google Play store, antivirus/malware defenses
Drive-by and WebView vulnerability	Exploits vulnerability in WebView interface, malware automatically downloads without user's knowledge or consent	Information gathering, malicious website gains remote shell system access	Affects any device running an Android version earlier than 4.2, restricted software patches due to carrier, upgrade hardware/new smartphone to mitigate risk
Phishing	Gathers sensitive data, such as login credentials and personal data	Impersonates an official or legitimate source, such as a banking website, fake emails, hoaxes, and web links to untrusted websites; this also expands on social engineering	Use antivirus/malware defenses to scan device, email, and web access regularly; monitor attempts to change/access system at the Kernel level; user education and awareness is vital; encryption of information

Continued

TABLE 2 Example of Android Attack Vectors/Actors and Possible Mitigation Strategies—cont'd

Potential Attack Vector/Actors	Description	Examples	Mitigation Strategies
Webpages	Trusted or untrusted webpages	Pop-up windows, shortened URL links that do not clearly show the website URL, users can be taken to an unknown website with malicious content that tricks users into downloading and installing various items	Similar mitigation strategies to phishing, monitor webpage port access, runtime analysis, clearing browser cache, do not auto save or store usernames and passwords for critical websites, be aware of clicking on URL links, do not allow suspicious installation prompts
Bluetooth	Spreading malicious content	Paired devices may share and spread malware and steal data if user is unaware and accepts transfer requests	Do not pair with unknown devices; make sure to disconnect/cancel previously connected devices as a safety measure; turn off/disable Bluetooth; be aware of apps wanting to use Bluetooth channel, which can disconnect one channel and connect to another; employ a notification system to prompt user of unintentional connections to a device
Physical attack/USB/ other peripherals	USB connectivity and syncing with external sources	Smartphones have a large storage capacity in which malicious content can be stored and used to spread across multiple devices; data theft involving removable SD cards and using them in other devices; a more advanced example would involve activating the Android Debug Bridge (ADB) feature, configuring the device to allow apps to be installed without permissions to accept prompts	Activate PIN code to prevent unauthorized access, do not leave phone unattended, be aware of surroundings, do not plug phone into unknown devices, use secondary password prompt for installing apps, only the owner can install/update, manufacturer firmware and security patches
Google Play store	Malware-infected apps, such as games	Limited verification process, lack of app code review	Bouncer, knowing what access is required and what permissions the app needs to function and why it needs certain access, individual permission acceptance, not just accept all
User admin permissions	Authorized to accept and grant permission to device	Allows malicious apps to install and access Android system, connects to unprotected networks due to admin privileges	User education, second prompt to challenge user and awareness of what access is being granted
App permissions	New/already installed apps request permission to install, update, or make a change; malicious app injections; third-party apps	IPC; data capture and loss through unencrypted transmission; notification pop-ups that are accepted but may not be what they seem; unusual permission requests, such as a weather app asking for camera access (not needed and potential threat); apps may have been repackaged as a free version that may contain malicious content (Pieterse and Olivier, 2012)	Know what apps are being/have been installed and their use, selective app permission acceptance, using Google Play instead of random untrusted app stores/websites, antivirus/malware defenses for prevention, introduction of a notification and alert system when IPC occurs

Remote app install	Various services are now available that allow apps to be installed remotely onto a device from an external website, such as Google Market (not official Google Play store)	No app permission acceptance or confirmation; an app could be installed directly onto a device without user intervention from a website offering the service, resulting in malicious code being installed alongside the app, although updated in v.2.3, older devices running lower Android versions are still at risk	Users of older Android devices should use the official Google Play store, practice due diligence on reputable remote app install websites, antivirus/malware defenses, upgrade and start using the latest Android OS release/version (update of physical handset device required)
Gateway to third-party workstation	Virtual Private Network (VPN) solutions, connecting to home or corporate networks, provided by third-party apps such as TeamViewer	Additional line into other sensitive networks, malicious content can spread	Enterprise Mobile Device Management (MDM) solutions, antivirus/malware defenses, close connections properly, encryption, latest patches and security updates, also relates to mobile internet access and physical attack mitigation strategies
Internet Relay Chat (IRC), instant messages apps, P2P file sharing networks	Third-party installed software	Connect to other devices and services, more vulnerable and open to further exploits	Avoid installing bundled unauthorized apps, device and port activity monitoring, antivirus/malware defenses, also relates to webpage mitigation strategies
Privacy	Manufacturers and apps gathering user data	Data being gathered includes GPS locations, system logs, account information and user interaction with the device, which can be used not for financial gain but for mass consumer production and research development	Turn off GPS through the physical device and in-app options, sign out of accounts (such as Gmail), create a dedicated and limited profile account just for Android use that has less private and confidential data exposure
Rooted device	Opens additional services and functionalities, can install apps currently forbidden by phone manufacturer and/or carrier, will allow full system access to Android OS	Malicious content can exploit a rooted device and gain core system access and control; view all personal information; gain access to gateways (e.g., VPNs); install Kernel modules, such as rootkits, and render them unusable; untrusted device (e.g., DroidKungFu threat (Spreitzenbarth, Forensic Blog, 2014))	Do not root device if unsure of consequences, analyze app permissions more closely, install antivirus/malware defenses

In addition, a recent report estimated "[w]ith an overall infection rate 0.65 percent [between 2013 and the first half of 2014], around 15 million mobile devices are infected worldwide at any time" (Alcatel-Lucent, 2014, p. 4).

Throughout the past couple of years, potentially unwanted programs (PUP), such as malware, have had a significant impact on the Android OS, with a worldwide market share of 78.9%, Android continues to be a top target for malicious threats. According to G DATA (2015), for example, in the first quarter of 2015, there were 440,267 brand new malware samples identified, compared to the fourth quarter of 2014, where 413,871 malware samples were identified, which is an increase of 6.4%. In relation to the first quarter of 2014, there were 363,153 malware samples identified, which is an increase of 21% in the first quarter of 2015.

As users are frequently using Android devices for everyday usage, such as taking advantage of Internet banking and online shopping on the move, there is a tendency for more PII information to be shared with various apps. Thus the malware efforts of cybercriminals are financially motivated and are targeting such interactions. For example, known Android malware identified in the first quarter of 2015 accounted for 50.3% being financially motivated, such as banking Trojans (i.e., Svpeng Trojan, which masquerades as Flash Player and includes a malicious combination of financial malware and ransomware) and SMS Trojans, where 49.7% were other malware attack vectors (see Table 2; G DATA, 2015).

As malicious apps aim to abuse the possible vulnerabilities in the Android platform, apps, and various services, a countermeasure would be to install antimalware software. Antimalware configuration is kept up to date by using signature repositories that include known malware threats and definitions, which allow antimalware to react quickly when a threat is discovered. Thus the speed with which antimalware reacts to the detection of malware will be based on how up to date the definitions are in the repository, which is similar to how antivirus definitions work. Antimalware is designed to scan files, emails, attachments, SMS messages, and websites to help protect against Trojans, viruses, worms, and rootkits (Shabtai et al., 2009).

Although traditional workstation environments have seen a significant evolution in malware detection systems, smartphone devices present a number of unique challenges, and traditional detection systems are not easily deployed in a mobile device environment. Smartphones are likely to store more sensitive data and PII (e.g., SMS messages, photos, and videos taken using the device's camera, as well as geolocation information stored by various apps) and therefore pose a greater security and privacy risk to users. The effectiveness of antimobile malware signature repositories is unclear, as such an approach may offer resource-constrained mobile devices limited protection against newer mobile threats, such as polymorphic and metamorphic code (Suarez-Tangil et al., 2014).

A study by AV-Test (2014) evaluated 36 Android security apps over a period of 6 months with a restricted dataset of approximately 2300 malware samples. Throughout the study, eight security apps achieved plausible and optimistic detection results. The security apps with positive results included Ahnlab, Avira, BitDefender, Cheetah Mobile (three versions), G data, Kaspersky, McAfee, Qihoo, Symantec, TrendMicro, and TrustGo. The findings provide an indication of how antimobile malware apps for Android are improving in performance and detection rates.

Having antimalware apps perform regular scans and signature updates will have an adverse impact on power consumption and the performance of the device. One promising approach is to have cloud-based signature repositories, where the heavy lifting is undertaken in the cloud rather than the lightweight client app. There are, however, privacy and confidentiality concerns about using cloud-based solutions (Suarez-Tangil et al., 2014). For example, will cloud-based antimalware providers be able to track the device users?

Awareness of app privileges and the number of permissions requests needed are becoming a primary focus point for reasonable protection against malware. For example, if the required antimalware app permissions requests are not fully accepted, the app will not be used to the best of its ability, thus leaving the smartphone unprotected. If all requested permissions are accepted, it would be difficult to fully understand what the permissions are doing or mean. The various protection methods available from an antimalware app may include a number of different detection and analysis methods, such as type of monitoring, granularity, and identification, all of which require various permissions granted by the user. This leads to further concerns related to privacy and confidentiality (Suarez-Tangil et al., 2014).

Thus new privacy apps for the general user are becoming popular, allowing control over permissions that an app is using, such as Privacy App by SnoopWall. Further development in regard to app permission control, security, and privacy measures may also include enterprise-wide solutions, such as GlobalProtect by Palo Alto Networks, where mobile users benefit from enterprise security features by connecting through a VPN connection.

With the increase in the popularity of Android devices and the subsequent growth of mobile malware, we have seen an increase in the number of antimalware apps in recent times. Major security companies, such as Intel Security (McAfee Mobile Security), AVG Mobile, AVAST, Symantec, and Kaspersky are offering free or paid (in-app purchase) antimalware apps. The Google Play install statistics identify that the two most popular downloaded antimalware apps are AVG Mobile and AVAST, each reaching between the region of 100,000,000 and 500,000,000 installs (as of Jul. 20, 2014). There are also new players catering for the Android market. For example, CM Security (Cheetah Mobile), and Lookout Security & Antivirus (Lookout Mobile Security) reportedly have between 50,000,000 and 100,000,000 downloads as of Jul. 20, 2014, and 360 Security (Qihu) and Antivirus Free (Creative Apps) have between 10,000,000 and 50,000,000 downloads respectively as of Jul. 20, 2014 (Google Play, 2014).

There are, however, challenges faced by Android and other mobile antimalware app designers due to the inherent differences between a mobile device and the "traditional" client device, such as a desktop and laptop. For example, mobile devices are typically resource constrained due to manufacturer restrictions. Thus timely core OS version and patch updates may not be released for older hardware devices. This leaves the devices vulnerable and more open to potential security threats and exploits (Husted et al., 2011). Another difference is how a user will inherently have higher permissions on a device, where they can unintentionally install any number of apps from untrusted sources. Therefore giving the user control over accepting all app permission requests that may be a potential risk to both the user and the device (Shabtai et al., 2009; Feth and Pretschner, 2012). This raises concerns about the potential security risks and threats related to interapp and resource communication such as IPC interactions (Ongtang et al., 2012). Any newly installed app may contain malicious app injections that will try to communicate with and affect other apps on the device.

Despite the increased attention to the threat of mobile malware and security companies offering both free and paid antimalware apps, the number of downloads is low in comparison to other apps such as games. Research conducted by TrendMicro shows that only 20%

of Android-based devices have security apps installed despite the increase in mobile malware (TrendMicro, 2012). Similarly, a survey of 250 university students and staff at a South Australian university found that the majority of the participants did not install an anti-malware app (Imgraben et al., 2014). The findings and those of a study by Zhou and Jiang (2012, p. 96), which found that mobile malware is "rapidly evolving and existing antimalware solutions are seriously lagging behind," suggested that more needs to be done to protect mobile device users.

The lack of adoption of antimalware apps is, perhaps, due to a lack of user awareness (as highlighted by Imgraben et al. (2014)) and the perception that antimalware apps will slow device performance and increase battery consumption. In comparison to existing antivirus solutions, there is a wider range of anti-malware apps to choose from, which may further confuse users. By conducting an evaluation of the top 15 most downloaded free antimalware apps, this research will facilitate users to making an informed decision.

2.3.2 Firewall

If configured in the correct manner, firewalls can be an essential part of protecting Android smartphone data. With the ability to control and keep a log of all inbound and outbound traffic through various connections, firewalls can guard against untrusted network resources and attacks to vital services of the OS and core framework. Once the firewall has been configured to monitor and manage communications within a set of access list rules, it will be able to detect whether an app is trying to send private and confidential data and block this communication (Shabtai et al., 2010).

Although firewalls are an effective solution, they are unable to block all communications such as SMS messages and attacks via the Internet browser, emails, and Bluetooth. Nevertheless, having the ability to manage app permissions and define what access they do and do not have is an important part of protecting data and private information (Shabtai et al., 2010).

2.3.3 Intrusion Detection System

An Intrusion Detection System (IDS) is a well-established security mechanism that has been implemented through information technology (IT) infrastructure and computer systems. Providing several security features, such as monitoring network and port activity, file protection and, notably, identification of suspicious activity, IDS capabilities have also been designed for smartphone security protection and monitoring. For IDS to be effective, a number of approaches are used to complement each other, which include Prevention-, Detection-, Anomaly-, and Signature-based approaches (La et al., 2013).

Each approach has a unique function for detecting malicious software or activities that is able to learn system behavior and alert the user if a suspicious anomaly is found. This is an effective measure if definitions are kept up to date and can identify unknown threats (Shabtai et al., 2010).

2.3.4 App Certification

App certification is specifically designed to counteract malware apps, as legitimate apps go through stringent testing and review before they are packaged in order to ensure appropriate functionality and determine their purpose. CA verifies a trust association, which is checked before an app is installed on a smartphone. Therefore, any malicious app that attempts an installation without a certification will be detected and removed (Shabtai et al., 2009). However, certifications can be a costly exercise for an app developer.

As Android is an open-source platform, there are several third-party app stores available where users can freely download any number of apps. This is an additional security threat, as apps may have a higher risk of containing malware that can bypass any CA authentication (Shabtai et al., 2009).

2.3.5 Selective Access Control

Given that installed apps have been granted certain permissions by the user, it is likely that these apps use the granted permissions as and when it suits their purpose. To prevent unnecessary granted permissions, it is entirely possible for the package installer to be modified so that advanced features can be installed to allow control over permissions. In this way, the user is fully aware of a request and has the ability to allow or deny the request without any interference to the usability of the smartphone or performance. By adding control of app permissions, malicious software is prevented from using unknowingly granted permissions and data as a whole is protected (Shabtai et al., 2010).

Limiting unnecessary app permissions will harden an Android device and will give the user the responsibility of becoming more aware of the functionalities of the device, thus allowing the user more control over what permissions are granted. Selective access control can be seen in corporate environments, where BYOD initiatives are managed and enforced by certain policy restrictions, ultimately protecting the corporate infrastructure, user, and personal data (Shabtai et al., 2009).

2.3.6 Context-Aware Security

There are a number of activities a smartphone can carry out in any moment. These include contextual activities, such as adjustments in local time, or wireless connections to other devices. Depending on the contextual circumstances, context-aware security is able to restrict or allow access based on predefined configurations that learn from the interaction and surroundings of its day-to-day operations based on user activity (Shabtai et al., 2010).

For example, if context awareness detects that a device has changed locations and is in a different time zone or country, it may be configured to lock down the smartphone, make it inaccessible, and encrypt its data. Although this is not an instant security measure and takes time to configure and set up, it does present an interesting method for protecting malicious access to resources and services based on predefined settings that help protect confidential content (Shabtai et al., 2010).

2.3.7 Data Encryption

Although the prevention of malicious software attacks is important, consideration must also be given to personal data protection because smartphones may be lost or stolen. As the amount of data being stored on a smartphone increases, data encryption has become a highly regarded factor for any event because the user is in control of managing access.

Throughout all Androids platforms, data encryption can include several techniques, such as a hardware access passcode, file-level password-based encryption, and a SIM personal identification number (PIN). Additional measures can include limiting the number of password attempts and locking the smartphone or file when the maximum attempts have been reached (Shabtai et al., 2010). Not only is this a reliable internal security measure, but such a measure can also be implemented with removable storage, such as an SD card. There are also additional features defined within apps themselves; for example, SMS and MMS apps may also include a separate passcode that can be set for further protection. With a variety of options, implementing data encryption can help prevent the exposure of sensitive and personal data (Wang et al., 2012).

However, newer releases of Android, namely Lollipop and Marshmallow, include a number of security enhancements to ensure data encryption to protect users. For example, full disk encryption was included, allowing the user to encrypt their device if they so choose. Smart Lock features, such as Trusted Face, was a feature released in earlier Android versions (Ice Cream Sandwich and above) and has since been updated to include Trusted Places and Trusted Devices. Lollipop also introduced multiuser, guest, and restricted profiles, allowing more control over the protection and encryption to keep data safe. Additional features within Marshmallow include fingerprint authentication and credentials authentication, which uses timeout variants based on when the device was last unlocked and used. Such security additions help to protect and encrypt data where required (Android Security Enhancements, 2015; Android Developers Guide, 2015).

Further data encryption and security features include the adaptation of remote device wiping and data backup and restore services through additional cloud anti-malware apps. Users are able to backup their data to personal cloud storage services and restore their data to another device when convenient. Remote device wiping is beneficial when a device is either lost or stolen to protect users (Walls and Choo, 2015; Di Leom et al., 2015). Additional data encryption and security features ensure data encryption to prevent data leakage.

3 EXPERIMENT SETUP

To determine the effectiveness and reliability of the 15 most popular (by number of installs) free antimalware apps available on Google Play store (Table 3).

To ensure the usefulness of this study, we obtained 15 popular Android malware samples for analysis by the antimalware apps. The malware samples were collected between Feb. 27 and Dec. 4, 2014 from the Contagio Mobile (2014) Malware Mini Dump database (Table 4). The malware sample SMS Sender (Xxshenqi-A.apk and com.android.Trogoogle.apk) includes two datasets from the same malware family, but most malware samples are from different malware families.

Three mobile test devices were used, each with their own Android OS (Ice Cream Sandwich, Jelly Bean, and KitKat) (Table 5). Each of the 15 antimalware apps will be installed on every test device, which will be used to scan against the 15 malware samples and conducted in 675 individual tests. The experiment process is designed to accommodate a typical day-to-day user. Therefore each test was conducted manually, as if a user was unknowingly installing a malicious app, which will hopefully give an indication and validate the effectiveness and reliability of the apps under examination, as the experiment process has been designed to be repeatable. While each individual antimalware app provides various configuration options, our study used default configurations as would most users, particularly non-IT-literate users.

TABLE 3 Antimobile Malware Apps for Android Devices (Information Correct as of Dec. 16, 2014)

Manufacturer	Antimalware App	Initial App Release Date	Current Version	License	Developer Website Source	Number of Installs (Google Play)
AVG Mobile	Antivirus Security	2011	v4.2.212757	Free	http://www.avg.com/au-en/for-mobile#android-tab	100,000,000–500,000,000
AVAST Software	Mobile Security and Antivirus	Dec. 2011	4.0.7871	Free	http://www.avast.com/en-au/free-mobile-security	100,000,000–500,000,000
Cheetah Mobile	CM Security and Find My Phone	Late 2012	v2.2.5.1040	Free	http://www.cmcm.com/en-us/cm-security	50,000,000–100,000,000
Lookout Mobile Security	Lookout Security and Antivirus	Nov. 2009	v9.9.1	Free	https://www.lookout.com/android	50,000,000–100,000,000
Doctor Web Ltd	Dr. Web v.9 Anti-virus	Dec. 2013	v9.02.1(2)	Free [14-day demo only]	http://download.drweb.com/android	10,000,000–50,000,000
Qihu	360 Security—Antivirus Free	Jun. 2013	v2.1.0.1032	Free	http://360safe.com/mobile-security.html	10,000,000–50,000,000
Creative Apps	Antivirus Free	2011	7.3.02.02	Free	http://en.nq.com/mobilesecurity	10,000,000–50,000,000
Norton Mobile	Norton Security and Antivirus	Jun. 2013	3.8.6.1653	Free [28-day demo only]	http://community.norton.com/t5/Norton-Mobile-Security/bd-p/NMS	10,000,000–50,000,000
TrustGo Inc.	Antivirus and Mobile Security	Feb. 2013	1.3.15	Free	http://www.trustgo.com/features	5,000,000–10,000,000
McAfee Mobile Security/Intel Security	McAfee Free Antivirus and Security	Oct. 2011	4.3.0.448	Free	https://www.mcafeemobilesecurity.com	5,000,000–10,000,000
Kaspersky Lab	Kaspersky Internet Security	Jun. 2011	11.6.4.1190	Free	http://www.kaspersky.com/android-security	5,000,000–10,000,000
BitDefender	Mobile Security and Antivirus	Apr. 2013	2.30.625	Free [14-day demo only]	http://www.bitdefender.com.au/solutions/mobile-security-android.html	1,000,000–5,000,000
MalwareBytes	MalwareBytes Antimalware Mobile	Oct. 2013	1.05.0.9000	Free	http://www.malwarebytes.org/mobile	1,000,000–5,000,000
Sophos Limited	Free Antivirus and Security	Jul. 2012	4.0.1433 (12)	Free	http://www.sophos.com/en-us/products/mobile-control.aspx	100,000–500,000
Pablo Software	Virus Scan	Jun. 2014	1.5.9	Free	https://play.google.com/store/apps/details?id=com.pablosoftware.virusscan	100,000–500,000

TABLE 4 Experiment Malware Samples

Malware Sample Date	Malware Sample Name	File Name	Description
Dec. 4, 2014	Deathring; preloaded malware	com.android. Materialflow.apk	DeathRing is a preloaded malware on brand new smartphones popular in Asia and African countries. DeathRing is a Trojan masquerading as a ringtone app that uses SMS and Wireless Access Point (WAP) vectors for malicious means. For example, SMS content may be used to phish PII data (The Register and Leyden, 2014)
Nov. 20, 2014	Notcompatible.C	Com.security.patch. apk	NotCompatible.C is a sophisticated botnet that used encryption and peer-to-peer communication, which has evolved from the earlier NotCompatible.A malware threat. NotCompatible.C has a botnet-like nature and is primarily aimed at network security, using Android as the attack vector to gain access. The malware can compromise vulnerable hosts and exploit exposed data inside the network. With such sophistication, NotCompatible.C is an example of how mobile malware has significantly matured (Lookout, 2014)
Oct. 30, 2014	Android SMS worm Selfmite	selfmite.apk	The Android Selfmite vulnerability previously surfaced early Jun. 2014 and was called Andr/Slfmite-A. The same vulnerability resurfaced in Oct. 2014, named Andr/Slfmite-B, and masquerades as a Google Plus app. The vulnerability uses a fake Google Plus icon as a botnet-style malware, which collects PII data and decides what to do with it. The fake app also installs with device administrator rights, making it difficult to uninstall and take over critical aspects of the smartphone, such as SMS and phone. The aim for this malware is to make money through affiliate revenue and pay-per-click icons (Sophos, 2014)
Oct. 8, 2014	Xsser mRAT (Android sample)	code4hk.apk	The code4hk malware is an app that exploits PII data from Android and iOS devices. The malware uses a fake mobile remote access tool (mRAT) app that claimed to coordinate the Occupy Central pro-democratic movement in Hong Kong. The app initiates through a link that is sent through a messaging service called Whatsapp, which then activates the malicious app if clicked. Activation leads to exploitation and extraction of data (Lacoon Security and Bobrov, 2014)
Aug. 3, 2014	SMS Sender	Xxshenqi-A.apk	The fake SMS Sender malware app is a combination of a worm plus a Trojan. The Trojan is effectively packaged within the worm and activated when the APK file has been installed, therefore two versions are from the same malware family. Shenqi-A malware targets all SMS messages made and received (McAfee Labs et al., 2014)
Aug. 3, 2014	SMS Sender	com.android. Trogoogle.apk [Torgle-A]	
Jun. 23, 2014	Google Cloud Messaging Trojan	smsgoogle.apk 05android (Google Cloud Messaging) / Android. Mobilespy / Agent-DBM	The Google Cloud Messaging Trojan prevents an affected user from uninstalling the malicious app and exploits PII and hardware informational data, such as IMEI serial and device ID. The data is sent to premium numbers via SMS, therefore charging the user and capturing data at the same time (F-Secure, 2014)

Date	Name	Package	Description
May 10, 2014	Android Monitor Spyware	com.exp.tele.apk (HGSpy.A/QlySpy.a)	Android Monitor Spyware comes in various forms of malware, such as HGSpy.A and QlySpy.a. The malicious app gains permission for a number of core processes and system preferences. Elevated permissions include location, Internet, Wi-Fi control, phone, messaging, and phone reboot control (Contagio Mobile, 2014)
May 6, 2014	Android SMS Trojan	Google-fake-installer.apk FakeInst (RuSMS-AH, Google.Services.Framework)	Android SMS Trojan, known as FakeInst, masquerades as an installer for other applications. However, this is a malware that sends SMS messages to premium-rate numbers or services without knowledge (Contagio Mobile, 2014)
May 6, 2014	Fake AV Se-cure MobieAV	Fake-av.apk Se-cure. Mobieav	FakeAV malware predominantly use visual payloads, enticing users to take action and pay a fee to protect their device. Known FakeAV apps do not have the same functionality as legitimate AV apps and do not offer the same protection (Contagio Mobile, 2014; Spreitzenbarth, Forensic Blog, 2014)
May 6, 2014	Android Samsapo.A	android.samsapo.apk (com.android.tools. system)	Android Samsapo.A is a worm that tries to hide within the Android system utilities. The malware is designed to spread through various means, such as email attachments and across a network. Permissions are escalated to exploit SMS, phone calls, and alarm settings and act as a downloader for other malware apps from different URLs (Contagio Mobile, 2014; Spreitzenbarth, Forensic Blog, 2014)
May 6, 2014	Android Fake Banker	fake-banker.apk (Sparkasse/Banker-Y)	Android Fake Banker malware is a fake mobile online banking app, which aims to exploit PII data. This specific malware sample masquerades as a well-known EU bank (Contagio Mobile, 2014)
Mar. 6, 2014	Dendroid.AndroidSpyware	com.parental.control.v4.apk	Dendroid is a well-known Android malware that targets a device's camera and audio, as well as access GooglePlay. The malware uses a remote-access Trojan to control the device and exploit data (Contagio Mobile, 2014)
Feb. 28, 2014	iBanking Android	iBanking.ing.apk (Security Space)	iBanking Mobile Bot malware masquerades as legitimate banking apps. Once the user accepts the permissions, the malicious app is able to capture incoming/outgoing calls, redirect numbers, capture audio, and send PII to a remote location. This specific malware sample masquerades as a well-known EU bank (Contagio Mobile, 2014)
Feb. 27, 2014	Android Tor Trojan	tor.video.mp4.apk (com.BaseApp)	Android Tor Trojan targets the Tor network and builds upon the anonymity of its users through a fake app (Contagio Mobile, 2014)

Source: Contagio Mobile, 2014. Mobile malware mini dump, viewed 08 August 2014. http://contagiominidump.blogspot.com.au.

TABLE 5 Specifications of Test Devices

Hardware/ Manufacturer	Android OS Version	Kernel Version	Chipset/Processor	Memory	Internal Storage
Samsung Galaxy Music S6010	Android 4.0.4 Ice Cream Sandwich (upgradable to 4.1.2 Jelly Bean)	3.0.15-1150453	850 MHz Cortex-A9	512 MB	4 GB
Samsung Galaxy Young NL 3G 850	Android 4.1.2 Jelly Bean	3.4.0-1140261	Qualcomm MSM7227A Snapdragon with 1 GHz Cortex-A5 CPU	768 MB	4 GB
Motorola Moto G X1033	Android 4.4 KitKat	3.4.42	Qualcomm Snapdragon 400 processor with 1.2 GHz quad-core CPU	1 GB	8 GB

Therefore the detection criterion will be based on antimalware app signature definition updates at the time of experiment (see Section 3.1), not based on behavioral factors. The antimalware apps were updated with the most recent signature repositories updates before any malware samples were tested and data recorded (see Table 3).

3.1 Experiment Process

To ensure both repeatability and reproducibility, which are key principles in scientific experiments, we outline the flow of our experiments below (Fig. 2):

1. The first step in the flow diagram is *Start*, which is where the experiment begins.
2. The next step is to create a new or use an existing *Google test account and link this account to Android test device.*
3. The next step in the process is to *Sign in to Google Play store and install free antimobile malware app on the Android test device.* Anti-malware apps will be installed based on their popularity (i.e., number of downloads) (see Table 3).
4. The next step is to *Confirm antimobile malware app version for Android test device.* This step is in place to confirm the actual version being tested on each Android test device, as some apps have a "varies with device" version release that is not defined in the Google Play store.
5. In order to have a consistent approach to testing individual antimalware apps using up-to-date signatures, the next step is to *Update definitions* and perform an initial scan of Android test device.
6. To prepare for the malwaresample.apk file transfer, the next step is *Connect Android test device to personal computer* via *USB.*
7. Using the Contagio Mobile (2014) Malware Mini Dump database, the next step is to proceed to *Download known malwaresample.apk file to desired location on test personal computer.*
8. The next step, *Decision on how to upload file*, is to upload the sample file that is based on user preference, which may be:

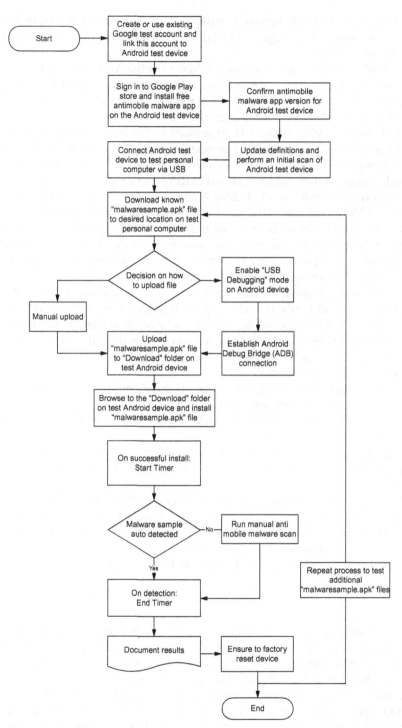

FIG. 2   Experiment process.

    a. *Manual upload*: Manually upload sample file to the *Downloads* folder of the Android test device. Note: The plugged-in test device will behave similarly to that of an external hard drive.

    b. *Enable USB Debugging mode on Android device*: On the Android test device, go to the home screen, select *Menu > Applications > Development*, and enable *USB Debugging*. Note: Android OS Jelly Bean and KitKat require "tapping" the *About* option a few times before the *Development* tab appears.

    c. *Establish Android Debug Bridge (ADB) connection*: The Android ADB feature is another way of communicating between a personal computer and an Android test device. As Android is based on Linux, it allows a terminal-based interface; therefore files can be uploaded using command line instead of drag and drop.

9. Depending on the decision made in Step 8, the next step is *Upload malwaresample.apk file to Download folder on test Android device* for testing the antimalware apps.

10. Now that the sample file has been uploaded, the next step is to *Browse to the Download folder on test Android device and install malwaresample.apk file*. This will initiate the installation of the sample file onto the Android test device, where a digital timer watch will be used to record accurate detection time results.

11. Once this has been initiated, the next process is *On successful install: Start Timer*. Being extremely attentive and critical in this approach is necessary, as the timer must be started precisely upon confirmation that the install has finished. If there is any doubt in starting the timer upon a successful install, this step has to be repeated for accuracy.

12. This step is a defining factor in the overall detection rate and time, where the *Malware sample auto detected* is recorded.

    a. No—*Run manual antimobile malware scan*—If the antimalware app did not detect the *malwaresample.apk* file, then a manual scan was run.

    b. Yes—*On detection: End Timer*—If the *malwaresample.apk* was detected, the time will be recorded.

13. Following the detection process, the next step is *Document results*, which involves recording the detection type, detection time in seconds, and detection rate (see Section 3.2).

14. No malicious sample files can be left on the device, so the *Ensure to factory reset device* process has been added to keep all Android test devices in the same clean environment.

15. The process for additional sample files can be repeated in the process named *Repeat process to test additional malwaresample.apk files*.

16. Finally, the terminal *End* represents the end of the experiment.

3.2 Metrics

In our study, bar graphs and cumulative distribution function (CDF) will be used across the three following areas of malware sample detection principles, which collectively analyze the reliability and effectiveness of the antimalware apps used in our experiment.

Type of Scan (Auto [A] or Manual [M]): The type of scan used to identify a malware sample. Auto mode refers to the app being able to automatically detect a threat. If there is no automatic detection, a manual scan is conducted to thoroughly test the sample malware. A bar graph is used to represent the type of scan value. An effective antimalware app should perform a scan automatically for any new app installation, hence a higher percentage of the auto scan type will result in a higher scan value percentage. The latter is computed as (number of the type of scan, auto or manual)/(total number of test cases performed against the antimalware app).

Detection Time: The time it takes for the malware sample to be detected. For the purposes of reporting data, the detection time is recorded in milliseconds. Where a malware sample is not detected or an automatic scan does not take place, the detection time is recorded as n.a. CDF is used to cumulatively represent all detection time values and displays how the antimalware apps are distributed. For example, the detection time values for each app are sorted in ascending order (i.e., smallest value to largest value), which in most instances include 45 data points: 15 malware samples tested on each individual antimalware app across all three Android OS; $15 \times 3 = 45$. The data points in this example are representative of $1/45$, which is 0.0222 (2.22%), up to 1.0 (100%). Each data point is representative of a percentage to determine the cumulative frequency of the detection time. While most apps have 45 data points, it is not true for all of the antimalware apps within this experiment. The apps that result in n.a. have fewer data points; however, they will still add up to 100%. Each data point on the graph show how results are distributed cumulatively for each antimalware app. Results with n.a. will not be included, as a figure is required to plot a result. Thus if any antimalware apps have n.a. across all 15 malware samples tested, they will not be shown, as they have no detection time due to their manual type of scan. Therefore antimalware apps that automatically detect a threat are considered more reliable and effective in detecting the malware samples used within this experiment.

Malware Sample Detected (Yes [Y] or No [N]): This identifies whether the tested malware sample was detected, as a percentage value. A bar graph is used to represent the malware sample detection value. A higher percentage means more malware samples were detected, resulting in a higher percentage. Malware sample detection percentage is computed as (number of malware sample detected)/(total number of test cases performed against the antimalware app).

4 FINDINGS

First, we looked at the type of scan results (automatic or manual) to determine and compare antimalware apps (Fig. 3). The way in which the malware samples were detected played a vital role in the findings, as the aim of this analysis is to determine the effectiveness and reliability of free antimalware apps that are available from the Google Play store.

At the time of research, Android versions used within this experiment (i.e., KitKat, Jelly Bean, and Ice Cream Sandwich) are still popular versions throughout the consumer market. For example, KitKat currently holds the majority of distribution share across all Android platforms. In addition, it is likely no further updates or releases will be provided for KitKat, Jelly Bean, or Ice Cream Sandwich due to newer Android versions such as Lollipop and Marshmallow. Any new updates will relate to a new version release upgrade and device compatibility factors.

Our experiment conducted within this chapter is relevant, as its focus is on versions of Android that are no longer supported but are still widely used, hence the need to protect devices and ensure PII security. It is not uncommon for malware threats to target older Android versions, such as Ice Cream Sandwich, Gingerbread, and Froyo, thus learning attack methods and possibly adapting to newer Android versions. Furthermore, the experiment process

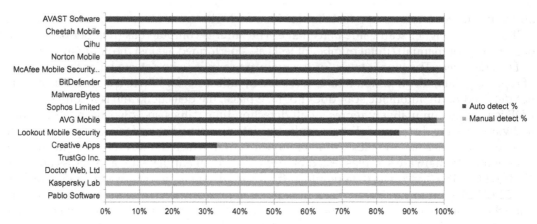

FIG. 3   Type of scan.

is designed to facilitate a manual procedure that is both repeatable and transparent, which can be used to test the effectiveness and reliability of any antimalware app across new or old Android versions with a range of collected malware samples from various sources (see Section 3.1).

Although Lollipop and Marshmallow have recently been released, they still have a lower distribution and are somewhat less stable and more in flux than previous Android versions, as mentioned previously. Therefore, Lollipop and Marshmallow will be considered in future experiments.

The apps with a higher automatic detection of malware samples are more reliable and effective in protecting an Android device against malicious threats, thus protecting the user intuitively through prompt notification to remove a detected threat. Those with manual detection of malware samples require additional user intervention, which may lead to a malicious threat to perform the attack, as it was not detected and mitigated in a timely manner.

With this in mind, the apps that automatically and consistently detected a threat and would immediately prompt the user to uninstall received a higher percentage. The top eight anti-mobile malware apps examined were AVAST Software, Cheetah Mobile, Qihu (360 Security), Norton Mobile, McAfee Mobile Security/Intel Security, BitDefender, MalwareBytes, and Sophos Limited. All eight antimalware apps received 100% each for automatic detection and removal of the malware samples used within this experiment. The results show that all eight apps performed extremely well and show promising signs of Android automatic malware protection.

Following closely at 97.78% was AVG Mobile, where the majority of scans were automatic with one manual intervention. A manual scan was needed, as AVG did not detect one of the malware samples used within this experiment. The type of scan used correlates with the malware samples detected, as some malware samples were not detected at all. In this instance, a manual scan is used to verify possible detection of the installed malware sample to show transparency and accurate findings across all antimalware apps (see Fig. 7).

Lookout Mobile Security (A: 86.67%/M: 13.33%), Creative Apps (A: 33.33%/M: 66.67%), and TrustGo Inc. (A: 26.67%/M: 73.33%) required more prompts and more manual intervention. The three remaining apps did not provide automatic detection for the possible removal of malware samples used—Doctor Web Ltd (A: 0%/M: 100%), Kaspersky Lab (A: 0%/M:

100%), and Pablo Software (A: 0%/M: 100%). Although Doctor Web Ltd provided a free app, it was a 14-day trial and did not include automatic scanning. An in-app purchase to upgrade to the full version was required to benefit from automatic scanning. Kaspersky Lab and Pablo Software had no automatic notification of malicious threats being installed and required manual intervention on all malware samples installed. However, Doctor Web Ltd, Kaspersky Lab, and Pablo Software performed very differently in the malware samples detected, albeit manual intervention was needed, which makes these apps less reliable and effective in protecting an Android device.

Second, we looked at the cumulative frequency of detection time results across all three Android platforms and hardware test devices. During the experiments, we observed that the scanning mode (Fig. 3) had a considerable impact on the detection time across the different Android platforms and test devices. Antimalware apps that included automatic detection received a time value. Those that required a manual scan received no detection time value, which impacted the results distributed cumulatively for each tool.

Throughout the experiment, it becomes apparent the detection time for the 15 antimalware apps improved across newer Android OS's and hardware devices (Figs. 4–6). An observation was that some antimalware apps, such as AVAST, Cheetah, and TrustGo, started a scan of a malware sample during install, while other apps started a scan after install. Starting a scan during install showed significant improvement in detection time. However, the response in prompting for an automatic detection and removal of the malware samples was different across each malware sample.

At the time of experiment, Doctor Web scanned apps during install, which prompted a threat alert only with no automated process to remove the threat. Although this allowed for quicker detection time, the Doctor Web app did not autoprompt the user to uninstall or stop the malware sample from being installed; therefore the installed malware sample could be activated if opened. In order to remove the malware sample, a manual scan was needed within the app itself to activate the removal of the detected malware sample. Qiho also scanned apps

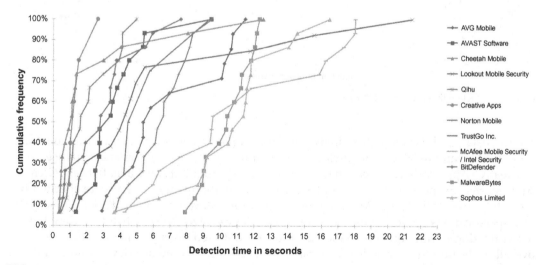

FIG. 4   Detection time: Android 4.0 (Ice Cream Sandwich).

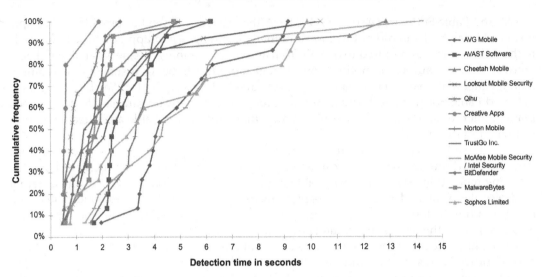

FIG. 5 Detection time: Android 4.3 (JellyBean).

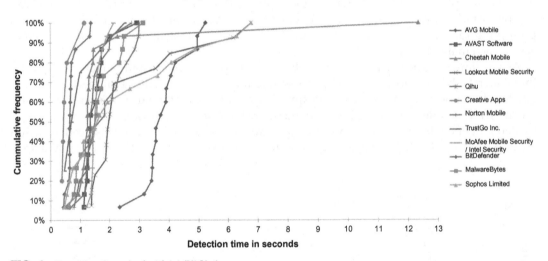

FIG. 6 Detection time: Android 4.4 (KitKat).

during install and detected all 15 malware samples (Fig. 7). Such an example demonstrates how effective and reliable antimalware apps are if they include an automatic response.

Creative Apps varied between malware samples. Throughout some installations, Creative Apps started to check malware samples during installation while others were checked immediately after installation. Manual scans were much slower on older devices, where device specifications are lower than that of newer devices. Device specifications may have a direct relation to how quickly malicious apps are detected, meaning better detection time overall. Detection time varied considerably over the three difference devices and Android OS platforms for Norton, McAfee, and Sophos. The lower specification device had slower

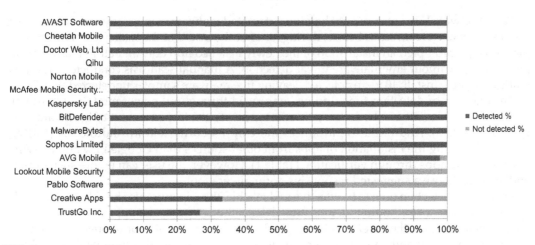

FIG. 7   Malware samples detected.

detection time overall; the detection time improved through later Android OS and hardware devices. Having a new and updated OS device proves to be a more reliable way in detecting malicious apps sooner rather than later. Lower detection times can be seen in Fig. 4, and a comparison in the improvement of detection time across all 15 anti-malware apps can be seen in Figs. 5 and 6.

Although TrustGo only detected four malware samples, the detection time was fairly responsive, as malware samples were scanned during installation. Once the malware sample was installed, a manual scan was run due to the low automatic malware sampled detection (Fig. 3). The manual scan adds to the experiment and analysis of the antimalware apps. If an automatic detection was missed, a manual scan, in theory, should detect any malicious activity. In this case, TrustGo did not detect 11 malware samples (Fig. 7).

Automatic scanning of a new app installation is not a feature of the free version of Kaspersky. App scanning during install is only available through the paid version, leaving vulnerabilities to the Android OS. Detection time was not taken into consideration, as the Kaspersky Lab app did not scan the malware samples on install. The malware samples could be installed and opened without any automated protection; therefore a manual scan was carried out on all malware samples and showed improved results (Fig. 7). Kaspersky did not have the option to change the default package installer, but if the option were available, detection time would increase significantly, as apps will be scanned before an installation begins.

BitDefender detected malware sample APK files on the first device scan, which is an added protection because no malware sample was installed. An antimalware app that scans and detects malicious APK files before an install has even started will have much higher detection time. However, this experiment process focuses on malicious threats that are installed. BitDefender did not prompt to change default package installer. Detection time improved over each test device. For example, older versions of Android and hardware performed slower than newer platforms. MalwareBytes detected all malware sample APK files when they were transferred to test devices. The detection time also improved over newer hardware devices and latest Android platforms (Figs. 4–6).

Pablo Software Virus scan did not have an automated malware scan for any malware samples installed. There were no scans before, during, or after the install of the malicious malware samples. The app prompted an installation of the newly installed app only and all 15 malware samples installed without any malware threat detection. A manual scan was conducted after each malware sample install; 10 were detected, leaving five malware samples undetected (Fig. 7).

The majority of detection time findings improved throughout newer models of hardware and Android OSs. The hardware may be a factor due to the improvement of hardware specification (Table 5). Android also introduces more app security within Android 4.4 (KitKat), such as restricting the installation of apps from other sources than Google Play and allowing or disallowing apps through verification (Table 1). However, the user can ignore such options and instead choose a suggested responsive antimalware tool.

In order for detection time to be effective and reliable, the app must also be able to remove the threat immediately. Our findings demonstrated that although particular apps were able to detect the malware samples, they were neither flagged as imminent threats nor removed upon detection. For example, the antimalware apps not included within the detection time results were Pablo Software, Kaspersky Lab, and Doctor Web. Due to a lack of automatic scan capability, no detection time could be recorded and the apps received a result of n.a (see Section 3.2). Nevertheless, the type of scan and malware sample detection results were taken into consideration.

Finally, we looked at the overall malware samples detected (Fig. 7), which include both automatic and manual detection across all Android platforms. Impressively, 10 out of the 15 antimalware apps used in this experiment achieved 100% detection of the malware samples used. The 10 top rated antimalware apps are AVAST, Cheetah, Doctor Web, Qihu, Norton, McAfee/Intel Security, Kaspersky, BitDefender, MalwareBytes, and Sophos.

With a large number of positive results, up-to-date malware definitions play a key role in detecting known malware. As mentioned earlier, malware samples were used from various malware families to test accuracy and transparency. Having up-to-date malware definitions are the sole responsibility of antimalware companies, which will depend on available infrastructure resources and technology (see Section 2.3.1). If a wide variety of malware families is known, then detection will undoubtedly improve. AVG performed very well and detected a very large number of malware samples, receiving 97.78%. Interestingly, the one malware sample recorded as not detected for AVG was the most recent sample and on Android 4.0 (Ice Cream Sandwich); AVG installed on newer Android platforms were able to detect all malware samples. Such a result demonstrates the vulnerability in older Android platforms and proves that upgrading to newer Android OSs and hardware devices is vital to ensure additional security measures (see Section 2.1.2).

Lookout Mobile Security received 86.67% and Pablo Security received 66.67%, which resulted in a large number of malware samples being detected. They showed promising results, and the detection would only improve if a wider range of malware families could be included in their definition updates. Of the remaining apps, Creative Apps detected 33.33% and TrustGo only detected 26.67%; both were unable to detect the majority of malware samples used in this experiment and therefore performed the at lowest levels.

A key observation throughout the experiment was how each antimalware app handled the detection of the malware sample APK files. As part of the experiment process, the malware samples (APK files) were manually transferred onto the smartphone devices in order to test each one. Antimalware apps such as AVAST, Lookout Security, BitDefender, and MalwareBytes were the only ones to actively detect that malicious APK files (malware samples) were being transferred onto the device. They also automatically prompted the removal of malicious APK files before any installation took place, which is a huge advantage in protecting any Android device. If the experiment process expanded the type of scans performed, such antimalware apps would have extremely good detection time over other antimalware apps in the Google Play market.

Initially, it seemed that hardware specification potentially had a role in improving detection times. As the experiment continued, however, this was not always the case, as Android 4.4 (KitKat) on the Motorola Moto G also presented slower detection times, as did older devices and Android platforms. Possible causes may relate to different Android versions and API's integrations.

The Motorola Moto G also has higher hardware specifications; there was a considerable difference to the time it took for the malware samples to complete installation. The malware samples were much quicker than older devices when installing malware sample APK files (Table 5); therefore this may contribute to the improved detection times of those antimalware apps used within this experiment. As the malware samples were installed more quickly, the detection of malicious activity would improve. However, this was not always true in all experiments. Older devices were able to detect some of the malware samples much more quickly. BitDefender and MalwareBytes were representative of this theory, as the detection time on newer Android platforms and hardware out-performed their predecessors.

After testing 15 anti-malware mobile apps, the major limitation in the majority of such apps tested is the inability to take control of the Google install manager system process. A unknowing user can begin the initial installation of a malicious app; once the malicious file has completed the installation, only then did the majority of antimalware mobile apps run a scan on the newly installed apps and only then were any malicious threats detected. Surprisingly, only three apps have an option that prompted to take control of the default Android package installer—AVAST, Lookout Mobile Security, and Norton Mobile. The Android package installer controls how APK files are installed. Having unknown APK files scanned would significantly increase the detection of any malicious threat, providing malware definitions are up to date. Within this experiment, the option was not selected because not all apps had the same option, so it would be an unfair advantage.

The aim of this experiment is to provide transparency between popular free antimalware apps by following an experiment process. Throughout this experiment, three vital observations were identified to significantly improve detection time, including the scanning of any APK files that are transferred to a smartphone, an option for changing the default installer package, and for a scan to immediately start during an app installation rather than after completion. If the antimalware apps used within this experiment have up-to-date malware definitions across a wide variety of malware families, all three observations will significantly improve malicious app detection times and detection rates.

5 CONCLUSION AND FUTURE WORK

While Android and other mobile devices may be seen by some as an extension of existing threats to the security and privacy of user data, the mobile threat landscape is an extremely fast-moving environment (Choo, 2011; Quick et al., 2013). A 2014 study by 26 privacy enforcement authorities in 19 countries examining 1211 popular mobile apps for both Android and iOS platforms found that nearly 60% of these apps raised privacy concerns even before they were downloaded, and 85% of the apps were reportedly accessing personal data without providing adequate information to users (Leyden, 2014; Privacy Commissioner of Canada, 2014). It is essential that users undertake proactive measures such as those identified in this chapter; only a decade ago, several criminologists warned that "those who fail to anticipate the future are in for a rude shock when it arrives" (Grabosky et al., 2004, p. 156).

In this study, we manually examined the 15 most popular antimalware apps installed on devices running the three most recent versions of the Android OS. They were evaluated against 15 malware samples taken from various malware families from the Contagio Mobile Malware Mini Dump database. This is, to the best of our knowledge, the first academic study that provides a systematic and transparent evaluation of free antimalware apps for Android devices.

Our findings suggested that detection type is paramount in the responsiveness of detecting a malicious threat before, during, or upon immediate completion of a new app installation, which will prevent any consequent threat activation. Findings also suggested that there is a constant race between malware developers and security providers. For example, we identified that a number of free antimalware apps have outdated signature repositories and fewer options to change the default Android package installer. However, having an antimalware mobile app with automatic threat detection and removal installed is a significant advantage in protecting an Android device against potential malicious threats.

Future work includes:

1. Evaluate a wider range of devices in a live environment that would include both known and unknown (zero-day) malware samples. For example, users of the test devices would click on untrustworthy links and dubious advertisements and download attachments from phishing or spam email messages. Such experiment setting could potentially uncover additional malware families that have not been detected as part of signature repositories. The Android OS includes manual security features that allow or disallow the installation of nonmarket-based apps, which is a protective measure against manual app installations. For example, options such as "unknown sources and verify apps" are now included within Android KitKat and Lollipop, which prevent manual app installations taking place if selected. Therefore future work within a live environment will provide in-depth analysis into the relationship between malware and the Android OS.

2. Survey antimalware app users regarding their perceived effectiveness and reliability of the apps and evaluate the perceived effectiveness and reliability against the experiments either in a controlled environment (such as ours) or in a real-world deployment.

3. The above experiment (see Section 3.1) was conducted manually through a step-by-step process, where results were recorded manually on a per millisecond basis. The time involved was lengthy due to the precision of following each step of the experiment process, therefore limiting the malware sample dataset to 15 across 15 antimalware apps. Development of an automated process will enable the experiment to increase the malware dataset and include samples from different categories, as well as increase a broader range of antimalware apps, gaining further evaluation of their capabilities and limitations.

4. In addition, a list of prerequisites can be organized that will benchmark a number of different features that a user should expect from an antimalware tool. For example, does an antimalware app have options to change the default Android package installer? What about the ability to locate or lock a smart phone remotely or to notify the user of suspicious activity? Additional features would improve the overall effectiveness of an antimalware app.

CONFLICT OF INTEREST DECLARATION

The authors are not affiliated with any security company or antimalware app provider. No personal recommendations or endorsement should be presumed from the apps selected in this study.

References

Alcatel-Lucent, 2013. Kindsight Security Labs Q4 2013 Malware Report. viewed 07 September 2014, http://resources.alcatel-lucent.com/?cid=172490.

Alcatel-Lucent, 2014. Kindsight Security Labs Malware Report H1. viewed 11 September 2014, http://resources.alcatel-lucent.com/?cid=180437.

Amadeo, R., 2014. The history of Android, follow the endless iterations from Android 0.5 to Android 4.4. viewed 05 July 2014, http://arstechnica.com/gadgets/2014/06/building-android-a-40000-word-history-of-googles-mobile-os/.

Android Developers Dashboards, 2015. viewed 11 October 2015, http://developer.android.com/about/dashboards/index.html.

Android Developers Guide, 2013. Signing your applications. viewed 24 October 2013, http://developer.android.com/tools/publishing/app-signing.html.

Android Developers Guide, 2014. viewed 21 June 2014, http://developer.android.com/about/index.html.

Android Developers Guide, 2015. Android 6.0 APIs. viewed 11 October 2015, https://developer.android.com/about/versions/marshmallow/android-6.0.html.

Android Security Enhancements, 2015. viewed 11 October 2015, https://source.android.com/devices/tech/security/enhancements/index.html.

Anti-Phishing Working Group (APWG), 2013. Mobile threats and the underground marketplace. viewed 5 Sep 2014, http://docs.apwg.org/reports/mobile/apwg_mobile_fraud_report_april_2013.pdf.

AV-TEST, 2014. The independent IT-Security Institute, 36 security apps for Android are put under constant fire. viewed 08 August 2014, http://www.av-test.org/en/news/news-single-view/36-security-apps-for-android-are-put-under-constant-fire.

Choo, K.-K.R., 2011. The cyber threat landscape: challenges and future research directions. Comput. Secur. 30 (8), 719–731.

Choo, K.-K.R., D'Orazio, C.J., 2015. A generic process to identify vulnerabilities and design weaknesses in iOS healthcare apps. IEEE, US.

Chu, H.C., Lo, C.H., Chao, H.C., 2013. The disclosure of an Android smartphone's digital footprint respecting the Instant Messaging utilizing Skype and MSN. Electron. Commer. Res. 13 (3), 399–410.

Contagio Mobile, 2014. Mobile malware mini dump. viewed 08 August 2014, http://contagiominidump.blogspot.com.au.

Delac, G., Silic, M., Krolo, J., 2011. Emerging security threats for mobile platforms. In: In MIPRO, 2011 Proceedings of the 34th International Convention. IEEE, Opatija, Croatia, pp. 1468–1473.

Dietz, M., Shekhar, S., Pisetsky, Y., Shu, A., Wallach, D.S., 2011. QUIRE: lightweight provenance for smart phone operating systems. In: In USENIX Security Symposium '11, San Francisco, CA.

Di Leom, M., DOrazio, C.J., Deegan, G., Choo, K.-K.R., 2015. Forensic collection and analysis of thumbnails in android. In: In Trustcom/BigDataSE/ISPA, Vol. 1. IEEE, Helsinki, Finland, pp. 1059–1066.

Enck, W., Ongtang, M., Mcdaniel, P., 2009. Understanding Android security. IEEE Secur. Privacy Mag. 7 (1), 50–57.

Feth, D., Pretschner, A., 2012. Flexible data-driven security for android. In: In Software Security and Reliability (SERE), 2012 IEEE Sixth International Conference, Gaithersburg, MD, USA. on. IEEE, pp. 41–50.

Fortinet, 2014. Threat landscape report. viewed 19 July 2014, http://www.fortinet.com/sites/default/files/whitepapers/Threat-Landscape-2014.pdf.

F-Secure, 2014a. Mobile threat report Q1 2014. viewed 19 July 2014, http://www.f-secure.com/static/doc/labs_global/Research/Mobile_Threat_Report_Q1_2014.pdf.

F-Secure, 2014b. Threat description Trojan-Spy: Android/Tramp.A. viewed 12 December 2014, https://www.f-secure.com/v-descs/trojan_android_tramp.shtml.

G DATA, 2015. Threat report: Q1/2015, mobile malware report. viewed 11 October 2015, https://public.gdatasoftware.com/Presse/Publikationen/Malware_Reports/G_DATA_MobileMWR_Q1_2015_US.pdf.

Google Play, 2014. Apps. viewed 20 July 2014, https://play.google.com/store.

Grabosky, P.N., Smith, R.G., Grabosky, P., Urbas, G., 2004. Cyber Criminals on Trial. Cambridge University Press, Cambridge.

Hou, O., 2012. A look at Google bouncer, TrendMirco. viewed 26 October 2013, http://blog.trendmicro.com/trendlabs-security-intelligence/a-look-at-google-bouncer/.

Husted, N., Saïdi, H., Gehani, A., 2011. Smartphone security limitations: conflicting traditions. In: In Proceedings of the 2011 Workshop on Governance of Technology, Information, and Policies. ACM, pp. 5–12.

Imgraben, J., Engelbrecht, A., Choo, K.R., 2014. Always connected, but are smart mobile users getting more security savvy? a survey of smart mobile device users. Behav. Inform. Technol. http://dx.doi.org/10.1080/0144929X.2014.934286.

Kashyap, A., Horbury, A., Catacutan, A., Uscilowski, B., Wueest, C., Mai, C., Mallon, C., O'Brien, D., Chien, E., Park, E., O'Gorman, G., Lau, H., Power, J.-P., Hamada, J., Ann Sewell, K., O'Brien, L., Maniyara, M., Thonnard, O., Johnston, N., Cox, O., Coogan, O., Vervier, P.-A., Liu, Q., Narang, S., Doherty, S., Gallo, T., Symantec Corporation, 2014. Internet Security Threat Report 2014. Viewed 5 Sep 2014, vol. 19. Symantec Corporation, Mountain View, CA, USA. http://www.symantec.com/content/en/us/enterprise/other_resources/b-istr_main_report_v19_21291018.en-us.pdf.

La, P.M., Martinelli, F., Sgandurra, D., 2013. A survey on security for mobile devices. IEEE Commun. Surv. Tutorials 15 (1), 446–471.

Lacoon Security, Bobrov, O., 2014. Android icon vulnerability can cause serious system-level crashes. viewed 12 December 2014, https://www.lacoon.com/chinese-government-targets-hong-kong-protesters-android-mrat-spyware/.

Leontiadis, I., Efstratiou, C., Picone, M., Mascolo, C., 2012. Don't kill my ads! balancing privacy in an ad-supported mobile application market. In: In Proceedings of the Twelfth Workshop on Mobile Computing Systems & Applications. ACM, New York, USA, pp. 2.

Leyden, J., 2014. This flashlight app requires: your contacts list, identity, access to your camera.... viewed 12 September 2014, http://www.theregister.co.uk/2014/09/11/mobile_app_privacy_survey/.

Liebergeld, S., Lange, M., 2013. Android security, pitfalls and lessons learned. 28th International Symposium on Computer and Information Sciences, 2013, Paris, France. In: Information Sciences and Systems 2013. Springer International Publishing, pp. 409–417.

Lookout, S.T., 2014. The new NotCompatible: sophisticated and evasive threat harbors the potential to compromise enterprise networks. viewed 12 December 2014, https://blog.lookout.com/blog/2014/11/19/notcompatible/.

McAfee Labs, Mobile Security, Zhang, M., 2014. Android icon vulnerability can cause serious system-level crashes. viewed 12 December 2014, http://blogs.mcafee.com/mcafee-labs/chinese-worm-infects-thousands-android-phones.

NakedSecurity by Sophos, D.P., 2014. Return of the Android SMS virus: self-spreading "Selfmite" worm comes back for more. viewed 12 December 2014, https://nakedsecurity.sophos.com/2014/10/10/return-of-the-android-sms-virus-self-spreading-selfmite-worm-comes-back-for-more/.

Nimodia, C., Deshmukh, H.R., 2012. Android operating system. Softw. Eng. 2229-4007. 3 (1), 10.

Ongtang, M., Mclaughlin, S., Enck, W., Mcdaniel, P., 2012. Semantically rich application centric security in Android. Secur. Commun. Netw. 5 (6), 658–673.

Pieterse, H., Olivier, M.S., 2012. Android botnets on the rise: trends and characteristics. In: In Information Security for South Africa (ISSA). IEEE, Johannesburg, Gauteng, South Africa, pp. 1–5.

Privacy Commissioner of Canada, 2014. Global Internet sweep finds significant privacy policy shortcomings. viewed 12 September 2014, https://www.priv.gc.ca/media/nr-c/2013/nr-c_130813_e.asp.

Quick, D., Martini, B., Choo, R., 2013. Cloud Storage Forensics. Elsevier Science, Burlington.

Rivera, J., Goasduff, L., 2015. Gartner says emerging markets drove worldwide smartphone sales to 19 percent growth in first quarter of 2015, Gartner. viewed 05 October 2015, http://www.gartner.com/newsroom/id/3061917.

Rivera, J., van der Meulen, R., 2015. Gartner says tablet sales continue to be slow in 2015. Gartner, viewed 05 October 2015, http://www.gartner.com/newsroom/id/2954317.

Shabtai, A., Fledel, Y., Kanonov, U., Elovici, Y., Dolev, S., 2009. Google Android: a state-of-the-art review of security mechanisms. arXiv. preprint arXiv:0912.5101.

Shabtai, A., Fledel, Y., Kanonov, U., Elovici, Y., Dolev, S., Glezer, C., 2010. Google Android: a comprehensive security assessment. IEEE Secur. Privacy Mag. 7 (2), 35–44.

Sky News, 2014. Mysterious fake mobile phone towers discovered. viewed 5 September 2014, http://news.sky.com/story/1329375/mysterious-fake-mobile-phone-towers-discovered.

Spreitzenbarth, Forensic Blog, 2014. Mobile phone forensics and mobile malware, current android malware. viewed 28 June 2014, http://forensics.spreitzenbarth.de/android-malware.

Suarez-Tangil, G., Tapiador, J.E., Peris-Lopez, P., Ribagorda, A., 2014. Evolution, detection and analysis of malware for smart devices. IEEE Commun. Surv. Tutorials 16 (2), 961–987.

Symantec Intelligence, 2012. Symantec intelligence report: September 2012. viewed 5 Sep 2014, http://www.symantec.com/content/en/us/enterprise/other_resources/b-intelligence_report_09_2012.en-us.pdf.

The Register, Leyden, J., 2014. DeathRing: Cheapo Androids pre-pwned with mobile malware. viewed 04 December 2014, http://www.theregister.co.uk/2014/12/04/cheapo_androids_prepwned_with_mobile_malware/.

TrendMicro, 2012. TrendLabs 2Q 2012 security roundup. viewed 22 July 2014, http://www.trendmicro.com.au/cloud-content/us/pdfs/security-intelligence/reports/rpt-its-big-business-and-its-getting-personal.pdf.

Vargas, R.J.G., Anaya, E.A., Huerta, R.G., Hernandez, A.F.M., 2012. Security controls for Android. In: Computational Aspects of Social Networks (CASoN). IEEE, Sao Carlos, Brazil, pp. 212–216.

Vidas, T., Christin, N., Cranor, L., 2011. Curbing android permission creep. In: In Proceedings of the Web. Vol. 2, pp. 91-96. W2SP 2011: Web 2.0 Security and Privacy 2011, Oakland, California. Held in conjunction with the 2011 IEEE Symposium on Security and Privacy. http://w2spconf.com/2011.

Walls, J., Choo, K.-K.R., 2015. A review of free cloud-based anti-malware apps for Android. In: In Proceedings of 14th IEEE International Conference on Trust, Security and Privacy in Computing and Communications (TrustCom 2015), Helsinki, Finland. 20–22 August 2015. IEEE Computer Society Press (ERA 2010/CORE 2014 A rank conference).

Wang, Y., Streff, K., Raman, S., 2012, Smartphone security challenges. In: Computer, Vol. 45(12), Dakota State University, USA. IEEE, pp. 52-58.

Zhou, Y., Jiang, X., 2012. Dissecting Android malware: characterization and evolution. In: 33rd IEEE Symposium on Security and Privacy, pp. 95–109.

Timeline Analysis for Digital Evidence on MTK-Based Shanzhai Mobile Phone

J. Fang*, Z.L. Jiang†, S. Li*, S.-M. Yiu‡, L.C.K. Hui‡, K.-P. Chow‡

*Jinan University, Guangzhou, China †Harbin Institute of Technology Shenzhen Graduate School, Shenzhen, China ‡The University of Hong Kong, HKSAR, China

1 INTRODUCTION

In the last decade, worldwide mobile phone usage has increased dramatically. Globally, the number of mobile cellular subscriptions reached 5.3 billion by the end of 2010, reported by the International Telecommunication Union (ITU). And vendors shipped 371.8 million units in Q1 2011, growing 19.8% year-over-year (IDC) (Wauters, 2011). At the same time, the computational power and storage of mobile phones are getting more and more powerful, especially the deployment of dual-core CPU and gigabytes of internal memory (Lomas, 2011). Due to their mobility and the portability, mobile phones have become second nature to people, and as a result are often quite involved in some criminal cases (Mislan, 2010). More seriously, the powerful mobile phone can be used as a criminal tool anytime and anywhere. In both cases, a lot of digital evidence may be stored inside the mobile phone, and so mobile phone forensics techniques are necessary for retrieving and investigating the information (Barmpatsalou et al., 2013).

Mobile phone forensics has been studied for quite a long time and there are several commercial products for investigating the mobile phones of world leading brands, such as Symbian (Mokhonoana and Olivier, 2007), Android (Vidas et al., 2011), Windows (Klaver, 2010), Blackberry, and iPhone. However, in China, a new category of mobile phone with a commonly known brand of "Shanzhai mobile phone" (Shanzhai phone for short) emerged from 2007 after China's government removed the license policy to manufacture mobile phones and now it is flooding in the global mobile phone market due to its high cost-performance ratios (Nanyang, 2010). The Chinese word "Shanzhai" originally means "mountain village," but now it has another meaning to refer to imitation, low-end and unprofessional brands and goods, particularly electronics. Contrast to the remarkable growth of "Shanzhai phone," there is less published research work related to Shanzhai phone forensics. The reason may lie in the shortage of the technical documents of Shanzhai phone and the great number of Shanzhai phone models. Benefit from the turnkey solution provided by MediaTek (MTK) (http://www.mediatek.com/en/index.php) and Spreadtrum (http://www.Spreadtrum.com) the development period for Shanzhai phone can be shortened from over one year to one month. It means that there will be thousands of models of Shanzhai phones appearing on the market during a single year. Unfortunately, such a quick change becomes a nightmare to researchers to perform digital forensics on Shanzhai phone. Since Shanzhai phones are spreading worldwide and there is trend of criminals using them as they perpetrate crimes, it is necessary to conduct a deeper investigation on Shanzhai phones. As a result, Shanzhai phone forensics unavoidably become more and more important.

In this paper, the method for retrieving data from the internal memory of a typical MTK-based Shanzhai phone is introduced. Data structures of storing call log, phone book, short message service (SMS) and some advanced media content are also parsed via reverse engineering. Furthermore, the extracted information is analyzed with historical information to reconstruct the sequence of operations for help determine a suspect's activity.

2 RELATED WORK

There has been some research on mobile phone forensics since the early 2000s. There is a wide range of mobile forensics tools developed to acquire data from the flash memory of mobile phones (Ayers et al., 2014; McCarthy, 2005). However, most of the tools use commands and response protocols to indirectly access the memory. These commands and protocols depend on the operating system (OS) and actually change the contents of the memory. Only data visible to the OS can be recovered. Also, such tools fail to retrieve data from dead or faulty mobile phones. Another problem with such tools is that they cannot recover deleted data.

Flasher tools are the easiest and noninvasive way to read flash memory data (Breeuwsma et al., 2007), which have been used in quite a few mobile forensics cases (Gratzer and Naccache, 2006; Purdue University, 2007). However, these approaches cannot ensure a complete dump of the memory and may depend a lot on the OS. Meanwhile, if the data connector of the mobile phone is not supported by flasher tools, electronic wiring of the communication pins on mobile phone's Printed Circuit Board (PCB) may be required for connection with flasher tools.

The physical extraction approach is to physically remove the internal flash memory chip from the mobile phone and read it with a memory reader. This procedure requires professional engineers because memory chips may be damaged during de-soldering. Joint Test Action Group (JTAG) is an embedded test technique to test automatically the functionality and quality of the soldered integrated components on PCB, which is a standard test access port and boundary-scan architecture. It controls the phone's microprocessor in debug mode to communicate with the memory chip, and dump the memory bit by bit. Therefore,

TABLE 1   Comparison of Three Internal Memory Acquisition Approaches

	Desoldering	JTAG	Flasher Tools
Risk of chip damage	High	Low	Low
Risk of data modification	Low	Low	Medium
Complexity of usage	High	Medium	Low
Electronic soldering	High	Medium	Not required in many cases
Completeness of data	High	Medium	Medium (may not be guaranteed)

it ensures the completeness of the forensics binary image and it is OS-independent. A brief comparison of these approaches is shown in Table 1.

In this paper, we go for the easier solution of using a flasher tool to obtain the memory instead of using JTAG because our focus is more on how the information is stored in the memory. Note that using JTAG should provide a lower level picture of the memory.

From the viewpoint of OS, there have been various forensic software or tools aimed at dedicated OS, such as Symbian (Mokhonoana and Olivier, 2007), Windows mobile (Klaver, 2010), Android (Vidas et al., 2011; Hoog, 2011), and iPhone (Hoog and Strzempka, 2011). A more detailed survey could be found in Barmpatsalou et al.'s review paper (Barmpatsalou et al., 2013). Since these tools are OS-dependent, they cannot be used directly to acquire data from Shanzhai phones. There has been some research work on mobile forensics using JTAG (Willassen, 2005; Zhang, 2010).

3 DIGITAL EVIDENCE IN SHANZHAI PHONE

In this paper, a typical model of Shanzhai phone is selected to be studied in the experiments. The model is an imitated version of iPhone4. This model is based on one low-end processor of MediaTek, MT6253, which is MediaTek's first monolithic GSM/GPRS handset chip solution that offers the highest level of integration with lowest power consumption and best-in-class features. Most of Shanzhai phone models were developed on this platform.

3.1 Physical Data Storage and Logical File System

Inside the Shanzhai phone, a 16M bytes NOR flash chip (Toshiba TC58FYM7T8C) integrated with a 4M bytes RAM is used to work as read-only memory (ROM) for OS and as non-volatile random access memory (NVRAM) for data storage. As shown in Fig. 1, the 16M bytes of NOR flash of the Shanzhai mobile phone is divided into two parts. The first 14M bytes (memory address from 0 to 0xDFFFFF) are used to store code and will be kept unchanged after the Shanzhai phone is produced. Noted that this is the default configuration in MTK development solution.

The remaining 2M bytes (memory address from 0xE00000 to 0xFFFFFF) are further divided logically into two areas. As shown in Fig. 2, both of the two areas can be seen as a

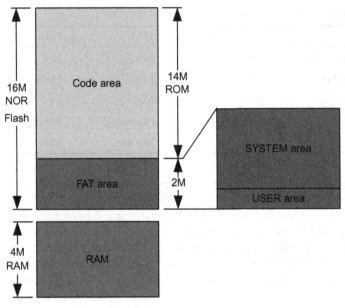

FIG. 1   The NOR flash memory for the Shanzhai phone.

FIG. 2   The directory as viewed from Windows.

removable drive under Windows OS when the Shanzhai phone is connected to a computer via USB data cable. Note that this is the only logical distribution of the two areas. Physically, the blocks in flash for the two areas are mixed and not separated as clearly as this figure. From the partition information, we know that both drives are formatted in FAT12 format, but only the drive (here is drive H:) corresponding to USER area can be accessed via Windows, the other one (drive I:) corresponding to SYSTEM area cannot be read, written, or viewed by a normal user. In general, the USER area is kept for the Shanzhai phone user as a storage to exchange data between the phone and a computer, while the SYSTEM area is kept for the OS of the phone as a virtual memory to save the data managed by OS. Note that some of the data saved in SYSTEM area can be viewed or edited by the user via the user interface (UI) of the Shanzhai phone, such as the settings of the phone, phonebook, call log, SMS, etc.

With the help of a flasher tool, the total 16M bytes of raw data in the flash memory can be retrieved as a memory dump and can be further investigated in a computer as a binary file.

3.2 Extracting Baseline Contents From Flash Dump of Shanzhai Phone

In this section, the flash memory dump of the Shanzhai phone is reverse engineered to sort out the format of storing three kinds of baseline contents of mobile phone including the phonebook, call log, and SMS.

In the MTK-based platform, the phonebook, call log, SMS and other system-related user information are organized as data items and stored as files in NVRAM. A data item management system is deployed to manage NVRAM data in the file system and maintains an internal lookup table to retrieve the data items. Fig. 3 shows the logical relationship between the data items and the files in NVRAM.

Usually, phonebook, call log and SMS are saved as data items named "NVRAM_EF_PHB_LID," "NVRAM_EF_PHB_LN_ENTRY_LID" and "NVRAM_EF_SMSAL_SMS_LID," respectively, under the subdirectory "NVD_DATA." While this high-level information can help us to understand the storage mechanism of MTK-based Shanzhai phone, since we cannot directly access to the file system of the phone, we must try to reverse engineer the binary dump to figure out the storing pattern of the data items as following.

Each kind of contents has a different data structure for storage. Phonebook saves the basic information of a contact as one entry, which is 86-byte length including 62 bytes for contact's

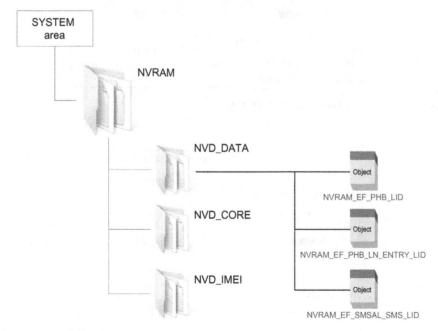

FIG. 3   Data items and files stored in NVRAM.

name and 20 bytes for contact's phone number in Binary-Coded Decimal coding. An example is illustrated in Fig. 4. Note that when one entry in the phonebook is deleted by a user, the logical memory space for that entry will be revoked and be filled in with a hexadecimal value of "0xFF."

Data item of call log saves each call event as one 92-byte length entry, including 32 bytes for caller's name, 7 bytes for the time of the call, 41 bytes for caller number and 4 bytes for call duration. An example is illustrated in Fig. 5. Note that when one entry in call log is deleted by user, the following call log will move one unit forward to replace the memory space of the deleted call log, and so on. Finally, all the entries later than the deleted entry will move one unit forward as a whole.

The data item of SMS saves each SMS as one 184-byte length entry containing a status byte and an 183-byte protocol data unit (PDU). The status byte is used to indicate the SMS is "new event," "read," "sent" or "draft." And the PDU part including the number of SMS Center (SMSC), the time of receiving the SMS (given by SMSC), the phone number of the sender and the content of the message. An example is illustrated in Fig. 6.

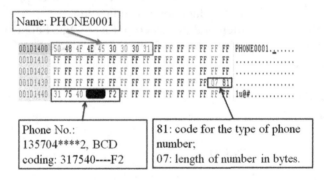

FIG. 4   Data format of phone book stored in NVRAM.

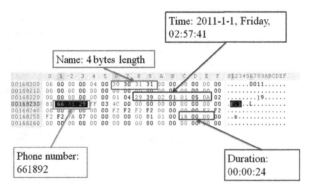

FIG. 5   Data format of call log stored in NVRAM.

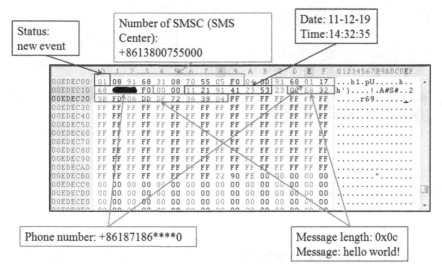

FIG. 6   Data format of SMS stored in NVRAM.

4 TIMELINE ANALYSIS OF THE DIGITAL EVIDENCE

In this section, we first investigate the recovery of content deleted by user's operations from the flash dump, then we discuss one characteristic of the data management of the MTK-based Shanzhai phone, with which one previous version of the file for storing data item will be kept every time the data item is modified. Based on this property of Shanzhai phone, we propose a timeline analysis method to retrace the suspect's activity.

4.1 Deleted Contents and "Snapshots" in the Flash Dump

In Section 3.2, when one entry in a data item is deleted or modified, or one entry is added to the data item, the memory space for storing data item will be modified accordingly. However, this may be still the understanding at the logical level of NVRAM files. When we go through the flash dump on the binary level, we find that there are multiple copies of data items. Some of them are the previous version of the data item before modification. This may be due to the fact of the flash file system: when the flash store is to be updated, the file system will write a new copy of the changed data to a fresh block, remap the file pointers, then erase the old block later when it has time. So, for example, when a phonebook entry is updated, the pointer to "NVRAM_EF_PHB_LID" will be changed from the gray block in Fig. 7 to the dark block. When a user accesses the phonebook via the UI of the phone's OS, the newest version of phonebook stored in the dark block will be displayed, while the previous version of the phonebook is still stored in the original flash memory block until the block needs to be recycled. We call the historical version of data items as "snapshot."

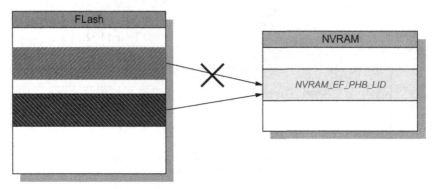

FIG. 7 Pointer remapping when data item modified.

4.2 Timeline Analysis on Phonebook

Since the previous data is just "erased" in the filesystem but not be really wiped from the physical storage, the recovery of deleted contents is possible. In our experiments, a tool was developed to automatically parse the flash memory dump to extract all versions of the data item using pattern matching techniques. An example is illustrated in Fig. 8. In this example, nine snapshots were found in the flash memory dump. Snapshot 7 should be the first version of phonebook file as it only contains one entry. Recall that one modification on the data item will generate one more snapshot. Then Snapshot 6 should be the second version as it only has one more operation compared to Snapshot 7 (the operation should be appending "jack1"). Following this logistic and comparing the entries in the snapshots, the operation sequence can be easily deduced as follows: Snapshot 7–Snapshot 6–Snapshot 5–Snapshot 4–Snapshot 3–Snapshot 2–Snapshot 1–Snapshot 9–Snapshot 8.

The above example shows a simple case of rebuilding the operation sequence of the phonebook. Note that the snapshots are continuous; that is, no snapshot is erased by flash recycling mechanism. When the case with some snapshots lost is considered, the situation becomes more complicated and algorithm needs to be applied in the analysis to help rebuild the timeline.

Next, we carry out an experiment with some snapshots lost and propose an algorithm to help analyze the timeline of the user's activity. First, we manually perform a series of operations on the Shanzhai phone with the following steps:

1. Add entry named "memory0"
2. Add entry named "memory1"
3. Add entry named "memory2"
4. Add entry named "memory3"
5. Add entry named "memory4"
6. Delete entry "memory1"
7. Delete entry "memory3"
8. Add entry named "memory5"
9. Add entry named "memory6"

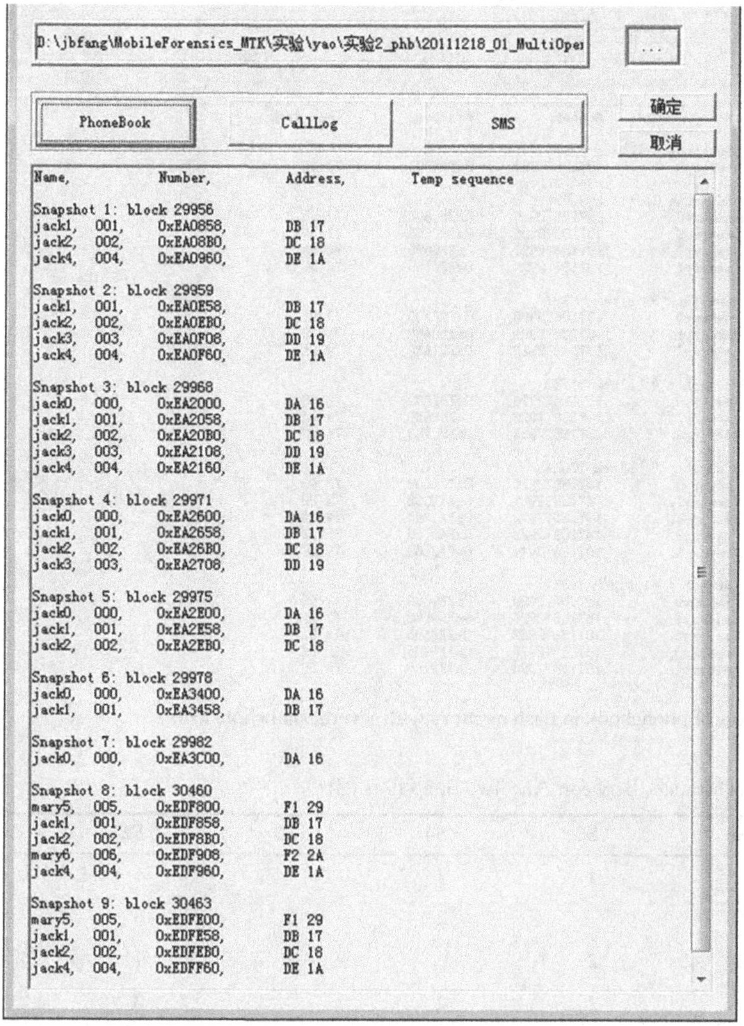

FIG. 8   All snapshots of a phonebook in flash memory.

The flash memory is dumped to a computer for investigation after the Step 9 is done. Running our tool on this flash dump, all the information of phonebook could be extracted as shown in Fig. 9. Note that snapshot 6 is the latest version of the phonebook. We define the distance (d) between two Snapshots A and B as the minimum number of operations to change A to B. Since one modification operation on the data item will generate one snapshot, the more similar the snapshots and the more closer the operations in time sequence. For example, in Fig. 9, since Snapshot 1 contains entry "memory0" and Snapshot 2 contains entries {"memory0," "memory2," "memory4," "memory5" }, changing from Snapshot 1 to Snapshot 2 requires three inserting operations, such that the distance between Snapshots 1 and 2 is three. All the distances between any two snapshots in Fig. 9 are calculated and shown in Table 2.

```
        ┌─────────────┐    ┌─────────────┐    ┌─────────────┐          确定
        │  PhoneBook  │    │   CallLog   │    │     SMS     │       ┌────────┐
        └─────────────┘    └─────────────┘    └─────────────┘       └────────┘
                                                                        取消
        ┌────────────────────────────────────────────────────────────────────┐
        │ Name,         Number,       Address,      Temp sequence            ▲ │
        │                                                                      │
        │ Snapshot 1: block 29984                                              │
        │ memory0,      18718672920,  0xEA4000,      72 D8                     │
        │                                                                      │
        │ Snapshot 2: block 30691                                              │
        │ memory0,      18718672920,  0xEFC600,      72 D8                     │
        │ memory5,      18718672925,  0xEFC658,      77 DD                     │
        │ memory2,      18718672922,  0xEFC6B0,      74 DA                     │
        │ memory4,      18718672924,  0xEFC760,      76 DC                     │
        │                                                                      │
        │ Snapshot 3: block 30997                                              │
        │ memory0,      18718672920,  0xF22A00,      72 D8                     │
        │ memory1,      18718672921,  0xF22A58,      73 D9                     │
        │ memory2,      18718672922,  0xF22AB0,      74 DA                     │
        │                                                                      │
        │ Snapshot 4: block 31763                                              │
        │ memory0,      18718672920,  0xF82600,      72 D8                     │
        │ memory2,      18718672922,  0xF826B0,      74 DA                     │
        │ memory4,      18718672924,  0xF82760,      76 DC                     │
        │                                                                      │
        │ Snapshot 5: block 32024                                              │
        │ memory0,      18718672920,  0xFA3000,      72 D8                     │
        │ memory1,      18718672921,  0xFA3058,      73 D9                     │
        │ memory2,      18718672922,  0xFA30B0,      74 DA                     │
        │ memory3,      18718672923,  0xFA3108,      75 DB                     │
        │ memory4,      18718672924,  0xFA3160,      76 DC                     │
        │                                                                      │
        │ Snapshot 6: block 32587                                              │
        │ memory0,      18718672920,  0xFE9600,      72 D8                     │
        │ memory5,      18718672925,  0xFE9658,      77 DD                     │
        │ memory2,      18718672922,  0xFE96B0,      74 DA                     │
        │ memory6,      18718672926,  0xFE9708,      78 DE                     │
        │ memory4,      18718672924,  0xFE9760,      76 DC                     │
        └──────────────────────────────────────────────────────────────────────┘
```

FIG. 9   Snapshots of phonebook in flash memory with several snapshots lost.

TABLE 2   The Distances Between Any Two Snapshots (S)

	S6	S5	S4	S3	S2	S1
S6		4	2	4	1	4
S5	4		2	2	3	4
S4	2	2		2	1	2
S3	4	2	2		3	2
S2	1	3	1	3		3
S1	4	4	2	2	3	

From Table 2 and the starting point, Snapshot 6, using the shortest path principle, so we can reconstruct the timeline of Snapshot 6, Snapshots 2 and 4, but leave three snapshots that cannot be determined with the shortest path principle. The partial sequence is shown in Fig. 10.

Since Snapshot 5 contains all three entries which also exist in Snapshot 4, Snapshot 5 should be the one nearer to Snapshot 4 than Snapshots 1 and 3. Then the Fig. 10 can be redrawn as Fig. 11 with all the sequences determined.

Thus, the timeline of the operations can be rebuilt with this method. Furthermore, the other kinds of contents stored in the Shanzhai phone also hold this characteristic and the method can be applied to the timeline analysis on the other kinds of contents.

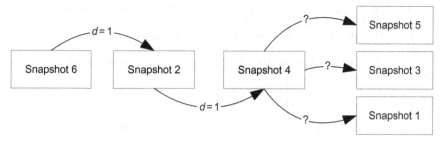

FIG. 10   Timeline of operations (partial).

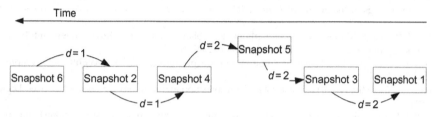

FIG. 11   Timeline of operations.

5 CONCLUSION

This paper presents work on the investigation of how phone call records and phonebook entries are stored in an MTK-based Shanzhai phone. The investigation reveals some important information on how the system handles the addition/deletion of phonebook entries and the phone call records. Although through the interface of OS, only the most recent entries of phone calls and phonebook are displayed, if the memory has not yet been overwritten, valuable evidence could still be retrieved. Furthermore, a deep analysis will be performed on the extracted information and the historical information to construct the corresponding timeline array to help determine a suspect's activity.

Acknowledgments

This work was partially supported by China State Scholarship Fund(No. 201506785014), National Natural Science Foundation of China (No. 61401176, 61402136, 61361166006), Natural Science Foundation of Guangdong Province (No. 2014A030310205, 2014A030313697), Science and technology projects of Guangdong Province (2016A010101017), Project of Guangdong High Education (YQ2015018), and NSFC/RGC Joint Research Scheme (N_HKU 72913), Hong Kong.

References

Ayers, R., Brothers, S., Jansen, W., 2014. Guidelines on Mobile Device Forensics. NIST Special Publication 800-101 Revision 1, pp. 1–87.
Barmpatsalou, K., Damopoulos, D., Kambourakis, G., Katos, V., 2013. A critical review of 7 years of mobile device forensics. Digit. Investig. 10 (4), 323–349.

Breeuwsma, M., Jongh, M.D., Klaver, C., Knijff, R.V.D., Roeloffs, M., 2007. Forensic data recovery from flash memory. Small Scale Digit. Device Forensics J. 1 (1), 1–17.

Gratzer, V., Naccache, D., 2006. Cryptography, law enforcement, and mobile communications. IEEE Secur. Privacy 4 (6), 67–70.

Hoog, A., 2011. Android Forensics: Investigation, Analysis and Mobile Security for Google Android. Elsevier, New York.

Hoog, A., Strzempka, K., 2011. iPhone and iOS Forensics: Investigation, Analysis and Mobile Security for Apple iPhone, iPad and iOS Devices. Elsevier, New York.

Klaver, C., 2010. Windows mobile advanced forensics. Digit. Investig. 6 (3), 147–167.

Lomas, N., 2011. Dual-core smartphones: The next mobile arms race. http://www.silicon.com/technology/mobile/2011/01/12/dual-core-smartphones-the-next-mobile-arms-race-39746799/.

McCarthy, P., 2005. Forensic analysis of mobile phones. BS CIS Thesis, Mawson Lakes.

Mislan, R., 2010. Cellphone crime solvers. IEEE Spectr. 47 (7), 34–39.

Mokhonoana, P.M., Olivier, M.S., 2007. Acquisition of a Symbian smart phone's content with an on-phone forensic tool. In: Proceedings of the Southern African Telecommunication Networks and Applications Conference. 8. Citeseer.

Nanyang, C., 2010. Fake iPhone 4G mobile phone hits Shanzhai market. http://www.suite101.com/news/fake-iphone-4g-mobile-phone-hits-shanzhai-market-a234058.

Purdue University, 2007. Expert: 'flasher' technology digs deeper for digital evidence. http://www.physorg.com/news95611284.html.

Vidas, T., Zhang, C., Christin, N., 2011. Toward a general collection methodology for android devices. Digit. Investig. 8, S14–S24.

Wauters, R., 2011. Worldwide mobile phone market grew 20% in q1 2011, fueled by smartphone boom. http://techcrunch.com/2011/04/28/worldwide-mobile-phone-market-grew-20-in-q1-fueled-by-smartphone-boom/.

Willassen, S., 2005. Forensic analysis of mobile phone internal memory. Advances in Digital Forensics. Springer, New York, pp. 191–204.

Zhang, Z.W., 2010. The research of MTK mobile phones flash file system recovery. Netinfo Secur. 11, 34–36.

CHAPTER

10

RESTful IoT Authentication Protocols

H.V. Nguyen, L. Lo Iacono

Cologne University of Applied Sciences, Cologne, Germany

1 INTRODUCTION

The Internet of Things (IoT) has evolved into an important building block for future IT visions such as Smart City, Smart Building, Smart Home, Smart Mobility and Industry 4.0. As those systems cover a large number of sensors and nodes that communicate frequently with each other, design concepts for developing IoT systems must be highly scalable (Atzori et al., 2010). One approach to fulfilling this requirement is the architectural style of the web known as representational state transfer (REST) (Fielding, 2000). REST is a guideline for designing large-scale distributed systems. Due to its strength in terms of scalability, interoperability, and efficiency, the application of REST has been adopted in areas such as service-oriented architecture (SOA) (Erl et al., 2012; Gorski et al., 2014a,b) and cloud computing (Lo Iacono and Nguyen, 2015a). Consequently, REST is gaining traction as an approved concept for implementing large-scale IoT systems (Shelby et al., 2014; Urien, 2015). Since IoT services and applications share sensible information, security is another prerequisite of paramount importance (Atzori et al., 2010). Hence, REST-Security for IoT-based environments is becoming relevant.

This chapter introduces an authentication concept for RESTful IoT protocols, which consider scalability and resource-restrictiveness constraints stemming from the architectural style REST and IoT networks and devices. The chapter is organized as follows: The foundations of REST are introduced in Section 2. Based on this background, Section 3 briefly introduces Constrained Application Protocol (CoAP) (Shelby et al., 2014) and Remote APDU Call Secure (RACS) (Urien, 2015), two RESTful protocols for the IoT domain. On the basis of the REST foundations and their technical instantiations, Section 4 proposes a methodology for developing security schemes for REST-based (IoT) systems of any kind. Following this methodology, Section 5 extends REST by an integrated authentication (Lo Iacono and Nguyen, 2015b) while remaining on the same abstraction level as REST itself. Section 6 utilizes the proposed security scheme as a guideline for implementing concrete authentication protocols to CoAP

(Nguyen and Lo Iacono, 2015) and RACS. Based on these results, Section 7 concludes this chapter with a summary, as well as a future research and development challenges.

2 REST FOUNDATIONS

Roy Fielding introduced the architectural style REST (Fielding, 2000) in his doctoral dissertation. The basic idea behind this concept is to provide a guideline proposing architectural constraints for designing highly scalable distributed software systems. These constraints are illustrated in Fig. 1.

The communication in REST is based on the *client-server* and request-response model. Therefore it is always the client who initiates the communication by issuing a request addressing a resource from a server. In the context of REST, a resource is an abstract definition of information intended for human interpretation or machine processing. Thus, a resource can have multiple representations. Moreover, a resource must be addressable by a unique resource identifier. Hence, each request must include a resource identifier. In conjunction with the requested action, both data elements define the intention and destination of a request. The resource identifier syntax and the request actions must be standardized and predefined by the *uniform interface* so that all components in a REST architecture can understand the purpose of a

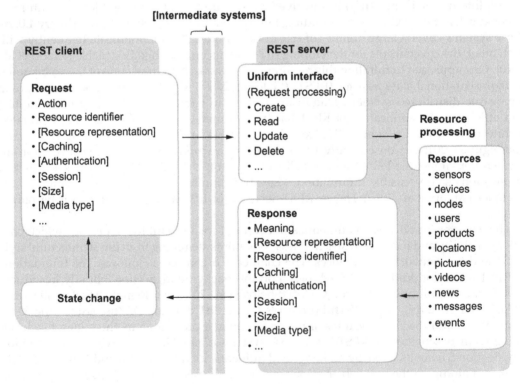

FIG. 1   REST constraints and principles (Gorski et al., 2014a).

request. Fielding does not specify any concrete actions for REST-based systems; the definition of a fixed set of actions is rather a matter of the implementation of the uniform interface. REST-based systems mostly use actions to create, read, update and delete a resource. Depending on the action, a request can comprise a resource representation such as that for creating or updating. In addition to the resource identifier syntax and request action, the uniform interface also defines a fixed set of further metadata elements describing, for example, the size and the media type of a resource representation. Since REST messages are constrained to be *stateless* and *cacheable*, metadata can also define state information such as authentication or session data and caching information. As requests in REST contain all required data elements including the action, the resource identifier, state and cache information, and further metadata, their semantics are *self-descriptive* for each server. This means that every server can understand the intention of a request without maintaining any particular state and without knowing the client in advance, since all requests are self-descriptive and all data elements are standardized.

The stateless and self-descriptive nature of REST messages makes them well suited for intermediate processing. Thus in many cases, the communication flow in REST-based systems is *layered* by multiple intermediate systems to ensure efficiency and scalability. For instance, intermediaries are utilized to cache messages, saving a server from replicated processing with the aim to reduce communication latency. A load balancer is another prevalent intermediate component to distribute workloads across multiple servers in order to provide scalability. Further intermediaries can be, for example, security gateways performing authentication, as well as access control or cross-protocol proxies encapsulating legacy or other related service systems.

Once a request receives a server, the endpoint returns a response including a response meaning informing about the result of a request. As with requests, a response can contain further metadata, such as authentication or caching information, and a resource representation accompanied by resource representation metadata. Moreover, the metadata and resource representation of a REST response may contain hypermedia elements defining application control information; that is, description of actions to be applied to resource identifiers, which are embedded in the metadata and resource representation.

The metadata and resource representation of the returned response triggers a state change inside the client. Based on hypermedia information within the response, a client can choose the next desired request, or state change, to repeat the described cycle. This kind of application control concept is called *hypermedia as the engine of application state*, one of the key interface constraints of REST.

All of these aforementioned constraints and principles describe a RESTful architecture that promotes scalability, generality of interfaces, and independent deployment of components, as well as reduces latency, enforces security, and encapsulates legacy and related systems.

Hypertext Transfer Protocol (HTTP) (Fielding and Reschke, 2014) is one protocol that is in conformance with the REST constraints and principles, as it is based on the client-server and request-response model. Moreover, it specifies a set of request actions (i.e., HTTP methods) and a set of further metadata such as header fields or status codes. Resources in HTTP can be addressed by a standardized resource identifier syntax, namely the URI (Berners-Lee et al., 2005) syntax. Also, HTTP messages can include a resource representation such as JSON (Crockford, 2006), HTML (Hickson et al., 2014), or XML (Bray et al., 2008). The metadata and resource representation may contain description on hypermedia relationships (i.e., links or resource identifiers) to describe the next possible state changes or requests for the client.

Additionally, HTTP messages are stateless and cacheable, so they can be processed in intermediate systems, such as proxies, cache servers, or load balancers, without saving any contextual information. HTTP was been originally invented as the technical foundation for the web, the world's largest distributed system.

3 RESTful IoT PROTOCOLS

Due to the success of the web and the strengths of REST, SOA, cloud computing, and the IoT domain have adopted principles and constraints of this architectural style to implement highly scalable service systems. For IoT, which aims at realizing a worldwide distributed and interconnected system, CoAP and RACS have been proposed as two RESTful protocols with a specified focus on constrained devices and networks.

3.1 RESTful CoAP

CoAP (Shelby et al., 2014) is binary application protocol based on HTTP. As for HTTP messages, CoAP message are divided in two parts: a header comprising metadata and a body (payload) containing a resource representation. Each CoAP header begins with a start header containing a version number (V), a message type (T), a token length (TKL), a code (C), and a message ID (MID). In contrast to HTTP, CoAP defaults to User Datagram Protocol (UDP) (Postel, 1980), an unreliable means of transport. To ensure transport reliability, CoAP messages can be confirmed. Such messages comprise the message type 0 (T=0). The reception of confirmable messages must be approved by an acknowledgement message (ACK), which is represented by the message type 2 (T=2). A receiver can also reject a confirmable message by sending a reset message (RST). These messages contain the message number 3 (T=3). Nonconfirmable CoAP messages contain the message number 1 (T=1). The token length describes the size of the token, which is used to match a response to its corresponding request. In case of a request, the code defines the method (i.e., the request action). CoAP provides four methods: GET (C=0.01), POST (C=0.02), PUT (C=0.03), and DELETE (C=0.04). These methods have the same functionality and properties as the methods in HTTP. CoAP responses use the code to represent the status code, such as Content (C=2.05), declaring that the response contains a resource representation, while Bad Request (C=4.00) or Internal Server Error (C=5.00) informs the client about a client-side or server-side error, respectively. The message ID concludes the CoAP start header. This ID is an identifier for linking a reset or an acknowledgement message to its respective confirmable message. Further metadata can be described by CoAP options. Important options for defining the resource identifier in a CoAP request are Uri-Path and Uri-Query. The Accept option is another crucial metadata element for declaring the desired media type being requested. Another mandatory option for defining the media type of a resource representation is content-format. The delimiter to separate the CoAP header from the body is 255 (11111111_2).

Fig. 2 depicts a CoAP request retrieving a resource representation in JSON (denoted by the number 50, which represents application/json) from a CoAP server. This request is given a so-called piggybacked response, which represents an acknowledgement as well as a response message. Such a response contains the same token value and message ID as the corresponding request.

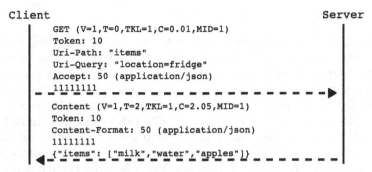

FIG. 2   CoAP request replied by piggybacked response.

FIG. 3   CoAP request replied by separate response.

If a server is not able to return a piggybacked response immediately, it can send a plain acknowledgement message instead to inform the client about the successful request reception (Fig. 3). This acknowledgement message contains an empty token value and same the message ID as the respective confirmable request. Once a server is able to return a response, it sends a confirmable response with the same token value as the corresponding request to the client. This so-called separate response contains a new message ID, as it represents a to-be confirmed message by itself. A client receiving a separate response must approve the reception of the message, with the new acknowledgement message containing the message ID of the separate response.

Since CoAP is based on HTTP, it contains all the characteristics for being a RESTful protocol. The communication in CoAP is stateless and follows the client-server and request-response models. CoAP requests always include a URI for identifying the requested resource. Moreover, CoAP specifies a set of request actions (i.e., CoAP methods) and further metadata describing caching information or the media type of the resource representation. In conjunction with the provided set of standardized metadata and stateless nature of CoAP, messages are self-descriptive so that they are optimized to be processed in layered systems.

3.2 RESTful RACS

RACS (Urien, 2015) is an application layer protocol designed according to REST. The goal of RACS is to remote control Secure Elements (SE) within a Grid of Secure Elements (GoSEs); that is, a RACS server. A SE is a tamper-resistant microcontroller, which provides secure storage and cryptographic operations in smart cards. As the name RACS implies, this protocol is also intended for transporting remote Application Protocol Data Unit (APDU) (The International Organization for Standardization (ISO), 1987) messages. An APDU is an independent protocol that specifies and manages the execution of application-oriented operations on SEs. RACS is a text-based protocol using the Transmission Control Protocol (TCP) (Postel, 1981) as means of transport secured by Transport Layer Security (TLS) (Dierks and Rescorla, 2008), whereas APDU is a binary protocol protected by its own standardized security specification. As with HTTP and CoAP, RACS uses the URI syntax for identifying resources such as GoSEs or SEs. A GoSE can be addressed by an IP address and a TCP port. Each SE within a GoSE has a unique identifier Secure Element Identifier (SEID), thus an SE is accessible by invoking a request with an URI composed of the IP address, TCP port, and SEID.

Each message in RACS is composed of a set of command lines, which are separated by a carriage return and line feed. A command may contain further parameters, which are separated by a space character. The first command of each RACS message must be BEGIN and the last must be END. The BEGIN command may contain a request identifier as a parameter, which can be any kind of string. The request identifier must be echoed by the response in its BEGIN command. The RACS protocol defines the following set of request action commands: GET-VERSION, SET-VERSION, LIST, RESET, SHUTDOWN, POWERON, ECHO, and APDU. A request can comprise multiple request action commands, each of which is in its own command line. In such a case, the corresponding response must only return the status line of the last request action command. To force a server into returning a status line for a distinct request action command, APPEND must be added as the last parameter of the request action command line.

Each request action command is responded by a status header, which indicates the status line. Thus, a RACS response may contain multiple status lines, each returning the process result of its corresponding request action command. In case of a successful request processing, the status line starts with a plus (+). If a request contains an error, then the status line begins with a dash (-). The second parameter of the status line is an integer defining the status code. This parameter is followed by a number indicating the command line of the request action command being processed. A status line may contain further parameters such as a status phrase explaining the status code in a human-readable form.

Table 1 depicts some example request-response communications in RACS. The first row shows a RACS request comprising one GET-VERSION request action command. This request action command is replied by a RACS response containing a successful status code, the command line of the corresponding request action command, and the requested version number. The second example illustrates a request including a request ID and LIST request action command. This request is given a response containing the corresponding request ID and status line expressing the meaning and requested list of SEIDs of the GoSE. In Row 4, a request performing one RESET request action command is shown. This request action command includes the parameter WARM, which triggers a warm reboot of the SE. The last example shows a request, which executes two request action commands. Here, two APDU requests

TABLE 1 Example RACS Requests and Responses

#	RACS Request	RACS Response
1	BEGIN GET-VERSION END	BEGIN +002 001 1.0 END
2	BEGIN myRequestID LIST END	BEGIN myRequestID +004 001 <SEID1> <SEID2> END
3	BEGIN RESET <SEID> WARM END	BEGIN +005 001 <SEID> Reset Done END
4	BEGIN APDU <SEID> <APDU Request1> APPEND APDU <SEID> <APDU Request2> APPEND END	BEGIN +006 001 <APDU Response1> +006 002 <APDU Response2> END

are sent. To inform the server on returning a status line for each request action command, the APPEND parameter is added at the end of each line.

RACS also supports an HTTP interface. To perform a RACS request via an HTTP interface, a URI with the following syntax must be created:

https://<GoSEAddr:port>/<path>?cmd0=param0,...,<paramN>&cmdN=paramN0..., paramNM

The following example shows a request including one RESET request action command, which performs a warm reboot.

https://GoSE.org/RACS?BEGIN=myRequestID&RESET=SmartCard1,WARM&END=

The returned HTTP response includes a resource representation, which describes the RACS response in an XML document.

```
<RACS-Response>
  <begin>myRequestID</begin>
  <Cmd-Response>
    <status>+005</status>
    <line>001</line>
    <parameters>
  <parameter>SmartCard1</parameter>
  <parameter>Reset</parameter>
  <parameter>Done</parameter>
</parameters>
</Cmd-Response>
<end></end>
</RACS-Response>
```

The current stage of the RACS draft specification does not specify which HTTP method must be used to perform a RACS request on the HTTP interface. Also, it does not specify the to-be returned HTTP status code of the HTTP response, which includes the RACS response. Moreover, the current version does not contain all required characteristics for being a RESTful protocol. The RACS protocol is based on a stateless client-server in addition to a request-response model and defines a set of predefined request actions, as well as standardized further metadata. Additionally, RACS servers and SEs within RACS servers can be addressed by an URI. However, RACS does not specify any metadata for caching or transferring resource representation. RACS requests can only include APDU calls. The aforementioned missing RESTful message properties might not be required for the application domain of RACS, or they may be defined in future versions.

4 SECURITY FOR RESTful IoT PROTOCOLS

Security is one fundamental requirement when it comes to design systems in IoT. In REST-based IoT systems transport-oriented security has been established as the de facto mean to secure the message exchange. CoAP uses Datagram TLS (DTLS) (Rescorla and Modadugu, 2006) for ensuring the confidentiality and integrity of the transport layer. Also, several works have been published to optimize DTLS for the deployment in constrained networks and environments (Park and Kang, 2014; Kang et al., 2015). The RACS protocol requires TLS as the mandatory security layer over TCP.

In layered systems, such as that by the adoption of REST, transport security with DTLS or TLS alone is, however, not sufficient to cope with requirements in large-scale distributed systems (Gorski et al., 2014a). Transport-oriented security protocols can only ensure the integrity, authenticity, and confidentiality of information during transit. If a message resides in an intermediate system, the data is unprotected, leaving the surface vulnerable to man-in-the-middle attacks (Lo Iacono and Nguyen, 2015b; Nguyen and Lo Iacono, 2015).

For this purpose, a more comprehensive set of security means needs to be developed in order to support software engineers in implementing message-oriented protection mechanisms that will supplement transport security. Therefore Gorski et al. (2014a) propose a required REST-Security stack comprising security components for REST-based service systems (see Fig. 4). This stack is adopted from the mature Simple Object Access Protocol (SOAP) security domain.

Besides the required security building blocks for developing a holistic protection of REST-based systems, this stack also shows the missing and fragmented work in REST-Security. Here, only approaches for authorization and message security are available so far. Solutions for secure conversation, federation, policy, trust, and privacy are still missing. Moreover, the schemes for authorization and message security include much vulnerability, as revealed in Lo Iacono and Nguyen (2015b), Nguyen and Lo Iacono (2015), Yang and Manoharan (2013), and Sun and Beznosov, 2012, showing that despite using these technologies, man-in-the-middle attacks are still possible. This indicates that none of them are mature enough to be applied in mission- and business-critical environments. Additionally, the available approaches are only designed for HTTP or CoAP, meaning that no message security technologies exist for RACS. HTTP, CoAP, and RACS merely represent three possible protocols for implementing REST-based systems. With the increased adoption of REST in, for example, SOA, microservices, cloud computing, and IoT, more RESTful protocols are expected to evolve perspectively. This requires the development of a general REST-Security framework, which provides safeguards for all REST-based systems, including current and prospective RESTful technologies.

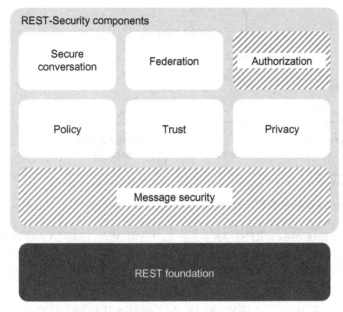

FIG. 4   REST-Security stack (Gorski et al., 2014a).

Based on this finding, this section proposes a methodology for defining REST-Security components, which relies on the same idea as REST itself: REST is an abstract model for designing large-scale distributed systems. This model can be adopted with suitable technologies of any kind, such as HTTP, CoAP, or RACS, to build highly scalable service systems such as the web, IoT, SOA, or cloud applications (see Fig. 5).

Following this concept, REST-Security schemes should rely on the same abstraction level as REST itself. These schemes then form a REST-Security abstract model building a set of guidelines for implementing security technologies for RESTful protocols of any kind (see Fig. 6), as REST is a guideline for designing high scalable distributed systems with RESTful technologies such as HTTP, CoAP, and RACS (see Fig. 5).

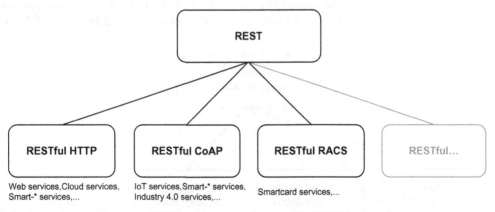

FIG. 5   Instantiation of the general REST architecture style to specific RESTful protocols.

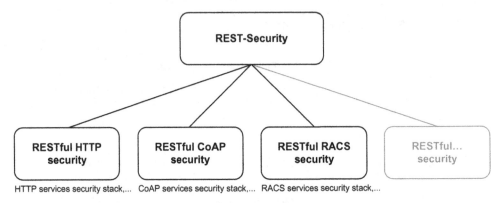

FIG. 6   Instantiation of a general REST-Security to specific RESTful protocols.

The next section proposes a REST Message Authentication (REMA) scheme, which follows this methodology. REMA marks the initial steps towards a REST message security, which build the foundation for further REST-Security components of the REST-Security stack (see Fig. 4).

5 REST MESSAGE AUTHENTICATION

A REMA must ensure the authenticity and integrity of the whole REST messages, making them immune to all kinds of man-in-the-middle-attacks. Following the introduced methodology, this section introduces an approach that augments REST by authentication scheme while remaining on the same abstraction level as REST itself. This generic scheme serves as a message authentication guideline for adopting a RESTful message authentication to distinct RESTful protocols including HTTP, CoAP, RACS, and other prospective protocols (see Fig. 7).

The key idea of REMA is to thwart the man-in-the-middle attacks revealed in Lo Iacono and Nguyen (2015b) and Nguyen and Lo Iacono (2015) by protecting the whole message at the application layer. To do so, a digital signature over all security-relevant message elements is computed. Therefore, a message signature algorithm and a message verification algorithm need to be defined. Before being able to sign and verify REST messages, a general policy defining what REST message elements to be authenticated is required. Note that this policy and this section use the abstract notation for the REST messages of Lo Iacono and Nguyen

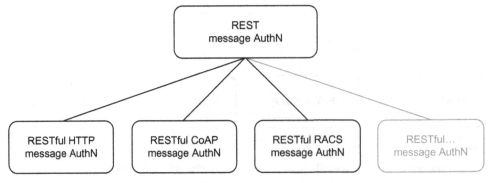

FIG. 7   Instantiation of a RESTful message authentication to RESTful protocols.

(2015b) and Nguyen and Lo Iacono (2015). For further details on these notations, the reader is referred to Lo Iacono and Nguyen (2015b) and Nguyen and Lo Iacono (2015).

1. A message $r \in R$ comprising a resource representation must include at least the two resource representation metadata entities, $m_{bl} \in M_b$ and $m_{bt} \in M_b$, describing the length and the media type of the contained resource representation, respectively.
2. A request $r \in R_c$ must contain at least one control data element, $m_{ca} \in M_{ca}$, and one resource identifier, $i \in I$, describing the action and the target of the action.
3. A response $r \in R_s$ must contain at least one control data element, $m_{cm} \in M_{cm}$, expressing the meaning of the response.
4. A read request must contain at least one resource representation metadata element, $m_{br} \in M_b$, describing the desired media type being requested. Moreover, this request must not include a resource representation.
5. A creation request must contain a resource representation.
6. An update request must contain a complete or partial resource representation.
7. A delete request does not require any additional prerequisite header element until further requirements. Moreover, this request must not include a resource representation.

Based on these definitions, this section proposes a generic signature and verification algorithm for REST messages. Further requirements are the matter of technical instantiation of the uniform interface and application domain.

5.1 REST Message Signature

Algorithm 1 defines the procedure for signing a REST message. Note that error conditions are not made because of readability reasons. This algorithm requires a REST message r, a description on application-specific, to-be signed header elements *desc* and a signature genreration key k as input.

ALGORITHM 1   REST MESSAGE SIGNATURE (LO IACONO AND NGUYEN, 2015B)

Input: REST message r, description *desc* of the application-specific, to-be signed header entries, signature generation key k

Output: Signature value *sv*, time-variant parameter *tvp*

1: $b \leftarrow getBody(r)$
2: $h \leftarrow getHeader(r)$
3: $\tilde{h} \leftarrow getTbsHeaders(h)$
4: $\tilde{h} \leftarrow \tilde{h} \,\|\, getTbsHeaders(h, desc)$
5: $tvp \leftarrow generateTimeVariantParameter()$
6: $tbs \leftarrow tvp$
7: $i \leftarrow 0$
8: **while** $i < |\, \tilde{h}\, |$ **do**
9: $tbs \leftarrow tbs \,\|\, delimiter \,\|\, normalize(\tilde{h}_i)$
10: $i \leftarrow i + 1$
11: **end while**
12: $tbs \leftarrow tbs \,\|\, delimiter \,\|\, hash(b)$
13: $sv \leftarrow sign(k, tbs)$

The first two statements extract the body b and the header h from the message r. The next step gathers security-relevant header entries from h and store them to $\tilde{h}$, which represents the header containing the security-critical header elements defined by the policy. After that, the application-specific, security-relevant header entities defined by *desc* are attached to $\tilde{h}$. In order to thwart replay attacks, the following step generates a time-variant parameter *tvp* and assigns it to the variable *tbs*. These two steps must not be omitted even when another time-variant is already available in $\tilde{h}$ because a considerable time span might exist between a message generation and signature generation. In the next step, all security-relevant header entries in $\tilde{h}$ are normalized and concatenated to *tbs*. Next, a cryptographic hash of the body b is computed and appended to *tbs*. The final step signs *tbs* with the signature generation key k. The algorithm then returns the signature value sv and time-variant parameter *tvp* as output.

To guide the receiver in verifying a signed REST message, an authentication control data $m_{cpa} \in M_{cp}$ must be created, which contains the signature algorithm name *sig*, the hash algorithm *hash*, a key id *kid*, the time-variant parameter *tvp*, the signature value sv, and the description on application-specific header elements *desc*. After the creation of m_{cpa}, this metadata is included to the header h.

5.2 REST Message Verification

Algorithm 2 describes the process for verifying REST messages, which are signed by Algorithm 1. Note that error conditions are not made due to readability reasons; this algorithm requires a signed REST message r as input only. As with Algorithm 1, the first two steps of Algorithm 2 extract the body b and header h from the message r. After that m_{cpa}, which contains all the information guiding the receiver in verifying the message, can be obtained from h. The statement in line 5 constructs $\tilde{h}$ according to the policy. The next step appends

---

ALGORITHM 2   REST MESSAGE SIGNATURE VERIFICATION (LO IACONO AND NGUYEN, 2015B)

Input: Signed REST message r
Output: Boolean signature verification result *valid*

1: $b \leftarrow getBody(r)$
2: $h \leftarrow getHeader(r)$
3: $m_{cpa} \leftarrow getAuthenticationControlData(h)$
4: $(sig, hash, kid, tvp, sv, desc) \leftarrow split(m_{cpa})$
5: $\tilde{h} \leftarrow getTbsHeaders(h)$
6: $\tilde{h} \leftarrow \tilde{h} \,||\, getTbsHeaders(h, desc)$
7: $tbs \leftarrow tvp$
8: $i \leftarrow 0$
9: **while** $i < |\tilde{h}|$ **do**
10:     $tbs \leftarrow tbs \,||\, delimiter \,||\, normalize(\tilde{h}_i)$
11:     $i \leftarrow i + 1$
12: **end while**
13: $tbs \leftarrow tbs \,||\, delimiter \,||\, hash(b)$
14: $verify \leftarrow getVerificationAlgorithm(sig)$
15: $valid \leftarrow verify(kid, tbs, sv)$

---

the application-specific header entries specified by *desc* to $\tilde{h}$. After building $\tilde{h}$, *tvp*, all elements in $\tilde{h}$ and a cryptographic of *b* are concatenated in the same order and manner as in Algorithm 1 to *tbs*. With *kid*, *tbs*, and *sv*, the signed message *r* can be verified. The result of this verification process is then returned as output.

6 RESTful IoT MESSAGE AUTHENTICATION

This section adopts the proposed authentication scheme to CoAP and RACS to show how it is implemented in concrete RESTful IoT technologies. Further instantiation to prospective RESTful IoT protocols can likewise be conducted.

6.1 RESTful CoAP Message Authentication (RECMA)

The two templates of the following table show the instantiation of the concatenation process of Algorithm 1 for building *tbs*. The left template describes construction rules for CoAP request and responses, where a time-variant parameter (*tvp*), all security-relevant header elements ($\tilde{h}$), and the body (*b*) are concatenated to byte array. The right one defines the concatenation process for acknowledgment (ACK) and reset messages (RST). Here, only *tvp* and $\tilde{h}$ are concatenated to a byte array as both message types do not contain a message body. The adopted and extended policy for constructing $\tilde{h}$ in CoAP is described in Nguyen and Lo Iacono (2015); the reader is referred to this paper for further reference.

tbs Constructing Template for CoAP request and responses	*tbs* Constructing Template for CoAP ACK and RST
Tvp	tvp
‖Version	‖Version
‖Type	‖Type
‖TokenLength	‖TokenLength
‖Code	‖Code
‖MessageID	‖MessageID
‖Token	
‖Options0	
...	
‖OptionsN	
‖hash(body)	

Assuming that the following request and acknowledgement message require to be signed:

Example CoAP request	Example CoAP ACK
POST (V=1,T=0,TKL=1,C=0.02,MID=1)	ACK (V=0,T=2,TKL=0,C=0.00,MID=1)
Token: 10	11111111
Uri-Path: "items"	
Content-Format: 60	
Payload-Length: 15	
11111111	
{"items":"pork"}	

According to the policy of Nguyen and Lo Iacono (2015), the *tbs* of both messages is constructed as follows:

tbs of Example CoAP request	tbs Constructing Template for CoAP ACK and RST
0x14D14486B51 #*tvp*	0x14D14486B57 #*tvp*
‖0x01 #Version	‖0x01 #Version
‖0x00 #*Type*	‖0x02 #*Type*
‖0x01 #TokenLength	‖0x00 #TokenLength
‖0x02 #*Code*	‖0x00 #*Code*
‖0x01 #Message-ID	‖0x01 #Message-ID
‖0x0A #*Token*	
‖0x00 #Uri-Host(3)	
‖0x00 #Uri-Port(7)	
‖hash(UTF8("items")) #*Uri-Path(11)*	
‖0x60 #Content-Format(12)	
‖0x00 #Max-Age(14)	
‖0x00 #Uri-Query(15)	
‖0xF0 #Payload-Length (65001)	
‖hash(UTF8({"item":"pork"})) #*Body*	

The concatenation order of the items of the CoAP start header follows the order of the predefined positions of these header entries. The CoAP are appended according the order of option numbers. After constructing both *tbs*, these two variables are signed by signature generation key k.

$$sv = sign(k, tbs)$$

The last step assigns the computed signature value sv and corresponding authentication metadata to newly introduced CoAP options: Signature-Value (sv), Signature-Algorithm (sig), Hash-Algorithm ($hash$), TVP (tvp), and Key-ID (kid). These options represent m_{cpa} and are included with the header h.

Signed CoAP request	Signed CoAP ACK
POST (V=1,T=0,TKL=1,C=0.02,MID=1)	ACK (V=0,T=2,TKL=0,C=0.00,MID=1)
Token: 10	11111111
Uri-Path: "items"	Signature-Algorithm: 1
Content-Format: 60	Hash-Algorithm: 1
Payload-Length: 15	TVP:
Signature-Algorithm: 1	Signature-Value: <sv>
Hash-Algorithm: 1	Key-ID: <kid>
TVP:	
Signature-Value: <sv>	
Key-ID: <kid>	
11111111	
{"items":"pork"}	

This CoAP implementation of REMA uses the numbers for declaring the signature and hash algorithm name. The number 1 within the Signature-Algorithm options stands for an HMAC-SHA256. The same number in the Hash-Algorithm option represents an SHA256. The description on application-specific header entries *desc* is omitted in these examples, because ACK and RST messages must not contain CoAP options and the example request does intend to include application-specific options to $\tilde{h}$. Moreover, this RECMA utilizes the Payload-Length option to define the size of the body. This option is not standardized metadata element; rather, it is draft specification, which has been expired yet. Still, RECMA uses this option and declares this metadata entry as an element of $\tilde{h}$ in order to both avoid man-in-the-middle attacks manipulating the body and to comply with *transport independence* constraint (Fielding, 2000; Nguyen and Lo Iacono, 2015).

6.2 RESTful RACS Message Authentication (RERMA)

The following table shows two templates for authenticating RACS messages. In contrast to CoAP, the RERMA utilizes a string concatenation instead of a byte concatenation, as it is a text-based protocol.

tbs Constructing Template for RACS request	*tbs* Constructing Template for RACS request
tvp + "\n" +	tvp + "\n" +
rid + "\n" +	rid + "\n" +
a0+ " " +p0+ " " + ... + pN + "\n" +	sc + " " + cl0 + " " + p0 + " " + ... + pN + "\n"+
...	...
aM + " " +pM0+ " " + ... + pMN + "\n"+	sc + " " + clM + " " + p0 + " " + ... + pMN + "\n"+

The left template describes the concatenation process for requests. According to Algorithm 1, the first parameter assigned to *tbs* is the time-variant parameter (*tvp*), followed by line break (\n). Next, the request ID (rid) with a line break is appended. If the request does not include a request ID, an empty string must be added instead. After that, each command line containing a request action command separated by a line break is appended to *tbs*. For each command line, the request action command (a) must be added first, then the parameters of the corresponding request action command (p) are appended. Each parameter must be separated by a whitespace. The right template denotes the concatenation process for RACS response. *tvp* and the request ID are added in same manner as in the left template. The status code (sc) followed by the processed command line of corresponding request action command (cl) and parameters are appended next. As the current stage of RACS does not define how to transfer and declare resource representation, this part is omitted in the current stage of RERMA. Further work will extend RERMA by this missing property, if transferring and declaring resource representation is defined in RACS.

Assuming that the following two RACS messages require authentication:

Example RACS request	Example RACS response
BEGIN APDU SmartCard1 <APDU Request1> APPEND APDU SmartCard1 <APDU Request2> APPEND END	BEGIN +006 001 <APDU Response1> +006 002 <APDU Response2> END

Based on Algorithm 1 and the templates in the previous table, the *tbs* of both messages is constructed as follows:

tbs of Example RACS request	*tbs* of Example RACS response
1455190341456 APDU SmartCard1 Base64(<APDU Request1>) APPEND APDU SmartCard1 Base64(<APDU Request2>) APPEND	1455190341556 +006 001 Base64(<APDU Response1>) +006 002 Base64(<APDU Response2>)

Then both strings are encoded to UTF8 and signed with a key k. As the RACS is a text-based protocol, the resulting binary signature value must be converted by a Base64 transformation to a string:

$$sv = Base64\left(sign\left(k, UTF8\left(tbs\right)\right)\right)$$

Finally, sv, along with the corresponding authentication metadata (m_{cpa}) is added to the request as a new command line, starting with the newly defined command action SIGNATURE. Note that this command action is considered experimental, as it does not exist in the current RACS specification. Therefore the representation of m_{cpa} may change in the future in order to be compliant with forthcoming versions of the RACS draft specification. In the RACS response, m_{cpa} is included into the status line, which is in conformance with the RACS specification, as a status header can contain additional response parameters.

Signed Example RACS request	Signed Example RACS response
BEGIN APDU SmartCard1 <APDU Request1> APPEND APDU SmartCard1 <APDU Request2> APPEND SIGNATURE RSA/SHA256 <kid> 1455190341456 null <sv> END	BEGIN +006 001 <APDU Response1> +006 002 <APDU Response2> +006 003 SIGNATURE RSA/SHA256 <kid> ⏎ 1455190341556 null <sv> END

Both messages do not include application-specific metadata elements to be signed. Therefore, the fifth parameter of the SIGNATURE command line is defined as null. If additional header elements need to be signed, a list containing the position number of the parameter separated by a comma must be included instead.

If the HTTP interface is utilized to perform a RACS request, the RESTful HTTP Message Authentication (REHMA) (Lo Iacono and Nguyen, 2015b) must be used to authenticate the HTTP messages.

7 CONCLUSION AND OUTLOOK

REST has established itself as an important architectural style for developing large-scale hypermedia distributed system. In IoT environments, the principles and constraints of REST have been adopted by several application domains including CoAP- and RACS-based systems. Other IoT areas with prospective RESTful protocols will eventually arise likewise. The increasing implementation of the REST concept in various technologies, as well as application domains, and the insufficient protection of transport-oriented protection demand generic security approaches augmenting REST on the same abstraction layer.

This chapter therefore proposes an approach that extends REST by an authentication scheme while remaining on the same abstraction layer of REST itself. This security scheme then serves as a guideline for implementing message authentication for RESTful (IoT) protocols. Based on this guideline, this chapter introduces a REST message authentication scheme for two RESTful protocols for the IoT domain, CoAP and RACS, respectively.

REMA, RECMA, and RERMA provide integrity and authenticity, as well as non-repudiation for REST messages and RESTful protocol when using asymmetric signature algorithms in conjunction with an appropriate public key infrastructure. Still, in order to approach a comprehensive message security, confidentiality must be considered as well. In layered systems, this security service is of specific importance, as many intermediate systems, such as cache servers, load balancers or content delivery networks are operated by third-party services. If REST messages are not encrypted, those intermediate services have plain-text access to traversing messages. This is especially critical for IoT environments, as sensitive information is transferred from node to node. Therefore a REST message confidentiality scheme needs to be developed. This scheme must follow the introduced methodology by defining a guideline for adopting and implementing confidentiality services for RESTful technologies including HTTP, CoAP, RACS, and prospective RESTful protocols (see Fig. 8).

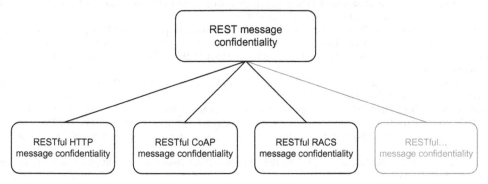

FIG. 8   General RESTful message confidentiality and its instantiation to concrete RESTful protocols.

Following this methodology, further security components for the REST-Security stack in Fig. 4 can be developed. All these steps will be elaborated in further work in order to build a generic and robust security framework for mission-critical REST-based (IoT) systems.

References

Atzori, L., Iera, A., Morabito, G., 2010. The Internet of Things: a survey. Comput. Netw. 54, 2787–2805. Available from: http://www.sciencedirect.com/science/article/pii/S1389128610001568.
Berners-Lee, T., Fielding, R., Masinter, L., 2005. Uniform Resource Identifier (URI): Generic Syntax. IETF, RFC 3986. Available from: https://tools.ietf.org/html/rfc3986.
Bray, T., Paoli, J., Sperberg-McQueen, C.M., Maler, E., Yergeau, F., 2008. Extensible Markup Language (XML) 1.0. World Wide Web Consortium (W3C) Recommendation, fifth ed. Available from: http://www.w3.org/TR/2008/REC-xml-20081126.
Crockford, D., 2006. The Application/json Media Type for JavaScript Object Notation (JSON). IETF, RFC 4627. Available from: http://www.ietf.org/rfc/rfc4627.txt.
Dierks, T., Rescorla, E., 2008. The Transport Layer Security (TLS) Protocol Version 1.2. IETF, RFC 5246. Available from: https://tools.ietf.org/html/rfc5246.
Erl, T., Carlyle, B., Pautasso, C., Balasubramanian, R., 2012. SOA With REST: Principles, Patterns & Constraints for Building Enterprise Solutions With REST, first ed. Prentice Hall Press, Upper Saddle River, NJ.
Fielding, R.T., 2000. Architectural Styles and the Design of Network-Based Software Architectures. (Doctoral dissertation). In: University of California, Irvine. Available from: https://www.ics.uci.edu/~fielding/pubs/dissertation/top.htm.
Fielding, R., Reschke, J., 2014. Hypertext Transfer Protocol (HTTP/1.1): Message Syntax and Routing. IETF, RFC 7230. Available from: https://tools.ietf.org/html/rfc7230.
Gorski, P.L., Lo Iacono, L., Nguyen, H.V., Torkian, D.B., 2014a. Service security revisited. In: 11th IEEE International Conference on Services Computing (SCC).
Gorski, P.L., Lo Iacono, L., Nguyen, H.V., Torkian, D.B., 2014b. SOA-readiness of REST. In: 3rd European Conference on Service-Oriented and Cloud Computing.
Hickson, I., Berjon, R., Faulkner, S., Leithead, T., Navara, E.D., O'Connor, E., Pfeiffer, S., 2014. HTML5—A Vocabulary and Associated APIs for HTML and XHTML. W3C Recommendation. Available from: http://www.w3.org/TR/html5/.
Kang, N., Park, J., Kwon, H., Jung, S., 2015. ESSE: efficient secure session establishment for Internet-integrated wireless sensor networks. Int. J. Distrib. Sens. Netw. 2015. http://dx.doi.org/10.1155/2015/393754.
Lo Iacono, L., Nguyen, H.V., 2015a. Towards conformance testing of REST-based web services. In: 11th International Conference on Web Information Systems and Technologies (WEBIST).
Lo Iacono, L., Nguyen, H.V., 2015b. Authentication scheme for REST. In: International Conference on Future Network Systems and Security (FNSS). Springer International Publishing, Switzerland.
Nguyen, H.V., Lo Iacono, L., 2015. REST-ful CoAP Message Authentication. In: International Workshop on Secure Internet of Things (SIoT), in Conjunction With the European Symposium on Research in Computer Security (ESORICS).
Park, J., Kang, N., 2014. Lightweight secure communication for CoAP-enabled Internet of Things using delegated DTLS handshake. In: International Conference on Information and Communication Technology Convergence (ICTC). http://dx.doi.org/10.1109/ICTC.2014.6983078.
Postel, J., 1980. User Datagram Protocol. IETF, RFC 768. Available from: https://tools.ietf.org/html/rfc768.
Postel, J., 1981. Transmission Control Protocol. IETF, RFC 793. Available from: https://tools.ietf.org/html/rfc793.
Rescorla, E., Modadugu, N., 2006. Datagram Transport Layer Security. IETF, RFC 4347. Available from: https://tools.ietf.org/html/rfc4347.
Shelby, Z., Hartke, K., Borman, C., 2014. The Constrained Application Protocol (CoAP). IETF, RFC 7252. Available from: https://tools.ietf.org/html/rfc7252.
Sun, S., Beznosov, K., 2012. The devil is in the (implementation) details: an empirical analysis of OAuth SSO systems. In: 19th ACM Conference on Computer and Communications Security (CCS). http://dx.doi.org/10.1145/2382196.2382238.
The International Organization for Standardization (ISO), 1987. Cards Identification—Integrated Circuit Cards With Contacts. ISO 7816.
Urien, P., 2015. Remote APDU Call Secure (RACS). IETF, Internet-Draft. Available from: https://tools.ietf.org/html/draft-urien-core-racs-05.
Yang, F., Manoharan, S., 2013. A security analysis of the OAuth protocol. In: IEEE Pacific Rim Conference on Communications, Computers and Signal Processing (PACRIM). http://dx.doi.org/10.1109/PACRIM.2013.6625487.

11

An Introduction to Various Privacy Models

X. Lu, M.H. Au

The Hong Kong Polytechnic University, Kowloon, Hong Kong

1 INTRODUCTION

Anonymity refers to the absence of identifying information of an individual. In the digital age, user anonymity is critically important since computers could be used to infer individuals' lifestyles, habits, whereabouts, and associations from data collected in different daily transactions (Chaum, 1985). However, merely removing explicit identifiers may not provide sufficient protection. The preliminary reason is that the released information, when combined with publicly available information, can also reveal the identity of an individual. A famous example is the Netflix crowdsourcing competition. In 2012, Netflix released a data set of users and their movie ratings. People could download the data and search for patterns. The data contained a fake customer ID, together with movie, customer's rating of the movie and the date of the rating. It is claimed that since customer identifiers have been removed, the released information would not breach user privacy. However, Narayanan and Shmatikov (2008) showed how customers can be identified when the dataset from Netflix is combined with some auxiliary data (such as data from IMDB).

Location privacy is also of great concern in the mobile setting. Here we briefly review a case related to the location privacy of a location-based social network (LBSN), namely, WeChat, as discussed in (Wang et al., 2015). By using a fake GPS position and mobile phone emulation, it is possible to reveal the exact location of any WeChat user with the nearby service turned on (Fig. 1).

The previous example raises a question: *what kind of information do we wish to protect when we talk about privacy protection?* In other words, how do we define privacy? Traditional models in dealing with data confidentiality are not applicable in this case, since we have to maintain data utility. In the Netflix competition example, the data set is released to the public for mining, while in WeChat Nearby service, the user should be able to obtain the list of users nearby.

Over the years, the research community has developed various privacy models, including *k*-anonymity (Sweeney, 2002) and differential privacy (Dwork, 2006). In this chapter, we discuss these definitions and implications and the techniques to achieve them.

FIG. 1   WeChat nearby people.

1.1 Organizations

This rest of this chapter is organized as follows. In Section 2, we present the definition of k-anonymity and discuss its practical implications. In Section 3, we discuss various techniques to achieve the definition. In Section 4, we discuss differential privacy, including its definition and implications. A differentially private mechanism that helps supporting differential privacy is reviewed in Section 5. We conclude in Section 6.

2 DEFINITION OF k-ANONYMITY

k-anonymity, proposed by Sweeney (2002), is a property of protecting released data from reidentification. It can be used, for example, when a private corporation such as a bank wants to release a version of data concerning clients' financial information to

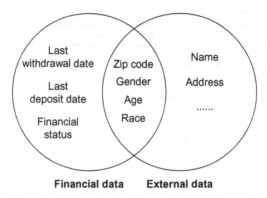

FIG. 2   Linking attack between released data and external data.

some public organizations for research purpose. Under this circumstance, released data should have the property that individual subjects of the data cannot be reidentified so as to protect their privacy. In other words, all the records in the released database should remain unlinkable to the clients. Clients' original data from a bank usually contains information such as name, address, and telephone number that can directly identify clients. One possible way to hide the identity is by directly removing the sensitive information from the database. However, it cannot guarantee clients' privacy. Information like zip code, gender, age and race, clients' identities still can be reidentified. Zip code provides an approximate location. Through searching by specific age, gender, and race, it is still possible to reveal clients' identities. Another possible way to achieve reidentification is called linking attack. Apart from attributes like name and address which can directly break the anonymity of data, there are also attributes called quasi-identifier (QID) which is used to link released data to external data. Gender, age, race and zip code is a typical tuple of QIDs and this tuple of QIDs from released data has high probability that also appears in some external data. If there are external tables like voter registration lists, then by linking the QIDs from released data to voter data, clients' identities may be revealed (Fig. 2).

k-anonymity requires that in the released data, each record can be mapped to at least *k* records in the original data. In another words, each record from the released data will have at least $k - 1$ identical records in the same released data. For example in Table 1, (a) is the original data and (b) is the data derived from (a). (b) has *k*-anonymity where $k = 2$. In Sweeney (2002), Latanya Sweeney presented the principle of *k*-anonymity and proved that if the released data owns the property of *k*-anonymity, then the linking attack which links the released data to other external data and tries to break the data anonymity can be defended. Intuitively, this is because each record in released data will have at least $k - 1$ same records.

TABLE 1   Example of *k*-Anonymity (*k* = 2)

(a) Original Data				
Name	**Gender**	**Race**	**Age**	**Zip Code**
Alice	Female	White	17	21103
Lucy	Female	Asian	22	21300
Daniel	Male	Black	27	21110
Kate	Female	White	15	21102
Rose	Female	Black	29	21109
Andy	Male	Asian	24	21304

(b) Sharing Data Derived From (a)			
Gender	**Race**	**Age**	**Zip Code**
F or M	White	15–19	211*
F or M	Asian	20–24	213*
F or M	Black	25–29	211*
F or M	White	15–19	211*
F or M	Black	25–29	211*
F or M	Asian	20–24	213*

3 MECHANISMS THAT SUPPORT *k*-ANONYMITY

After *k*-anonymity was proposed, various attempts had been made in designing a good algorithm that turns a database into a form that satisfied this definition. The main two techniques used to enforce *k*-anonymity in released data are generalization and suppression. Generalization consists of replacing attributes considered to be QIDs with a more general value. In Table 1, the values of gender, age, and zip code from (a) are all substituted by a generalized version in (b). Generalization can be applied in levels from a single cell to a tuple of attributes to achieve *k*-anonymity. Suppression consists of removing sensitive attributes to reduce the amount of generalization when achieving *k*-anonymity. Same as generalization, suppression can also be applied in cells or whole attributes. The combination of generalization and suppression has been used to construct different algorithms to help data satisfy *k*-anonymity. The conventional framework of such an algorithm always starts by suppressing several sensitive attributes and then partitions tuples of remaining attributes into groups and substituting accurate QIDs' values into generalized ones for each group, which are also called equivalent classes. This kind of generalization is homogeneous generalization and has been used to address *k*-anonymity in Iwuchukwu and Naughton (2007), Ghinita et al. (2007), and LeFevre et al. (2008). A property of homogeneous generalization is that if an original record t_i matches the released record t'_j whose corresponding original record is t_j, then t_j also matches t'_i. This property is called reciprocity. The most significant point for homogeneous generalization is how to divide the equivalent classes. The partitioning strategy will directly influence the utility of released data. There are two ways to do the partitioning job: global recording (full-domain anonymization) (LeFevre et al., 2005, 2006; El Emam et al., 2009) and local recording (Xu et al., 2006; Aggarwal et al., 2010). Global recording means that within a column, the same generalization strategy is applied to the equal value. So if two tuples in the original data have identical QID values, then they must have the same released value. However, in local recording, two tuples with identical QID values may have different generalized values. Incognito algorithm proposed in LeFevre et al. (2005) uses dynamic programming and is shown to be outperformed by previous algorithms on two real-life databases. The main idea of Incognito is that any subset of the tuple of QIDs with *k*-anonymity should also have the property of *k*-anonymity. Mondrian algorithm presented in LeFevre et al. (2006) uses a strategy called multidimensional global recording. In Mondrian, each attribute in the dataset represents a dimension and each record represents a point in the space. Instead of partitioning each records, Mondrian algorithm partitions the space into several regions and in each region, there are at least *k* points.

Algorithms using local recording may guarantee more anonymity in specific situation (Ninghui Li and Su, 2011).

Another generalization method is called nonhomogeneous generalization (Wong et al., 2010; Xue et al., 2012; Doka et al., 2015). For nonhomogeneous generalization, the property of reciprocity does not necessarily hold for all records. In Table 2, (b) is the released data derived from (a) using homogeneous generalization, and it is clear that (t'_1, t'_2, t'_5) is an equivalent class and (t'_3, t'_4) is another . In an equivalent class, all the generalized QID values are the same. However, in a nonhomogeneous generalized table (c), t'_1, t'_2 and t'_5 have different

TABLE 2   Example of *k*-Anonymity (*k* = 2) From Homogeneous and Nonhomogeneous Generalization

(a) Original Data			
Tuple ID	Gender	Age	Zip Code
t_1	Female	17	21103
t_2	Male	29	21110
t_3	Male	27	21210
t_4	Male	15	21202
t_5	Female	22	21109
(b) Sharing Data Generated by Homogeneous Generalization			
Tuple ID	Gender	Age	Zip Code
t'_1	F or M	17–29	211*
t'_2	F or M	17–29	211*
t'_3	Male	15–27	212*
t'_4	Male	15–27	212*
t'_5	F or M	17–29	211*

Continued

TABLE 2   Example of k-Anonymity ($k = 2$) From Homogeneous and Nonhomogeneous Generalization—cont'd

(c) Sharing Data Generated by Nonhomogeneous Generalization			
Tuple ID	Gender	Age	Zip Code
t'_1	Female	17–22	2110*
t'_2	Male	22–29	211*
t'_3	Male	15–27	212*
t'_4	Male	15–27	212*
t'_5	F or M	17–29	211*

generalized QID values. While both table (b) and (c) have 2-anonymity, (c) offers higher data utility since the generalized QID ranges in (c) is either smaller or equivalent to the corresponding ones in (b). This illustrates that by using nonhomogeneous generalization, one may achieve a higher data utility on the released data.

In Wong et al.'s work (Wong et al., 2010), original data and released data are seen as a graph and records from data are vertices. To achieve k-anonymity, each vertex from the graph should have exactly k matches in the same graph including the vertex itself. If we consider a matching between two vertices as an edge, then the former sentence can be rewritten as each vertex in the graph should have out degree and in degree k. So in such graph, there are k disjoint assignments can be extracted and each assignment represents a correspondence between vertices. Even though Wong et al.'s work use nonhomogeneous generalization, there is still the requirement that the generalized graph should form a ring in their strategy which causes redundancy.

Recently Doka et al. (2015) proposed a new algorithm called freeform generalization to implement k-anonymity in a nonhomogeneous way. They defined the problem as how to obtain high data utility in k-anonymity and wanted to solve this problem as an assignment problem in a bipartite graph that has two parts, namely, original and released. Each vertex from original part should have exactly k matches in the released part, and each vertex in the released part should also have k matches in the original part. Doka et al. (2015) proposed an approach to constructing the bipartite graph which contains k disjoint components. To construct such graph, the idea is choosing k different perfect matchings from all the possible matchings including the self-matching from original data to released data for vertices. After choosing, each vertex in the released graph should have k possible identities. The construction is secure since each disjoint assignment has the same probability $1/k$ to be the true one for an adversary. So, each time the adversary wants to find the identities of the released records, he/she will have k possible results. In the construction, each edge between two vertices will be assigned a weight based on Global Certainty Penalty (GCP). GCP is used to measure the information loss of matching an original record to a released record. The released data should keep k-anonymity and data utility. So when choosing the k perfect matchings, the total GCP should be kept as small as possible. Finally, a greedy algorithm was presented in Doka et al. (2015). The input to the greedy algorithm is a weighted completed bipartite graph $G = (S,T,E)$, and the output is a perfect match with a total weight close to the minimum. S represents vertices in original data and T represents in released data. A successful running of the algorithm is called an iteration. In each iteration, the algorithm tries to find perfect matching from S to T with a low total weight. And the self-matching from original data to released data with zero GCP will be found out in the first iteration. After one iteration, all the selecting edges will be removed from the bipartite graph and all the weights (GCP) on the edges will be redefined. After k iterations, k disjoint perfect matchings with low GCP will be presented. The algorithm can be used in the real word for a practical value k and the complexity for all k iterations is $O(kn^2)$, where n is the number of records in the original data.

4 DIFFERENTIAL PRIVACY

Since the introduction of k-anonymity, weaknesses of it as a model have been discussed, and these weaknesses lead to the proposal of stronger models including ℓ-diversity (Machanavajjhala et al., 2007), t-closeness (Li et al., 2007), or β-likeness (Cao and Karras, 2012). In this chapter, we do not go into details of these definitions and refer interested readers to the respective papers. Informally speaking, the main weakness in k-anonymity is that it does not guarantee proper protection of the sensitive attributes. For example, from Table 1(b), an adversary can safely conclude that if a target user is of age from 20-29 living in a place with zip code starting with 211, the target user is an African American with high probability. Since in the table, only Asians and African Americans are of age from 20-29 and all the Asians' zip codes start with 213.

4.1 Overview

Differential privacy, introduced by Dwork (2006), is an attempt to define privacy from a different perspective. This seminal work consider the situation of privacy-preserving data mining in which there is a trusted curator who holds a private database D. The curator responses to queries issued by data analysts. Differential privacy guarantees that the query results are indistinguishable for two databases that differ only in one entry. From an individual point of view, it means that inclusion of one's information in the private database D would not cause noticeable changes in the observed query outcome; thus, privacy is protected. This is made possible via adding noise to the query result. The setting is shown in Fig. 3:

Note that it is possible to create a synthetic database by issuing a query that output the private database D, as discussed in Chen et al. (2011). However, as pointed out in Clifton and Tassa (2013), the utility of this synthetic database maybe too low for it to be useful.

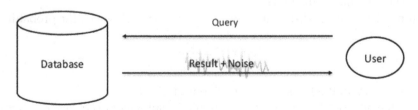

FIG. 3   Privacy-preserving data mining.

4.2 Definition of Differential Privacy

Now we can recap the definition of differential privacy (Dwork, 2006). We first establish the notation. Let $\mathcal{M} : D \rightarrow R$ be a randomized algorithm with domain D and range R. In concrete terms, we can think of $\mathcal{M}$ as a mechanism that answers a query to a database. Then we can formally define whether or not $\mathcal{M}$ provides differential privacy as follows.

Definition 1. A randomized algorithm $\mathcal{M}$ is ϵ-differentially private if for all possible subrange of $\mathcal{M}$, say $S \subset R$, and for all databases $D_1, D_2 \in D$ that differs by only one record, the probability that $\mathcal{M}$ gives the same output on input D_1 and D_2 with similar probability. More formally,

$$Pr(\mathcal{M}(D_1) \in S) \leq e^{\epsilon} Pr(\mathcal{M}(D_2) \in S).$$

Here ϵ controls how much information is leaked. For a small ϵ, the answer given by mechanism $\mathcal{M}$ on two databases that differ by one record is very likely to be the same. In other words, whether or not an individual's information is included in the database would not affect the outcome of the query significantly.

Example. Suppose the query we would like to make is whether or not Alice is a smoker. Consider mechanism $\mathcal{M}$ defined as follows. $\mathcal{M}$ first flips a fair coin $b \in \{0,1\}$. If $b = 0$, return the true answer. Otherwise, flip another coin $b' = \{0,1\}$. If $b' = 0$, return "yes," otherwise return "no." Now that there are two possible databases, namely, Alice is a smoker or Alice is not a smoker. If Alice is a smoker, $\mathcal{M}$ output "yes" with probability 3/4 and "no" with probability 1/4. If Alice is not a smoker, $\mathcal{M}$ output "yes" with probability 1/4 and "no" with probability 3/4. For any possible outcome, namely, "yes," or "no," the probability difference is at most three times. In other word, $\mathcal{M}$ is (ln 3) differentially private.

Remarks. Perhaps one of the most useful properties of this definition is that differential privacy holds during composition. Suppose we have a database D. The data owner releases the query result $\mathcal{M}_1(D)$. Later, he releases another query result $\mathcal{M}_2(D)$. If $\mathcal{M}_1$ and $\mathcal{M}_2$ are ϵ_1 and ϵ_2 differentially private, the outcome of releasing both $\mathcal{M}_1(D)$ and $\mathcal{M}_2(D)$ is $(\epsilon_1 + \epsilon_2)$ differentially private.

5 LAPLACE MECHANISM TO ACHIEVE DIFFERENTIAL PRIVACY

In general, the more noise we add, the more privacy we can guarantee. However, one should bear in mind that one usually aim to get as little noise as possible so as to maintain data utility. For query that returns real numbers as response, the Laplace mechanism is one of the basic mechanisms to provide differential privacy. We first recall the definition of Laplace distribution (Dwork and Roth, 2014).

Definition 2. The Laplace distribution with constant b is defined by the probability density function:

$$Lap(x \mid b) = \frac{1}{2b} e^{-\frac{|x|}{b}}.$$

Fig. 4 shows a plot of the Laplace distribution with $b = 0.045$:

Intuitively, the noise added to the answer should be sufficient to cover the maximum effect of a single data on the query outcome. Let F be this value. The Laplace mechanism is defined

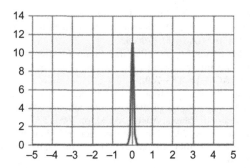

FIG. 4 Laplace distribution with $b = 0.045$.

as follows: if f is the actual query result, return $f + \textit{noise}$, where *noise* is drawn from the Laplace distribution with $b = F/\epsilon$. This mechanism is ϵ-differentially private.

Example. Suppose the database contains the grade point average (GPA) of all students. Assume the goal is to release the average GPA of the students in the database. We further assume that there are 1000 students and that the maximum GPA is 4.5. One could easily see that the maximum effect F of one record on the final outcome is $4.5/1000 = 0.0045$. Assume we would like to guarantee 0.1-differential privacy. We add noise following Laplace distribution with $b = F/\epsilon = 0.0045/0.1 = 0.045$. The distribution of the noise is given in Fig. 4.

6 CONCLUSION

In this chapter, we presented various definitions in relation to user privacy protections. We also discussed the various mechanisms to support these definitions. For an in-depth treatment of the subject, readers are referred to the book by Dwork and Roth (2014).

References

Aggarwal, G., Panigrahy, R., Feder, T., Thomas, D., Kenthapadi, K., Khuller, S., Zhu, A., 2010. Achieving anonymity via clustering. ACM Trans. Algor. 6 (3), 1–19.

Cao, J., Karras, P., 2012. Publishing microdata with a robust privacy guarantee. PVLDB 5 (11), 1388–1399.

Chaum, D., 1985. Security without identification: transaction systems to make big brother obsolete. Commun. ACM 28 (10), 1030–1044.

Chen, R., Mohammed, N., Fung, B.C.M., Desai, B.C., Xiong, L., 2011. Publishing set-valued data via differential privacy. PVLDB 4 (11), 1087–1098.

Clifton, C., Tassa, T., 2013. On syntactic anonymity and differential privacy. Trans. Data Privacy 6 (2), 161–183.

Doka, K., Xue, M., Tsoumakos, D., Karras, P., 2015. k-anonymization by freeform generalization. In: Bao, F., Miller, S., Zhou, J., Ahn, G.J. (Eds.), Proceedings of the 10th ACM Symposium on Information, Computer and Communications Security (ASIA CCS'15), April 14–17, 2015, Singapore. ACM, pp. 519–530.

Dwork, C., 2006. Differential privacy. In: Bugliesi, M., Preneel, B., Sassone, V., Wegener, I. (Eds.), Proceedings of 33rd International Colloquium, Automata, Languages and Programming (ICALP 2006), July 10–14, 2006, Venice, Italy. Part II, Lecture Notes in Computer Science, 4052. Springer, pp. 1–12.

Dwork, C., Roth, A., 2014. The algorithmic foundations of differential privacy. Found. Trends Theor. Comput. Sci. 9 (3-4), 211–407.

El Emam, K., Dankar, F.K., Issa, R., Jonker, E., Amyot, D., Cogo, E., Corriveau, J.P., Walker, M., Chowdhury, S., Vaillancourt, R., Roffey, T., Bottomley, J., 2009. Research paper: a globally optimal k-anonymity method for the de-identification of health data. JAMIA 16 (5), 670–682.

Ghinita, G., Karras, P., Kalnis, P., Mamoulis, N., 2007. Fast data anonymization with low information loss. In: Koch, C. (Ed.), Proceedings of the 33rd International Conference on Very Large Data Bases, 23-27 September 2007, University of Vienna, Austria. ACM, pp. 758–769.

Iwuchukwu, T., Naughton, J., 2007. K-anonymization as spatial indexing: toward scalable and incremental anonymization. In: Koch, C. (Ed.), Proceedings of the 33rd International Conference on Very Large Data Bases, September 23–27, 2007, University of Vienna, Austria. ACM, pp. 746–757.

LeFevre, K., DeWitt, D.J., Ramakrishnan, R., 2005. Incognito: efficient full-domain k-anonymity. In: Özcan, F. (Ed.), Proceedings of the ACM SIGMOD International Conference on Management of Data, June 14–16, 2005, Baltimore, MD. ACM, pp. 49–60.

LeFevre, K., DeWitt, D.J., Ramakrishnan, R., 2006. Mondrian multidimensional k-anonymity. In: Liu, L., Reuter, A., Whang, K.Y., Zhang, J. (Eds.), Proceedings of the 22nd International Conference on Data Engineering (ICDE 2006), April 3–8, 2006, Atlanta, GA. IEEE Computer Society, p. 25.

LeFevre, K., DeWitt, D., Ramakrishnan, R., 2008. Workload-aware anonymization techniques for large-scale datasets. ACM Trans. Database Syst. 33 (3), 1–47.

Li, N., Li, T., Venkatasubramanian, S., 2007. t-closeness: Privacy beyond k-anonymity and l-diversity. In: Chirkova, R., Dogac, A., Özsu, M.T., Sellis, T. (Eds.), Proceedings of the 23rd International Conference on Data Engineering (ICDE 2007), April 15–20, 2007, The Marmara Hotel, Istanbul, Turkey. IEEE Computer Society, p. 106–115.

Li, N., Qardaji, W.H., Su, D., 2011. Provably private data anonymization: or, k-anonymity meets differential privacy. CoRR. Abs/1101.2604.

Machanavajjhala, A., Kifer, D., Gehrke, J., Venkitasubramaniam, M., 2007. L-diversity: privacy beyond k-anonymity. ACM Trans. Knowl. Discov. Data 1 (1) Article 3.

Narayanan, A., Shmatikov, V., 2008. Robust de-anonymization of large sparse datasets. In: Proceedings of the 2008 IEEE Symposium on Security and Privacy (S&P 2008), May 18–21, 2008, Oakland, CA. IEEE Computer Society, pp. 111–125.

Sweeney, L., 2002. k-anonymity: a model for protecting privacy. Int. J. Uncertain. Fuzz. Knowl. Based Syst. 10 (5), 557–570.

Wang, R., Xue, M., Liu, K., Qian, H., 2015. Data-driven privacy analytics: a wechat case study in address-based social networks. In: Xu, K., Zhu, H. (Eds.), Proceedings of 10th International Conference on Wireless Algorithms, Systems, and Applications (WASA 2015), August 10–12, 2015, Qufu, China. Lecture Notes in Computer Science, 9204. Springer, pp. 561–570.

Wong, W.K., Mamoulis, N., Cheung, D.W.L., 2010. Non-homogeneous generalization in privacy preserving data publishing. In: Elmagarmid, A., Agrawal, D. (Eds.), Proceedings of the ACM SIGMOD International Conference on Management of Data (SIGMOD 2010), June 6–10, Indianapolis, IN. ACM, pp. 747–758.

Xu, J., Wang, W., Pei, J., Wang, X., Shi, B., Ada Wai-Chee, F., 2006. Utility-based anonymization using local recoding. In: Eliassi-Rad, T., Ungar, L., Craven, M., Gunopulos, D. (Eds.), Proceedings of the Twelfth ACM SIGKDD International Conference on Knowledge Discovery and Data Mining, August 20–23, 2006, Philadelphia, PA. ACM, pp. 785–790.

Xue, M., Karras, P., Chedy Raïssi, J.V., Tan, K., 2012. Anonymizing set-valued data by nonreciprocal recoding. In: Yang, Q., Agarwal, D., Pei, J. (Eds.), The 18th ACM SIGKDD International Conference on Knowledge Discovery and Data Mining (KDD'12), August 12–16, 2012, Beijing, China. ACM, pp. 1050–1058.

ABOUT THE AUTHORS

Xingye Lu received a bachelor's degree from the School of Computer Science and Engineering, Southeast University, China, in 2014. Currently she is a PhD student at the Department of Computing at Hong Kong Polytechnic University.

Man Ho Au received his undergraduate and graduate degrees from the Department of Information Engineering, Chinese University of Hong Kong, in 2003 and 2005, respectively, and a PhD from the University of Wollongong, Australia, in 2009. Currently, he is an assistant professor in the Department of Computing at Hong Kong Polytechnic University. Dr. Au's research interests include public key cryptography, information security, accountable anonymity, and cloud security. He has published over 90 papers in these areas. He has served as a program committee member for over 30 international conferences. He is an associate editor of the *Journal of Information Security and Applications*, Elsevier.

Performance of Digital Signature Schemes on Mobile Devices

D.Y.W. Liu*, G.Z. Xue†, Y. Xie†, X.P. Luo*, M.H. Au*
*The Hong Kong Polytechnic University, Kowloon, Hong Kong †Xiamen University, Fujian, China

1 INTRODUCTION

Mobile devices such as smartphones, PDAs, and tablets are so popular that they are indispensable to humans these days. Large amounts of digital information are being exchanged among the devices. The malicious access or utilization of this information might result in financial loss or the loss of other advantages. Particularly, people are concerned about the *authentication, integrity,* and *nonrepudiation* of the information. Authentication ensures that the communicating entity is legitimate, meaning that the entity is the one that he/she claims to be. Data integrity ensures that the information being received is the same as the one sent by an authorized entity, while nonrepudiation ensures that the parties in a communication cannot deny their participations in the process.

Inspired by handwritten signatures, cryptographers invented the term "digital signatures" to fulfill the authentication, integrity, and nonrepudiation requirements of digital communications. As an analogy to handwritten signatures, digital signatures provide a clue to the origin of a piece of digital information or a commitment of a piece of digital information by the sender (signer). Digital signatures also provide an integrity guarantee of a piece of digital information since the piece of digital information is "signed."

The idea of a "digital signature" first appeared in Diffie and Hellman's seminal paper, "New Directions in Cryptography," Diffie and Hellman (1976). A signer, say A, would like to protect his/her digital information, say m, against threats to authentication, integrity, and nonrepudiation. Two keys are being generated, namely a "public key" (pk) and a "private key" (sk). sk is kept secretly by A, who uses this key to produce signatures on messages. pk is used to verify the *validity* of a given digital signature σ on m, signed by A. pk is therefore accessible by public users. Here, *validity* refers to two concepts, namely, (1) the signature is created by A (authentication and nonrepudiation) and (2) the integrity of the message is maintained. The public key is normally derived from the private key and thus, the two keys are correlated. However, it is not feasible to derive the private key when only the public key

Mobile Security and Privacy
http://dx.doi.org/10.1016/B978-0-12-804629-6.00012-2

is known. Besides, it is impossible to forge signatures without the knowledge of *sk*. The study of digital signature schemes is an important subfield of public-key cryptography, initiated by Rivest et al. (1978). Since the signing key (*sk*) and the verifying key (*pk*) are different, this kind of cryptosystems is also known as *asymmetric* cryptosystems. We remark that being asymmetric is a necessary condition for a cryptosystem to provide nonrepudiation. The reason is that for any symmetric cryptosystems, the same key is used for both signing and verification processes. Consequently, both the signer and the verifier can be the origin of the signature and in this sense, both parties can deny having participated in the process. In other words, the signer must hold some "secret" information to achieve nonrepudiation.

One drawback of public-key cryptosystems is that they usually involve computations that are relatively heavy (e.g., modular exponentiations). The reason is that the security of these schemes relies on the difficulty of solving certain number-theoretic problems. Many digital signature schemes in practice fit the description. Well-known examples include the schemes, whose difficulties depend on the hardness of the Integer Factorization Problem (e.g., Rabin (1979)) and the Discrete Logarithm Problem (e.g., ElGamal (1985), Schnorr (1991), Pointcheval and Stern (1996), and DSS (National Institute of Standards and Technology, 1991, 1992)). Such intensive computations might not be desirable in mobile devices, in which the computational capability and battery capacity are limited.

1.1 Our Contribution

We present a performance analysis of two well-known digital signature schemes from pairing-based cryptography on mobile devices with Android (Google, 2016) platform. The two schemes are from Boneh et al. (2004b) (BLS) and Paterson and Schuldt (2006) (PS). The efficiency of these schemes is evaluated in terms of computation time and energy consumption during signature generation and verification, as well as the time to generate the message digest. Various types of information which reflect the practical settings, in terms of size and information type, are adopted in our experiments. We present the results and discuss their implications.

2 RELATED WORK

Digital signature is the de facto way to ensure the authentication, integrity, and nonrepudiation requirements. The Guidelines for Managing the Security of Mobile Devices in the Enterprise (Souppaya and Scarfone, 2013), developed by National Institute of Standards and Technology (NIST), suggested that digital signatures should be adopted for two purposes, namely, to ensure that only applications from trusted entities can be installed and to protect the integrity of the codes of these applications. A digital signature variant called mobile signature was defined by the European Telecommunications Standards Institute (ETSI) (2003). A number of models are proposed for the generation of digital signatures in the mobile environment. Specifically, digital signatures can be generated either on a mobile phone or on a SIM card on a mobile phone (Samadani et al., 2010). Digital signatures can be adopted in various mobile applications, including payment platforms (Wu et al., 2016), file transfer systems (Sayantan et al., 2015), and location proofs (Saroiu and Wolman, 2009). A survey of electronic signature solutions in mobile devices was carried out by Ruiz-Martínez et al. (2007), which discovered that mobile clients were able to generate digital signatures.

Recently, pairing-based cryptography (Paterson, 2005) has gain considerable attention thanks to its efficiency and improved security guarantees. For instance, Boneh et al. (2004a) introduced a short signature scheme (BLS) based on the Computational Diffie-Hellman (CDH) assumption on certain elliptic and hyper-elliptic curves. The signature length is half the size of a DSA signature (National Institute of Standards and Technology, 1992) for a similar level of security. Paterson and Schuldt (2006) proposed an efficient identity-based signature scheme (PS) based on Bilinear Decision Diffie-Hellman (BDDH) and Decision Linear (DL) assumptions with short signatures. This scheme enjoys the advantage that it is secure without relying on the so-called random oracle assumption (Bellare and Rogaway, 1993). In this chapter, we choose to investigate the practicality of these two well-known signature schemes on mobile devices.

3 THE EXPERIMENT

We experimented with the BLS and PS schemes on the Android (Google, 2016) platform. We adopted the Java Pairing-Based Cryptography Library (JPBC) (De Caro and Iovino, 2011) to develop the performance testing application on the Android platform.

3.1 Cryptographic Settings

In our experiment, we adopted Type A pairings, which is a standard bilinear pairing setup for cryptosystems. Type A pairings are constructed on the curve $y^2 = x^3 + x$ over the field $\mathbb{F}_q$ for some large prime q satisfying the constraint that $q \bmod 4 \equiv 3$. Both $\mathbb{G}_1$ and $\mathbb{G}_2$ are group of points on the elliptic curve $E(\mathbb{F}_q)$ having the same group order, say r. It is also required that r is a prime factor of $q + 1$. In other words, $q + 1$ is divisible by r. For a security level comparable with 1024-bit RSA encryption, q and r should be large prime numbers of 512 and 160 bits, respectively. For more information about this setting, please refer to PBC Library (Lynn, 2006).

3.2 Testing Environment

We examined the computation time (in terms of milliseconds) and energy consumption (in terms of joules) of information with diverse types and sizes reflecting practical scenarios. Table 1 shows the details of the data file being signed in the test application. For each type,

TABLE 1   Information Type and Size

Type	Size (kB)
Text string	0.144
Document (.docx)	14[a]
Image (.jpg)	2547
Movie (.mp4)	40217

[a]This corresponds to a one-page text document of about 400 words on Microsoft Word version 15.22.1.

TABLE 2   Testing Platform Specifications

	Device 1	Device 2
Operating system	Android OS, v5.0.1	Android OS, v4.1
Chipset	Qualcomm MSM8974AC Snapdragon 801	TI OMAP 4470
CPU	Quad-core 2.5 GHz Krait 400	Dual-core 1.5 GHz
GPU	Adreno 330	PowerVR SGX544
Memory (internal)	32 GB and 2 GB RAM	16 GB and 1 GB RAM
Card slot	microSD	microSD
Standard voltage	3.8 V	3.8 V
Battery capacity	3000 mAh	2100 mAh
Max energy	41040 J	28728 J

we test the time on (1) signature generation, (2) signature verification, and (3) message digest generation based on SHA-256 algorithm (NIST FIPS PUB 180-2, 2001). For each test, one of the information types (text string, document, image, or movie) was used. Each involved 10 trails, and the number presented for each type was the average of these 10 trails.

These tests were carried out on an experimental testbed which measures the computation time and energy consumption of two Android devices with specifications shown in Table 2. Device 1 has a more powerful hardware configuration in terms of processing power and memory than Device 2.

As shown in Fig. 1, the testbed consists of three elements: (1) power monitor, (2) Android device, and (3) laptop computer. As a core element, the power monitor (Monsoon FTA22D) connects the Android device and the computer laptop (Intel i5-2560M processor, 2.5 GHz, 3 MB cache, and 4 GB memory). The power monitor provides the DC electrical source with 3.8 V to the Android device, which avoids the influences of the unstable voltage when the battery continuously discharges. It also records the read-time voltage and current of the Android device at an interval of 0.2 ms. The power trace, including the time and the instant power, is sent to the laptop computer via USB interface communication in real time. A customized software is executed on the laptop computer to calculate the energy computation according to the measured data from the power monitor and the timestamps from applications.

As an integral preparation for the measurement, a testing app is designed to test the BLS and PS schemes which supports three processes, signature generation, signature verification, and message digest generation, in the sequence of $i = 1, 2, 3$. The app provides these functions: (1) record the beginning time t_0 of each test, and simultaneously send a signal packet to the laptop, (2) record the beginning time t_{2i-1} and the ending time t_{2i} of each process, which are used to calculate the computation time, (3) sleep for 30 s after each process to make sure that the device voltage returns a stable value.

The testing steps are as follows:

1. Carry out one test by executing the testing app after the voltage values of the device are stable for 5–10 s.

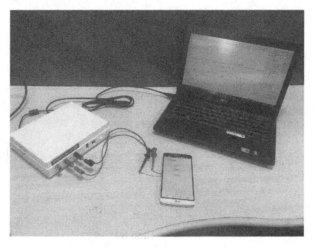

FIG. 1   Structure of the energy consumption measurement testbed.

2. Upon receiving the signal packet, the laptop records the current time $\overline{t}_o$ of the power monitor, which is used to synchronize the power trace.
3. The app records the timestamps of three processes. The power monitor measures the energy trace during the whole test.
4. The customized software in the laptop collects the timestamps from the app and the power trace from the power monitor. The computation time and energy consumption of the device in each process can be calculated after combining the two sets of measurements.

First, the computation time T_i of three processes can be obtained by $T_i = t_{2i} - t_{2i-1}$, $i = 1, 2, 3$. Next, the energy consumption of the device caused by the BLS and PS schemes is obtained after eliminating the basic energy consumption, which is caused by the screen and OS. The power trace of the device is shown as Fig. 2. Here, the basic power consumption is computed as the average of the power values before each test for a few seconds, shown as the red base line with 1850 mW in Device 1 (which is 2250 mW in Device 2). Then the energy consumption during signature generation/signature verification/message digest generation can be computed from the area between the power curve and the base line during the computation time from $t_{2i-1} + (\overline{t}_o - t_o)$ to $t_{2i} + (\overline{t}_o - t_o)$, $i = 1, 2, 3$.

3.3 Experiment Results and Observations

The experimental results are shown in Tables 3 and 4. We would like to highlight a few observations.

- Signature scheme BLS is more efficient than PS in both signature generation and verification. This is natural because BLS assumes the existence of a PKI, while PS is purely identity-based. Secondly, PS is proven to be secure in the standard model, while BLS's security analysis relies on the random oracle heuristic.

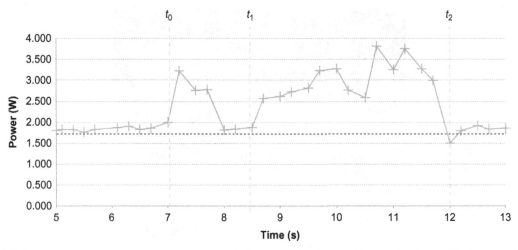

FIG. 2   Calculation of the energy consumption of device 1 in signature generation ($i = 1$).

- The size of data affects the time in message digest generation but not signature generation nor verification. This is because we adopt the common practice that the signature is generated and verified with respect to the message digest instead of the original message. As the message digest has a constant size (256 bits), the time spent on signature generation and verification for all types of data is similar in our experiment.
- The time required for message digest generation cannot be ignored. For a movie file of approximately 40 MB, 4 and 15 s are required in the message digest process in Devices 1 and 2, respectively. This is reasonable because a message digest is merely the hash value of the data while the computation of the hash for large data files is time consuming (Sravan Kumar and Saxena, 2011).
- We note that signature verification is more expensive than signature generation in general. Both devices take more time and energy to complete the process of signature verification.

Discussion. It is fair to say mobile devices nowadays possess comparable processing power to desktop/laptop computers. Incorporating cryptographic features into mobile applications does not impose too much of a burden on the computation time and energy consumption. Even though operations like hashing for relatively large files are still time consuming, such operations are not frequent for mobile agents. Our experiments show that it is feasible for mobile application developers to incorporate cryptographic techniques.

4 CONCLUSION

In this chapter, we provide a performance analysis of two well-known digital signature schemes on Android mobile devices. The efficiency of these schemes is evaluated in terms of computation time and energy consumption in signature generation and verification,

TABLE 3 Testing Results of Device 1

	BLS		PS	
Signature generation (time—millisecond)	String	569.5	String	518.1
	Document	400.9	Document	395.1
	Image	520.5	Image	502.2
	Movie	447.7	Movie	428.6
Signature verification (time—millisecond)	String	1096.3	String	887
	Document	1020	Document	915.8
	Image	1143.5	Image	1150.2
	Movie	955.6	Movie	932.1
Message digest generation (time—millisecond)	String	~0	String	~0
	Document	1.6	Document	1.8
	Image	305.7	Image	291.9
	Movie	4057.2	Movie	4186.9
Signature generation (energy consumption—joule)	String	0.824	String	0.721
	Document	0.766	Document	0.623
	Image	0.722	Image	0.648
	Movie	0.644	Movie	0.59
Signature verification (energy consumption—joule)	String	1.271	String	1.033
	Document	1.344	Document	1.214
	Image	1.346	Image	1.212
	Movie	1.373	Movie	1.263
Message digest generation (energy consumption—joule)	String	~0	String	~0
	Document	~0	Document	~0
	Image	0.337	Image	0.341
	Movie	4.197	Movie	3.988

as well as message digest generation. Our experiments involve various types of information, including text string, document, image, and movie files, which simulate realistic application scenarios. We realize that the main cost in applying digital signatures is in fact the generation of the message digest. Nonetheless, we have demonstrated that it is feasible to execute pairing-based signatures on mobile devices. Therefore we feel comfortable concluding that the use of cryptographic techniques in mobile applications is feasible to enhance security.

TABLE 4   Testing Results of Device 2

	BLS		PS	
Signature generation (time—millisecond)	String	850	String	582.4
	Document	724.2	Document	543.6
	Image	532.8	Image	342
	Movie	603.4	Movie	378.4
Signature verification (time—millisecond)	String	1901.2	String	2511.8
	Document	1582.8	Document	2663.6
	Image	1259.2	Image	1997.2
	Movie	1246.6	Movie	1826.8
Message digest generation (time—millisecond)	String	0.2	String	~0
	Document	5	Document	10.4
	Image	988.6	Image	1005.6
	Movie	15420	Movie	15543.6
Signature generation (energy consumption—joule)	String	0.836	String	1.033
	Document	0.825	Document	1.037
	Image	0.548	Image	0.968
	Movie	0.656	Movie	1.021
Signature verification (energy consumption—joule)	String	2.69	String	2.273
	Document	2.142	Document	1.705
	Image	1.712	Image	1.364
	Movie	1.868	Movie	1.42
Message digest generation (energy consumption—joule)	String	~0	String	~0
	Document	~0	Document	~0
	Image	1.095	Image	1.137
	Movie	16.858	Movie	17.51

Acknowledgments

We acknowledge the support from the National Natural Science Foundation of China (No. 61271242, 6137915), the Scientific Research Fund of Sichuan Provincial Department Science and Technology (No. 2015GZ0333), the Innovation Method Fund of China (No. 2015IM020500).

References

Bellare, M., Rogaway, P., 1993. Random oracles are practical: a paradigm for designing efficient protocols. In: Proceedings of the First ACM Conference on Computer and Communications Security (CCS'93), New York, NY. ACM, pp. 62–73.

Boneh, D., Boyen, X., Shacham, H., 2004. Short group signatures. In: Advances in cryptology—CRYPTO 2004, Volume 3152 of Lecture Notes in Computer Science. Springer, New York, pp. 41–55.

Boneh, D., Lynn, B., Shacham, H., 2004. Short signatures from the weil pairing. J. Cryptol. 17 (4), pp. 297–319.

De Caro, A., Iovino, V., 2011. JPBC: Java pairing based cryptography. In: Proceedings of the 16th IEEE Symposium on Computers and Communications (ISCC), Kerkyra, Corfu, Greece, June 28–July 1. pp. 850–855.

Diffie, W., Hellman, M., 1976. New directions in cryptography. IEEE Trans. Inform. Theory 22 (6), 644–654.

ElGamal, T., 1985. A public key cryptosystem and a signature scheme based on discrete logarithms. IEEE Trans. Inform. Theory 31, 469–472.

European Telecommunications Standards Institute (ETSI), 2003. Mobile commerce (m-comm); mobile signatures; business and functional requirements. Technical report TR 102 203.

Google, 2016. Android. https://www.android.com/.

Lynn, B., 2006. The Pairing-Based Cryptography Library. PBC Library Manual 0.5.14. https://crypto.stanford.edu/pbc/manual.pdf.

Majumdar, S., Maiti, A., Bhattacharyya, B., Nath, A., 2015. Advanced security algorithm using qrcode implemented for an android smartphone system: A-QR. Int. J. Adv. Res. Comput. Sci. Manage. Stud. 3 (5), 21–31.

National Institute of Standards and Technology (NIST), 1991. A proposed federal information processing standard for digital signature standard (DSS). Technical report.

National Institute of Standards and Technology (NIST), 1992. The digital signature standard, proposal and discussion. Commun. ACM 35 (7), 36–54.

NIST FIPS PUB 180-2, 2001. Secure hash standard.

Paterson, K.G., 2005. Chapter X. Cryptography from Pairings. In: Advances in Elliptic Curve Cryptography, Volume 317 of London Mathematical Society Lecture Notes. Cambridge University Press, pp. 215–251.

Paterson, K., Schuldt, J., 2006. Efficient identity-based signatures secure in the standard model. In: Proceedings of the 11th Australasian Conference on Information Security and Privacy (ACISP), July 3–5, 2006, Melbourne, Australia. pp. 207–222.

Pointcheval, D., Stern, J., 1996. Security proofs for signature schemes. In: Proceedings of EUROCRYPT'96, Volume 1070 of Lecture Notes in Computer Science, pp. 387–398.

Rabin, M., 1979. Digitalized signatures as intractable as factorization. MIT Laboratory for Computer Science. Technical report MIT/LCS/TR-212.

Rivest, R.L., Shamir, A., Adleman, L., 1978. A method for obtaining digital signatures and public-key cryptosystems. Commun. ACM 21 (2), 120–126.

Ruiz-Martínez, A., Sánchez-Martínez, D., Martínez-Montesinos, M., Gómez-Skarmeta, A., 2007. A survey of electronic signature solutions in mobile devices. JTAER 2 (3), 94–109.

Samadani, M.H., Shajari, M., Ahaniha, M.M., 2010. Self-proxy mobile signature: a new client-based mobile signature model. In: Proceedings of 24th IEEE International Conference on Advanced Information Networking and Applications Workshops (WAINA 2010), April 20–13, 2010, Perth, Australia, pp. 437–442.

Saroiu, S., Wolman, A., 2009. Enabling new mobile applications with location proofs. In: Proceedings of the 10th Workshop on Mobile Computing Systems and Applications (HotMobile 2009), February 23–24, 2009, Santa Cruz, CA.

Schnorr, C.P., 1991. Efficient identification and signatures for smart cards. Journal of Cryptology 4 (3), 161–174.

Souppaya, M., Scarfone, K., 2013. Guidelines for managing the security of mobile devices in the enterprise. http://dx.doi.org/10.6028/NIST.SP.800-124r1. Special Publication (NIST SP) 800-124 Rev 1.

Sravan Kumar, R., Saxena, A., 2011. Data integrity proofs in cloud storage. In: Third International Conference on Communication Systems and Networks (COMSNETS 2011), January 4–8, 2011, Bangalore, India, pp. 1–4.

Wu, J.L., Liu, C.L., Gardner, D., 2016. A study of anonymous purchasing based on mobile payment system. In: Proceedings of the 7th International Conference on Ambient Systems, Networks and Technologies/the 6th International Conference on Sustainable Energy Information Technology, May 23-26, 2016, Madrid, Spain, pp. 685–689.

ABOUT THE AUTHORS

Dennis Y.W. Liu received his BSc, MPhil, and PhD degrees in Computer Science from City University of Hong Kong in 2005, 2007, and 2014, respectively. Dr. Liu is currently a Teaching Fellow in the Department of Computing at Hong Kong Polytechnic University. His research interest is applied cryptography.

Guozhi Xue is a graduate student in computer science at Xiamen University, China. He received his B.S. in 2013 from Nanjing University. Mr. Xue's research interests include network security, network analysis and performance evaluation.

Yi Xie received her B.S. and M.S. from Xian Jiaotong University, China, as well as her PhD from Hong Kong Polytechnic University, Hong Kong SAR of China. Currently, she is an assistant professor in Xiamen University, China. Dr. Xie's research interests include high performance communication, network protocol analysis, network security, and modeling. She has published over 30 papers in these areas. Corresponding author: csyxie@xmu.edu.cn.

Xiapu Luo is a research assistant professor in the Department of Computing at Hong Kong Polytechnic University. His research focuses on mobile networks, smartphone security, network security and privacy, and Internet measurement. Dr. Luo obtained his PhD in computer science from Hong Kong Polytechnic University.

Man Ho Au received his undergraduate and graduate degrees from the Department of Information Engineering at Chinese University of Hong Kong in 2003 and 2005, respectively, and his PhD from University of Wollongong, Australia, in 2009. Currently, he is an assistant professor in the Department of Computing at Hong Kong Polytechnic University. Dr. Au's research interests include public-key cryptography, information security, accountable anonymity, and cloud security. He has published over 90 papers in these areas and he has served as a program committee program committee member for over 30 international conferences. Dr. Au is an associate editor of the *Journal of Information Security and Applications*, Elsevier.

Index

Note: Page numbers followed by *f* indicates figures and *t* indicates tables.